Richard Barrett is one of the most pr[ofound thinkers of] our day. With *A New Psychology of Human [Wellbeing]* his and our journey a step further. Bringing together numerous strands of research and theory with his visionary perspective he succeeds in "building a theory of human well-being that unites psychology with spirituality and science". This is a book whose time has come for many reasons; not least of all because it reminds us of the interrelatedness of all beings at a time when some forces still seek to tear us apart.

                      Ruth N. Steinholtz, Founder, AretéWork LLP.

A brilliant synthesis of the psychology of the future.

                      John Gray, author of *Men Are From Mars, Women Are From Venus.*

Richard Barrett offers the world an exciting new approach to the understanding of well-being: an approach that aligns with ancient wisdom and cutting-edge theories in science and psychology. He brings together Eastern and Western approaches to consciousness in a unifying model of reality that unites the material and energetic worlds. A brilliant book that will challenge your understanding of who you are and the world in which you live. Highly recommended.

            John Mackey, co-Founder and co-CEO, Whole Foods Market.

Everyone wants love, joy and happiness, but few realize that well-being is the foundation of them all. Richard's brilliant book redefines the meaning of well-being for the 21st century. A must read!

           Patricia Aburdene, author of *Megatrends 2010: The Rise of Conscious Capitalism* and *Conscious Money.*

Richard Barrett is a visionary. He unifies the soul wisdom of the ages with the science of modern medicine to reveal a path to human health and well-being. Never before have we seen a road map so clear to that which everyone seeks: a deep sense of well-being and fulfillment, and vibrant mental and physical health. This groundbreaking work provides the keys to the kingdom wherein lies true self-realization.

Sandra de Castro Buffington, Founding Director, Global Media Centre for Social Impact, UCLA Fielding School of Public Health.

One hundred years from now this will be the book that people cite as a major force in catalysing the transformation of human consciousness. The answers to many of the scientific materialists' "hard problems" are contained in these pages. A must read for anyone who suspects there is more to life than the current three-dimensional, physical explanation suggests.

Tom Evans, author of *New Magic for a New Era* and *Managing Time Mindfully*.

One of the most thought-provoking books I've read in years. Each concept, each proposal and each assertion invites the reader to step beyond the safety of learned historical views and expand their thinking with each chapter. A wonderful book!

T.S. Redmond, author and Behavioural Specialist.

"All you need is love!" These words from Richard Barrett's thought-provoking, scholarly new book sum up the positive energy of his transformational thinking, which brilliantly challenges orthodoxy about how to promote well-being. He legitimizes the use of the term "soul" enabling the reader to redefine who they are and their purpose on this planet. He brings together evidence from numerous sources supporting his convincing argument that for well-being (human flourishing) to develop we have to gain fulfilment at each stage of our psychological development. I am delighted to commend Richard's book, as its content makes a profound and unique contribution to the understanding of how we as humans can live aligned to our soul's purpose. A must read!

Dr. Neil Hawkes, Founder, International Values Education Trust.

This inspired and highly comprehensive work is a must read for anyone sincerely interested in advancing not only their understanding, but also their awareness of their inner nature. The correlations between our nature and the way we all go through life are a beacon by which one can navigate life much more effectively and with a greater sense of fulfilment.

Ron Hulnick, Ph.D, President, University of Santa Monica, and co-author of *Loyalty to Your Soul: The Heart of Spiritual Psychology.*

In this book, Richard Barrett provides a unique, unified model of physiology, psychology and spirituality. It shows how the realms of body, mind and soul are in an integrated ecosystem that affects our health, inner peace, relationships and our ability to know and fulfil our purpose on earth. Whatever gifts and challenges we were born with, we have the power to make choices to be our most joyful, loving and creative selves.

Phil Clothier, CEO, Barrett Values Centre.

I love this book. It is a terrific piece of work with which I resonate strongly. The subject of leadership is tired and broken. Richard Barrett's latest work combines rigorous research and original thinking, which he offers (to those bold enough) as a fresh way of seeing the wholeness of humanity—the key to restoring greatness in our organizations and well-being in our lives.

Lance Secretan, Founder & CEO, The Secretan Center Inc.

Richard Barrett's work is important. He feels the pulse of evolution. Through his evolving progression of books, he is claiming an important place in mapping and helping to chart the next great leaps of our evolutionary story. Barrett does not merely tell us who we are and where we come from, he invites us to consider who we might become and where we might go.

  Dr. Marc Gafni, President, Center for Integral Wisdom.

Richard's ground-breaking holistic approach will establish a new paradigm of well-being. This book bridges the divide of the spiritual and the physical, the mental and emotional and returns us to our wholeness. A must have for any practitioner working in the human potential movement.

  Karen Downes, Founder and Director, the Flourish Intitiative.

That our consciousness is important and gives us meaning in our life, and play an important role when growing healthy cultures, is well known to most of us. But understanding the importance it has on our psychological and physiological well-being is not that obvious to all. This book provides many new and valuable perspectives on this topic. Backed up with grounded researched from former and current thought leaders. I think this is the best book Richard has ever written!

  Tor Eneroth, Network Director, Barrett Values Centre.

The ultimate goal of human evolution is to live in harmony through love and wisdom. Richard Barrett's contribution is ground-breaking. He looks beyond form and matter, drawing on natural law and ancient wisdom, to build an integrated vibrational model for health and well-being.

  Fiona, Lady Montagu.

Richard Barrett's new book is an invaluable guide to the landscape for evolving travellers.
Barnet Bain, Director of *Milton's Secret* and author of *The Book of Doing and Being: Rediscovering Creativity in Life, Love, and Work.*

So many people these days are feeling a sense of unease, or lack of alignment, although they find it hard to put words to what's missing in their lives. Others succumb to illness or emotional problems that prevent them from living out their deepest purpose. In *A New Psychology of Human Well-Being*, Richard Barrett describes a larger, more integrated picture of life and shows us how the tributaries of psychology, science and spirituality all converge into the river of optimum well-being. This book provides a detailed and practical map of how we can each live our lives to the full. Regardless of where you are in your journey, you will find yourself in this book and will receive clear guidance on your next steps.
Judi Neal, Ph.D., author of *Edgewalkers* and *Creating Enlightened Organizations.*

Richard's description of the psychology of human well-being has been a real eye opener in helping me understand my own lived experience of anxiety fuelled depression and how a more soul-centred existence is essential to my well-being. The most remarkable aspect of this book is that Richard's description of our journey to psychological well-being is absolutely congruent with my own felt experience as I journey this path to a more soul-centred existence. A must read for all those interested in enhancing their own and others well-being in our very anxious world.
Geoff McDonald, former Global VP HR Unilever, Global Advocate and Campaigner for Mental Health, and Associate Director of Connecting with People

Books by Richard Barrett

The Metrics of Human Consciousness (2015)
Evolutionary Coaching (2014)
The Values-Driven Organization:
Unleashing Human Potential for Performance and Profit (2013)
What My Soul Told Me (2012)
Love, Fear and the Destiny of Nations (2011)
The New Leadership Paradigm (2010)
Building a Values-Driven Organization (2006)
Liberating the Corporate Soul (1998)
A Guide to Liberating Your Soul (1995)

A NEW PSYCHOLOGY OF HUMAN WELL-BEING

An Exploration of
the Influence of
Ego-Soul Dynamics
on Mental and
Physical Health

RICHARD BARRETT

Copyright © 2016 Richard Barrett.

All rights reserved. No part of this book may be reproduced, stored, or transmitted by any means—whether auditory, graphic, mechanical, or electronic—without written permission of both publisher and author, except in the case of brief excerpts used in critical articles and reviews. Unauthorized reproduction of any part of this work is illegal and is punishable by law.

Scripture taken from the King James Version of the Bible.

ISBN: 978-1-3265-9145-8 (sc)
ISBN: 978-1-4834-5310-1 (e)

Because of the dynamic nature of the Internet, any web addresses or links contained in this book may have changed since publication and may no longer be valid. The views expressed in this work are solely those of the author and do not necessarily reflect the views of the publisher, and the publisher hereby disclaims any responsibility for them.

Any people depicted in stock imagery provided by Thinkstock are models, and such images are being used for illustrative purposes only.
Certain stock imagery © Thinkstock.

Richard Barrett Fulfilling Books
19 Buckland Crescent London NW35DH
+447408879409
Fulfilling Books

Richard Barrett Fulfilling Books

rev. date: 06/23/2016

DEDICATION

I am dedicating this book to the memory of the founding fathers of the discipline of psychology—the study of the mind and behaviour—on whose shoulders we stand, particularly the memory Abraham Maslow, Carl Jung and Roberto Assagioli whose writings inspired me to embark on the activation of my soul.

Contents

List of Figures xiii
List of Tables xv
Quotations xvii
Acknowledgements xix
Preface xxi
Introduction xxix

Chapter 1	A larger jurisdiction for psychology	1
Chapter 2	The problem with perception	19
Chapter 3	The filtering of awareness	34
Chapter 4	The motivations of the ego and the soul	52
Chapter 5	The stages of psychological development	68
Chapter 6	Notes on the stages of psychological development	83
Chapter 7	Understanding needs and desires	101
Chapter 8	A theory of emotions and feelings	114
Chapter 9	Progression through the stages	127
Chapter 10	Energetic instability	135
Chapter 11	The impact of energetic instability	154
Chapter 12	The human energy field	183
Chapter 13	The impact of psychology on physiology	203
Chapter 14	Suicide and the stages of development	253
Chapter 15	A model of human well-being	271
Chapter 16	Loyalty to your soul: key principles	287
Chapter 17	A Decathlon of Flourishing, from age 60 to 80	289
Chapter 18	Cultural world views	290

Index 301

List of Figures

Figure I.1: The creation of three-dimensional awareness. xxxii
Figure 1.1: Stages of psychological development and levels of consciousness. 7
Figure 2.1: The projection of five fingers into two-dimensional awareness. 24
Figure 3.1: Filtering from the one-mind to the body-mind. 44
Figure 3.2: The expansion of conscious awareness. 46
Figure 4.1: The impact of love and fear on ego development................... 54
Figure 4.2: The impact that meeting your soul's desires has on your life. 56
Figure 5.1: The Seven Stages of Psychological Development and three evolutionary stages of the ego-soul dynamic..........69
Figure 6.1: Proportion of people in the UK choosing the value of friendship as one of their top ten value priorities. ... 88
Figure 6.2: Proportion of people in the UK choosing the value of honesty as one of their top ten value priorities......... 88
Figure 6.3: The percentage of people with genius level creativity by age. 90
Figure 6.4: Normal developmental process. 93
Figure 6.5: Accelerated developmental process. 94
Figure 12.1: The human energy field, the chakras and levels of consciousness...188
Figure 12.2: Linkages between the ego and soul layers of the energy field. 196
Figure 13.1: Proportion of people with Alzheimer's disease in the US, 2015. 217
Figure 13.2: Prevalence of strokes in Australia, 2009. 217

Figure 13.3: Number of people suffering from Parkinson's
disease in the UK in 2009. 218
Figure13.4: New cases of ovarian and prostate cancer in
Sweden in 2012. 221
Figure 13.5: New cases of prostate cancer by age in the UK,
2009–2011. 223
Figure 13.6: New cases of prostate cancer by age in Sweden in 2012. 223
Figure 13.7: New cases of ovarian cancer in Sweden in 2012. 224
Figure 13.8: New cases of breast cancer in the UK, 2009–2011. 227
Figure 13.9: New cases of breast cancer in Sweden in 2012. 227
Figure 13.10: New cases of breast and ovarian cancer in
Sweden in 2012. 228
Figure 13.11: Number of deaths from respiratory problems
Sweden in 2012. 229
Figure 13.12: Number of US adults per 100,000 diagnosed
with a heart attack by age and gender in 2014. 233
Figure 13.13: Number of deaths by gender from heart
related diseases in the US in 2012. 234
Figure 13.14: Number of deaths by gender from heart-
related diseases in the UK in 2014. 234
Figure 13.15: Number of deaths from liver disease in Sweden in 2012. .. 237
Figure 13:16: Number of deaths from diabetes in the US in 2012. 238
Figure 13.17: Percentage of population in the US considered obese. 239
Figure 13:18: Percentage of population in the US considered
obese by age grouping in 2012. 239
Figure 14.1: Incidence of suicide in the UK by age and gender in 2012. 259
Figure 14.2: Incidence of suicide in Sweden by age and
gender in 2012. 263
Figure 14.3: Incidence of suicide in the US by age and gender in 2009. 263
Figure A2.1: The emergence of new world views (years ago). 293

List of Tables

Table 1.1: From Maslow's hierarchy of needs to Barrett's levels of consciousness. 5
Table 3.1: Properties of the ego's and soul's awareness. 48
Table 3.2: The ego's and soul's experience of reality. 48
Table 4.1: The motivations of the ego. 53
Table 4.2: The motivations of the soul. 55
Table 5.1: The tasks, motivations and developmental focus associated with each stage of psychological development. 73
Table 6.1: Concerns and issues associated with each level of consciousness. 85
Table 6.2: Feelings and thoughts associated with a lack of mastery of levels of consciousness. 86
Table 8.1: The six basic emotions. 117
Table 8.2: Feelings/sensations experienced by the body-mind, ego-mind and soul-mind. 122
Table 8.3: Intensity of feelings. 122
Table 8.4: The relative levels of frequency of vibration of different "emotions." 124
Table 10.1: Stages of development, levels of consciousness and dominant minds. 137
Table 11.1: Summary of potential sources of energetic instability. 155
Table 11.2: The impact of the satisfaction of needs on our four minds..179
Table 12.1: Characteristics of over active and under active chakras.......186
Table 12.2: The human energy field, the chakras, stages of psychological development and levels of consciousness. 188
Table 12.3: Linkages between the lower and upper chakras and parts of the body. 197

Table 13.1: The leading causes of death in five industrialized nations.. 205
Table 13.2a: Causes of death by stage of psychological development in the US in 2013. 207
Table 13.2b: Causes of death by stage of psychological development in the UK in 2014. 208
Table 13.3: Stages of psychological development, ages at which physiological dysfunctions begin to appear and the age beyond which they peak. 211
Table 13.4: Physiological issues associated with each stage of psychological development. 212
Table 13.5: Characteristics of the serving stage of psychological development 214
Table 13.6: Characteristics of the integrating and conforming stages of psychological development 219
Table 13.7: Characteristics of the self-actualizing stage of psychological development 225
Table 13.8: Characteristics of the individuating stage of psychological development 230
Table 13.9: Characteristics of the differentiating stage of psychological development 235
Table 13.10: Characteristics of the conforming stage of psychological development 243
Table 13.11: Characteristics of the surviving stage of psychological development 245
Table 13.12: Stages of development and the onset of physiological disorders. 249
Table 14.1: Highest suicide rates by age range and gender for UK countries in 2012. 260
Table 14.2: Suicides among gifted writers.. 265
Table 15.1: Planes of being and scales of organization. 279
Table A2.1: The evolution of cultural world views. 291
Table A2.2: Stages of individual psychological development and cultural world views. 296

Quotations

I have included the following quotations because they are pertinent to the topics I will be discussing in this book.

Quotations from Abraham Maslow

"All the evidence that we have indicates that it is reasonable to assume in practically every human being, and certainly in almost every new-born baby, there is an active will towards health, and an impulse towards growth and actualization."

"Self-actualizing people have a deep feeling of identification, sympathy and affection for human beings in general. They feel kinship and connection as if all people were members of a single family."

"If the essential core of the person is denied or suppressed, he gets sick, sometimes in obvious ways, sometimes in subtle ways, sometimes immediately, sometimes later."

Quotations from Carl Jung

"Your visions will become clear only when you can look into your own heart. Who looks outside, dreams; who looks inside, awakens."

"There is no coming to consciousness without pain. People will do anything, no matter how absurd, to avoid facing their Soul."

"The privilege of a lifetime is to become who you truly are. Where wisdom reigns, there is no conflict between thinking and feeling."

Acknowledgements

It can be a lonely life writing a book: months of dedication, focus, and the hardest part of all, isolation. But when you share your life with someone who understands the importance of the relentless impulse you feel to create, it is so much easier. In this regard, I want to thank my wife and my primary counsellor, Christa Schreiber, whose support and words of wisdom I constantly treasure.

I also want to thank the source of my inspiration, the originator of my insights: my soul. I am frequently in awe of the ideas that arrive unannounced, usually around 4 or 5 in the morning, and the never-ending series of synchronistic experiences that guide my life. These moments, these flashes of insight, light me up inside. They make me glow.

On a more practical level, I want to thank Pete Beebe, the person who designs the covers for my books, all those who volunteered to proofread my book, my editor Louise Morgan and my team at the Barrett Values Centre.

PREFACE

To everything there is a season, and a time to every purpose under the heaven.[1]

Something significant happened to me as I started writing this book. I had a profound insight: I realized that I could not have written this book any sooner in my life because who I am has never stopped changing. My core has always been the same, but decade after decade of subtle shifts have gradually brought my personality into closer alignment with my core. Only now, with hindsight, can I look back on seventy years of life and see how the stages of psychological development led me into soul consciousness.

This insight made me realize that the way we are in the world, what we think about, what we consider important, what we include and exclude from the narrative we tell ourselves about who we are and why we do what we do, is determined by the lenses we wear. Our lenses are personal and dynamic. They are conditioned by multiple factors: the world view of the culture we were brought up in, the impact that our life's experiences, particularly those of our childhood, had on the formation of our beliefs, and most importantly, the stage of psychological development we have reached.

Although I was already aware of the importance that the stages of psychological development have on our lives, it was not until I read George E. Vaillant's book, *Triumphs of Experience*,[2] which reports on the longitudinal Harvard Grant Study of Social Adjustments, that I fully recognized how important the successful mastery of the stages of psychological development is to the level of happiness, meaning and fulfilment we find during the different seasons of our lives.

The Grant Study

The Harvard Grant Study of Social Adjustments began in 1938, four years after George Vaillant was born. Vaillant became the study director in 1972 and retired from his post more than three decades later in 2005. The purpose of the Grant Study, as it is popularly known, was to learn something about the conditions that promote optimum health by following the lives of 268 men, all Harvard graduates. This study is one of the longest running prospective longitudinal studies of adult male development that has ever been attempted.

One of the criticisms levelled at the Grant Study was that it focused on an elite group of men. Vaillant responds to this criticism by admitting that this was also one of his reservations when he became involved in the study and that his concerns had subsequently been allayed. He states:

> I have had the opportunity and privilege of studying the life courses of two contrasting groups [to the Grant Study]—a cohort of very underprivileged inner-city men and a group of gifted women. The results from both groups, each of which was studied prospectively for more than half a century, have confirmed [significant similarities to the results of the Grant Study].[3]

After reviewing the results of the three studies, Vaillant came to the conclusion that the advantages we attribute to the male gender and social class in America do not show up as being significant when we follow the life stories of gifted women and underprivileged men. In other words, gender and social class do not necessarily correlate with living a "successful" life. I suspect this is also true for people living in liberal democracies all over the world. For those living in autocratic regimes, where ethnic and social prejudices prevent certain genders, religions and social classes from getting the opportunities they need to express fully who they are, living a "successful" life can be full of challenges.

Prospective studies

Unlike retrospective studies, prospective studies follow a cohort in real time. This means that the results of prospective studies are not flawed by the lens of the stage of psychological development participants are at when they attempt to answer questions about their past. Prospective studies make our shifting subjectivity transparent. They enable us to see that what we regard as important changes with the passage of time. As Vaillant points out, time is a great deceiver. He considers our age filters to be so significant that he calls the first chapter of *Triumphs of Experience: Maturation makes liars of us all*.[4]

As indicated, the Grant Study was not the only longitudinal prospective study to have been carried out in the twentieth century. Other studies included the Inner City cohort of the Glueck study of juvenile delinquency[5] and the Terman study of gifted women.[6,7]

The Glueck study followed a group of 500 delinquent schoolboys and a contrasting group of 500 schoolboys who had not brushed up against the law. The study began in 1939 when the boys were teenagers; the final interviews were carried out in 1975 when the study participants had reached their 50s.

The Terman Study followed a group of talented women for eighty years from 1922. Most of the 672 women were born between 1908 and 1914. The key findings of this study are reported in *The Longevity Project*.[8]

Objectifying subjectivity

What I admire about George Vaillant's reporting is not just the stories he tells of the insights that the Grant Study yielded, but his refreshing honesty in making public his age/development-related biases in the way he approached his research. Time after time, Vaillant explains that what he considered important was proven wrong.

What Vaillant does, very explicitly in my opinion, is illustrate how wrong our assumptions can be when we fall into the trap of objectifying our subjectivity. We all do this; we can't help it. The rationale for everything we do is based on what we believe is important at the particular moment we make a decision or pass judgement. What we fail to recognize is that what is important to us depends on multiple factors: the influence of our parents, our cultural conditioning, our religious beliefs, the stage of psychological development we are at, and the needs of the stages of psychological development we have failed to master.

Depending on these biases you could easily be drawn into dismissing as unimportant some of the ideas expressed in this book, or any other book for that matter because they do not align with what you believe is important at the stage of psychological development you have reached. This is why I stated at the beginning of the book that I could not have written this book any earlier in my life because it would have been biased by what I considered important at the stage of psychological development I had reached.

This is still true today, but having spent at least a decade in what I regard as the last stage of psychological development, I can now look back at my life with a deeper understanding of how what was important to me during the earlier stages of my development influenced my decision-making and brought me to the larger perspective I now have.

I am not asking you to accept the thoughts and ideas contained in this book; I am asking you to recognize that your reaction to what I have written depends on many factors, most importantly the stage of psychological development you have reached, the level of consciousness you normally operate from, and your parental and cultural conditioning. What I would like you to notice, as you move through the chapters, is how this book makes you feel. What thoughts does it bring up for you? Which ideas you accept, and which ideas you reject?

My hope is that you resonate with most of the ideas and that you find the book enjoyable and entertaining, fully recognizing that it is just one person's attempt to understand what he believes is necessary to live a happy, meaningful and fulfilling life.

Denying the soul

What is different about this book compared to almost all other works on the topics of stages of development and human well-being is that it explores psychological development from the perspective of the ego-soul evolutionary dynamic. You will not find this approach in any scientific papers because the soul (sometimes called the higher-self or the inner core), along with the topic of consciousness, for the most part, is ignored by the academic world. Let me recount an anecdote that illustrates my point.

In 2015, I gave an opening keynote address at a conference put on by one of the top business schools in Europe. My title was *The Spiritual/*

Psychological Dimension of Creativity and Flow. The audience of close to 300 people was comprised of academics, coaches and business people. At the beginning of my speech, I conducted an experiment with the audience: I asked them to stand if any of the statements I was going to make were true for them.

I started by saying "I have a car", and most of the audience stood up. Then I said "I am a car," no one stood up. Then I said, "I have an ego" and after that "I am an ego." Most people stood up when I said "I have an ego" and sat down when I said "I am an ego." Then I said "I have a soul," everyone stood up. After that, I said "I am a soul" and everyone remained standing.

What I had half expected, but was amazed to see, was that everyone stood up for both of the final statements. Not just one, both of them! After jokingly pointing out the high level of confusion they must have about who they are, I suggested to the audience that having a soul was the stage of development that preceded being a soul, but the ultimate truth was that your soul has you! Since that occasion, I have repeated this exercise with diverse audiences in many parts of the world and each time I got the same result: the vast majority of people believe they have a soul, and they are a soul.

But it was what happened next that made me realize there is something wrong with the mainstream scientific approach. The next speakers, two very bright and influential academics were talking about neuroscience research.

They had a statement on their first slide that read "Assumptions we make: There is no soul". When I saw this statement, I could not help smiling to myself. The entire audience of academics, coaches and business people had just indicated that they believed they not only had a soul, but they were souls.

What this experience clearly pointed out to me, and I think the rest of the audience, was how the objective, scientific approach has a tendency to deny our inner knowing. Fortunately, if you care to look beyond mainstream academic circles you will find a plethora of serious writings that paint a very different picture of the world. You will also find an increasing number of universities promoting interdisciplinary approaches. This is to be welcomed.

One of the few academic institutions that embrace Spiritual Psychology is the University of Santa Monica (USM) in California. The founding faculty of USM, Drs. Ron and Mary Hulnick, have established a globally recognized and highly experiential Master's Degree Program (now offered in a non-degreed format) that seeks practical answers to life's essential questions. The text book they use for their programs is called *Loyalty to Your Soul: The Heart of Spiritual Psychology*.[9] Their key principles for living a life devoted to your soul are reproduced in Annex 1.

I believe there are two problems that arise from the objective scientific approach: the dualistic notion that the body and the mind belong to different realms, and the plethora of disciplines that keep our minds blinkered from the larger realities of life. In this respect, the following words written by Peter D. Ouspensky (1878–1947) early in the last century are almost as meaningful now as they were then:

> We fail to understand many things because we specialize too easily and too drastically, philosophy, religion, psychology, natural sciences, sociology, etc. each has their special literature. There is nothing embracing the whole in its entirety.[10]

However, all the different areas of knowledge must have significant interrelationships. We need to identify and explore these linkages if we are to develop theories that unify psychology, spirituality and science.

The proposition I set out in this book is that there is a unifying model. Furthermore, we can only grow to understand this model by removing our blinkers, embracing self-knowledge, and acknowledging the limits of our three-dimensional physical perception. The unifying model I propose transcends birth and death and leads us into an energetic dimension of reality where we encounter the soul.

My approach to writing this book, therefore, has been to bring together ideas from many disciplines, not limiting myself to academic research, but incorporating the thoughts and ideas of recognized thought leaders, most of whom lived during the past two hundred years. Also, you will find references to ancient wisdom; insights that have been handed down through generations. Interspersed throughout the book, and gluing it all together, you will find my thoughts and ideas.

References and notes

1. The Bible, Ecclesiastes 3, Verse 1, King James Version.
2. George E. Vaillant, *Triumphs of Experience* (Boston: Harvard University Press), 2012.
3. George E. Vaillant, *Adaptation to Life* (Boston: Harvard University Press), 1977, Preface to the 1995 Edition, p. x.
4. George E. Vaillant, *Triumphs of Experience* (Boston: Harvard University Press), 2012. pp. 1–26.
5. Sheldon Glueck and Eleanor Glueck, *Unravelling Juvenile Delinquency* (New York: Commonwealth Fund), 1950.
6. Lewis M. Terman and Melita H. Olden, *The Gifted Child Grows Up: Genetic Studies of Genius*, vol. 4 (Stanford: Stanford University Press), 1947.
7. Melita H. Oden, *The Fulfilment of Promise: Forty-Year Follow-up of the Terman Gifted Group*, Genetic Psychology Monographs 77, 1968; Carole K. Holahan and Robert R. Sears, *The Gifted Group in Maturity* (Stanford: Stanford University Press), 1955.
8. Howard S. Friedman and Leslie R. Martin, *The Longevity Project* (New York: Hudson Street Press), 2011.
9. H. Ronald Hulnick and Mary R. Hulnick, *Loyalty to Your Soul: The Heart of Spiritual Psychology* (Carlsbad: Hay House), 2010.
10. Peter D. Ouspensky, *Tertium Organum: A Key to the Mysteries of the World* (New York: Vintage Books), 1982, pp. 262–263.

Introduction

To make progress at this stage of human evolution, we need to stand on the shoulders of those who have gone before, not continually reinvent everything. We need to unite the various disciplines of human knowledge into an undifferentiated whole.

Although the study of the mind and human behaviour go back to the early Greek civilization, the discipline of psychology is a relatively recent addition to human knowledge. Until the close of the nineteenth century everything to do with the mind was regarded as a branch of philosophy.

The first person to refer to himself as a psychologist was Wilhelm Wundt (1832–1920). In 1879, in Leipzig, Wundt created the first laboratory dedicated exclusively to psychological research. Other early contributors to the field of psychology included William James (1842–1910), the first educator to offer a course in psychology in the United States, Ivan Petrovich Pavlov (1849–1936), a Russian physiologist, primarily known for his work on conditioning, and Hermann Ebbinghaus (1850–1909), a German psychologist who pioneered the experimental study of memory.

Shortly after experimental psychology took off, various kinds of applied psychology began to appear; among them was a new approach to the study of the mind known as psychoanalysis. This approach, pioneered by the Sigmund Freud (1856–1939), involved a set of theories and therapeutic techniques for treating mental disorders that involved bringing repressed fears and conflicts into the conscious mind to affect healing. Some of the central ideas in Freud's approach to psychoanalysis were:

- A person's development is mostly determined by forgotten events in early childhood.
- A person's behaviour is mostly determined by unconscious drives.

- Neurosis and other mental disturbances are driven by conflicts between a person's conscious and unconscious drives.
- Conflicts can be healed by bringing unconscious drives into conscious awareness and giving them a new meaning.

From these early foundations, many psychological theories and approaches to the treatment of mental disorders arose, each one reflecting the particular philosophical orientation of an individual or group of like-minded individuals. Such approaches are sometimes referred to by the name of the originator, for example, Jungian psychology, and sometimes, when different people agreed on a particular approach, by the name of a movement, for example, behaviourism, cognitivism, humanism, existentialism and transpersonal psychology.

Each time a new movement formed, within a few years it would splinter into new branches. The originators of the new branches validated their particular approach by linking it to the movement. For example, transpersonal psychology originally gained its acceptance by being recognized as a branch of humanistic psychology.

Abraham Maslow (1908–1970), one of the founding fathers of humanistic psychology, regarded transpersonal psychology as the "fourth force" in psychology, to distinguish it from the three other forces: psychoanalysis, behaviourism, and humanism. In other words, he tried to elevate the status of transpersonal psychology to a movement by differentiating it from humanistic psychology.

The key factor in differentiating transpersonal psychology from other movements was the inclusion of experiences and world views that extended beyond the personal level—experiences involving a larger sense of identity and an expansion of consciousness—that represented a more spiritual approach to life.

When we survey the evolution of psychology over the past 130 years we see a continuing divergence of thinking and theories explaining the operation of the human mind; a constant splitting and branching of approaches with occasional convergences, such as the coming together of behaviourism and cognitivism into the approach known as cognitive behavioural therapy (CBT).

If we trace the divergence of different approaches to psychology back to their philosophical roots we arrive at the concept of dualism—the splitting of the study of human experience into two ontologically separate categories—the study of matter (the body) and the study of mind (the psyche).

Before dualism there was monism. Whereas the proponents of dualism maintain that neither mind nor matter can be reduced to each other in any way, the proponents of monism maintain that only one thing is ontologically basic or prior to everything else. If we trace monism back to its philosophical roots we arrive at the origins of religion: a system of "magical" thinking that our early ancestors used to explain natural phenomena and give meaning to the events that occurred in their lives. At the source of all magical thinking were spirits; non-human entities onto which our early ancestors projected human motivations. From the perspective of evolutionary psychology, at the source of all human religions, we find the concept of spirituality.

Monism

This book is my attempt to rediscover the roots of monism: not religious monism, but a form of monism that is consistent with the ideas we find in science, psychology, and spirituality. In other words, what I am attempting to do is define a larger jurisdiction for psychology that reunites the disciplines of knowledge we have split apart, back into a unified whole. At the core of this whole, is energy: energy that displays the property of awareness. Energy that displays the property of awareness is called mind. I will argue that the mind energy is the basis of all life, and everything we perceive in our universe is comprised of mind energy.

I will also argue that consciousness arose from awareness when aspects of the unified whole separated from the whole. The separated aspects had to become conscious—have their own mind—to manage their separation. To manage their separation they had to limit their conscious awareness to the specific environment in which they found themselves so they could manage their internal stability and external equilibrium of their energetic identity.

Viewed through the lens of psychology, separation—the splitting off of parts and the limiting of the conscious awareness of those parts—is known as repression. Repression leads to distortions of reality and mental disorders. When monism evolved into dualism, we split apart the human psyche—the soul (spirituality)—into two parts: body (science) and mind (psychology), and we created the mental disorder or distortion of reality we call three-dimensional material awareness. This schema is shown in Figure I.1.

Figure I.1: The creation of three-dimensional awareness.

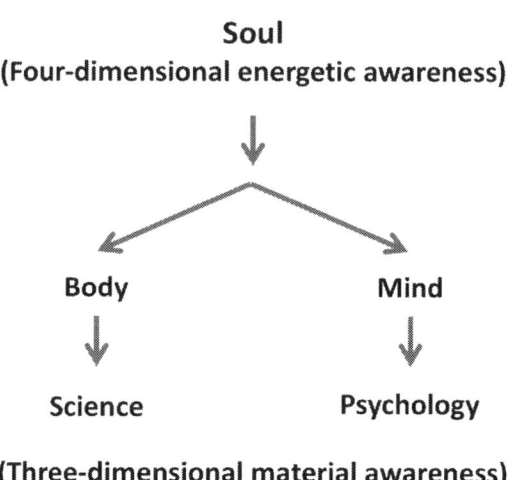

Viewed through the lens of psychology, healing occurs when what has been repressed is reintegrated into conscious awareness and given a new, more holistic meaning. This is exactly my purpose in defining a larger jurisdiction for psychology. I propose to reunite body and mind with soul. I shall be calling this new awareness, four-dimensional energetic awareness or the awareness of the soul.

I will begin by exploring and developing ideas that enable us to reunite psychology with spirituality—heal the split in mind that resulted in the distortion of reality we call three-dimensional material awareness, and then heal the split between psychology and science—heal the split that anchored our minds in three-dimensional material awareness. In so doing, I will also show how it is possible to heal the split between the Western material approach to medicine and Eastern energetic approach to medicine. In a nutshell, this is what the book is about: defining a psychological theory that integrates body, mind and soul.

Structure of the book

I have structured the book in the manner previously described, focusing first on healing the split between psychology and spirituality and then healing the split between psychology and science. In the last third of the book, I focus on healing the split between Western and Eastern medicine.

The first chapter explores the idea that there could be a larger jurisdiction for psychology and introduces the model of psychological development that I will be using to reintegrate spirituality with psychology: the Seven Levels of Consciousness Model. I also introduce the idea that we live in a multi-dimensional world. We think we live in a material world, but we live in an energetic world.

Chapter 2 explores the dichotomy between our material and energetic worlds in more detail. Only when we realize that our three-dimensional material world is contained within a four-dimensional energetic world, can we appreciate our true reality. I provide arguments and evidence to support this assertion.

Chapter 3 takes my exploration one stage further. It explains the evolution of consciousness and mind energy from the Big bang to the present day. It also explains the differences between three-dimensional reality—the reality of the ego, and four-dimensional reality—the reality of the soul.

In Chapter 4, I explain how our three-dimensional reality conditions the motivations of the ego and how our four-dimensional reality conditions the motivations of the soul. To flourish and thrive, we must learn to align the motivations of the ego with the motivations of the soul. We must recognize that mind is the higher order reality, and that mind influences matter.

Chapter 5 provides a detailed account of the seven stages of psychological development: the evolution of the needs of the ego and the desires of the soul.

Chapter 6 provides an in-depth understanding of how the stages of psychological development unfold in our lives.

In Chapter 7, I define what needs and desires are and what they are not. I also describe the difference between deficiency sensations in the body-mind and feeling deficiencies in the ego-mind.

Chapter 8 describes our six basic emotions: the link between our energetic reality and our physical reality. I show how emotions originate, how they lead to feelings and how our emotions and feelings are linked to the satisfaction or non-satisfaction of our needs.

Chapter 9 explains the fundamental importance of meaning-making to staying present in three-dimensional material reality. I also describe how imprints and beliefs—the sources of our meaning-making—are formed and how they condition our reality.

Chapter 10 deals with the concept of energetic stability: the basis of all life in three-dimensional material reality, and explains how we create stability and instability in our energy field through meaning-making. The link between energetic instability and pain is also explored.

Chapter 11 explains how and why the soul creates the ego. I also explain how the emotions of fear, anger and sadness relate to needs and why not getting our needs met creates energetic instabilities that in turn lead to physical and mental disorders.

In Chapter 12 I describe the structure of the human energy field: how the layers of the human energy field relate to the seven stages of psychological development, and how the seven levels of consciousness relate to the chakra system.

Chapter 13 identifies the leading causes of death in the UK and US and shows how the energetic instabilities associated with difficulties in mastering the stages of psychological development are linked to our physiological health.

Chapter 14 explains how energetic instabilities associated with difficulties in mastering the stages of psychological development are linked to the incidence of suicide in the UK, US and Sweden.

Finally, Chapter 15 summarizes the whole book. It explains how the Seven Levels of Consciousness Model unites different psychological approaches, and how science, spirituality and psychology can be unified into a single philosophy that provides a larger jurisdiction for psychology and a more comprehensive understanding of human well-being and flourishing.

If you want to get to the punch line before reading the whole book, I have two suggestions for you. First: read this chapter and the last chapter. Second: read the summaries of important points at the end of each chapter. The summaries are also useful if you put down the book for a few days and want to refresh your mind on where you have got to.

Definitions

Because the discipline of psychology is still in its infancy, there is no universal agreement on the terminology used to explain the structure and operation of the human psyche. Therefore, before going any further, I think it would be useful to provide some definitions for the terminology I will be using in this book.

Psyche

The term "psyche" has a long history of use, dating back to ancient times. In the days of the Ancient Greek Civilisation (800 B.C.–146 B.C.), the term "psyche" was used to refer to the soul. The idea of the soul was central to the philosophy of Plato. Plato considered the psyche to be immortal. In modern times, the meaning of the term psyche has been subject to significant change.

Carl Jung makes a distinction between psyche and soul. He refers to the psyche as the totality of all human mental processes, conscious as well as unconscious. He refers to the soul as a clearly demarked functional complex that has a unique personality. For Jung, the soul was an aspect of the psyche, and, therefore, Jung's approach to psychoanalysis included not just the ego aspects of our personality but also the soul aspects. For Jung, the soul was part of our unconscious.

In recent decades the terms "psyche" and "soul" have fallen into disuse, mainly because modern science cannot deal with what cannot be perceived by the senses or originates from a domain that is regarded as the unknown. What is not known, and cannot be scientifically proven, does not exist as far as modern psychologists are concerned. Unconscious content that percolates into conscious awareness and synchronistic experiences are not given the attention they deserve. These impulses originating in the four-dimensional energetic world of the soul are mostly disregarded.

In this book, I will be aligning myself with the position of Carl Jung. I will be using the term "psyche" to refer to the totality of our mental processes—conscious, subconscious and unconscious, and I will be using the term "soul" to refer to the functional complex that contains our own unique, life transcending personality—the source of our four-dimensional awareness.

The ego

Your ego is a field of conscious awareness that identifies with your physical body. Because the ego believes it inhabits a body and lives in a material world, it lives in three-dimensional reality and thinks it can die. Because it thinks it can die, it thinks it has needs, and because it thinks it has needs, it develops fears about not being able to get its needs met. The principal needs of the ego are survival, safety and security. The ego-mind is the creation of the soul-mind. The soul creates the ego to protect itself from the pain (energetic instability) it experiences being present in three-dimensional material awareness.

The ego is not *who* you are; it is who you think you are. It is the mask you wear to get your needs met in the physical, social and cultural framework of your material existence. The ego represents your sense of identity in relation to others and the social context in which you live. Your ego identity begins to form during the first two-to-three years of your life, and if all goes well, it reaches a natural resolution during your early 20s as you become a viable and independent member of your community in the cultural framework of your existence. When you get to this stage in your life, you normally respond to the question "Who am I?" by stating your age, gender, role/occupation, race, religion and nationality. These are the things that define your ego identity.

When the content and memories of the ego-mind are known to us in our present moment awareness, they are said to be conscious. When the content and memories of the ego-mind are not known to us in our present moment awareness, they are said to be either subconscious or unconscious. Subconscious content and memories can be easily brought into the consciousness awareness of the ego-mind. Unconscious content and memories fall into two categories: those that can be brought into the conscious awareness through specific, directed psychotherapeutic interventions, and those that cannot be brought into consciousness awareness.

In the former category are the traumas we experience *in utero* and during the first two years of our lives when the reptilian mind-brain is the dominant decision-making authority. In the latter category is the content and memories of the reptilian mind-brain that control the homeostatic (biological) functions that keep us alive. We only become conscious of our homeostatic functions when the body's survival needs are not being met: whenever we experience uncomfortable physical sensations or physiological pain.

The soul

Your soul is a field of conscious awareness that identifies with your energy field. It is who you are. You don't have a soul, you are a soul. Your soul and the soul of every other human being is an individuated aspect of the universal energy field from which everything in our physical world arises. Because the soul identifies with your energy field and not with your physical body, your soul lives in four-dimensional energetic reality. The soul knows it cannot die and consequently, has no fears. Not only does the soul have no fears, it also has no needs. The reason it has no needs is that at the energetic level of its existence it creates what it desires through its thoughts.

Because our souls are individuated aspects of the universal energy field, they feel a sense of connectedness to every other soul. Consequently, at the soul level, we live in oneness. There is no separation. When you live in a world of oneness, giving is the same as receiving: when you give to others, you give to yourself.

Even though the soul has no needs in the way that the ego has needs, it does have desires. The soul's principal desires are self-expression, connection and contribution. The soul incarnates into three-dimensional material awareness to fulfil these desires. The purpose of the soul's desires is to recreate its four-dimensional (4-D) reality in three-dimensional (3-D) awareness. You know your soul's desires are being met when you feel your life has meaning; when you can connect with others at a deep level, and when you can use your gifts and talents to contribute to making a difference in the world. The only things preventing the soul from fulfilling its desires are the ego's fears about meeting its deficiency needs: our survival, safety and security needs. The ego's fears about meeting its deficiency needs keep it firmly attached to its physical, social and cultural identity.

The soul incarnates into a human foetus by willing itself to be present in three-dimensional material reality. The soul's will to be present in three-dimensional material reality is the source of the ego's will to survive.

The universal energy field

The universal energy field, sometimes called the Great Field or the Zero-Point Energy Field, is the ground of all being, from which everything in our material world arises. The origin of this ground of all being is referred to by the scientific establishment in our three-dimensional material reality as the "big bang", the cosmological event that occurred 13.8 billion years ago, that gave rise to our physical universe.

> The Big bang produced, from nothing, a universe composed of photons, energy-packed radiations, unimaginably hot and compressed beyond description, a soup of energy, nearly homogenous throughout. The universe was born as an undifferentiated unity.[1]

The universal energy field is the energetic container for everything that exists. It is a field of universal awareness that forms the background from which everything in our physical world emerges.

The personal conscious

The personal conscious is the executive decision-making centre that interprets what is happening in our world. It contains the memories of which we are immediately aware. We use our conscious awareness to make what we believe are logical and rational decisions about how to respond to changes in our external environment so that we can get our needs met. As adults, the processes, content and memories of the personal conscious are related to the operation of the neocortex mind-brain.

The personal subconscious

The personal subconscious supports conscious mind in making decisions when the personal conscious is engaged in thinking about other matters. The personal subconscious contains memories, which although not immediately accessible, can be brought into conscious awareness. The content and memories held in the personal subconscious can affect how we react to situations when a present moment experience triggers an emotional memory stored in the subconscious mind. As adults, the processes, content and memories of the personal subconscious are related to the operation of the limbic mind-brain, which I also refer to as the subconscious ego-mind.

The personal unconscious

The personal unconscious supports the conscious mind in making decisions about the regulation of the functioning of the body. The personal unconscious contains memories or imprints that are not readily available for inspection. It requires special therapeutic skills or hypnotherapy to access this content. The content and memories held in the personal unconscious not only affect our moods, behaviour and decision-making, they also affect our physical and mental health. The processes, content and memories of the personal unconscious are related to the operation of the reptilian mind-brain, which I also refer to in this book as the body-mind.

All living creatures have some form of body-mind that controls the body's functioning. The awareness and processes that control the body-mind are not accessible to the conscious mind. The body-mind communicates with the conscious mind through sensations that are felt in the body. The key channels of communication between the body-mind and the conscious ego-mind are physical sensations, pain and bodily discomfort.

Mind/brain

You will note that throughout this book I refer to decision-making modalities of the conscious, subconscious and unconscious mind as belonging to a "mind/brain". I do this because I believe the mind is part of our energetic existence, and the brain is part of our material existence. The brain can die, but the mind lives on in the energy field of the soul. The brain, like the body, belongs to what I will be referring to as our three-dimensional (3-D) material reality. Three-dimensional reality is the world the ego-mind identifies with, even though its home is in the energetic world. The soul-mind belongs to what I will be referring to as our four-dimensional (4-D) energetic reality.

Instincts

Instincts are the beliefs of the body-mind that exist at the level of the species mind. They are designed to meet the body's survival needs. An organism does not need a brain to have instincts, but it does need a mind. Cells, for example, do not have a brain, but they have instinctual responses that enable them to react to threats, protect themselves and find energy sources that enable them to survive. Wherever there is awareness, there is mind, and the mind is always in the energy field.

Beliefs

Beliefs are always personal. Some of them may originate at the cultural level, but they always belong to the individual. Beliefs are assumptions we hold to be true. They may or may not be true; that is why they are called assumptions.

Beliefs are always contextual. Our principal beliefs are formed in the specific physical, social and cultural frameworks of existence that we are brought up in during the first twenty-four years of our lives, when our minds and brains are growing and developing and when we are learning how to get our deficiency needs met. Beliefs can be unconscious, subconscious or conscious.

Unconscious beliefs

These are the beliefs (I will also be calling them imprints) we learn while the reptilian mind/brain is growing and developing. The reptilian mind/brain is dominant—the main interface between "self" and the external world, and the executive decision-making authority—from the first trimester of gestation up to around the age of two. Our personal imprints are triggered whenever we experience an event that reminds us of a trauma or a time when we struggled to get our survival needs met during the period when the reptilian mind/brain was growing and developing.

Subconscious beliefs

These are the beliefs we learn while the limbic mind/brain is growing and developing. The limbic mind-brain is dominant from around the age of two until the age of about seven. Our subconscious beliefs are triggered whenever we experience an event that reminds of us of a situation that occurred while the limbic mind/brain was growing and developing, both positive experiences, where we got our safety needs met, and negative experiences when we struggled and failed to get our safety needs met.

Conscious beliefs

These are the beliefs we learn while the neocortex mind/brain is growing and developing. The neocortex mind/brain is dominant from around the age of eight onwards. Our conscious beliefs are triggered whenever we experience changes in our lives. We use our beliefs to understand what is happening so that we can make a decision as to whether the situation we are experiencing is a threat to our security or an opportunity to increase our security.

Rapid emergent learning

I call the learning that takes place during the first 24 years of our lives, rapid emergent learning because we are learning at the same time as our mind/brains are forming. Consequently, the imprints and beliefs we learn during this period of our lives tend to become hard-wired into our brains in the form of synaptic connections. What we learn, particularly during the first two years of life when the reptilian mind/brain (body-mind) is growing and developing and the next five years when the limbic mind/brain (emotional mind) is growing and developing, conditions our reactions and responses to life events for the rest of our lives. Normal emergent learning takes place after our rational mind/brain has become fully functional around our mid-20s.

Values

Whatever we consider to be important that is missing from our lives or whatever we want more of, is what we value. The three main things the ego values are staying alive, safety and security. The three main things the soul values are self-expression, connection and contribution.

Our values can be positive or potentially limiting. Positive values, such as friendship, trust and creativity, help us to build relationships, connect with others and make a contribution to the world. Potentially limiting values do just the opposite. They may help us meet our ego's short-term needs, but in the long-term they are divisive. They are counterproductive to the desires of the soul; they suppress self-expression and prevent connection and contribution. Potentially limiting values are sourced from the fears the ego has about getting its needs met. Potentially limiting values support the ego's self-interest. Examples of potentially limiting values include greed, blame and status-seeking.

While the ego-mind is dominant, during at least the first half of our lives, we let our beliefs guide our decision-making; when the soul-mind starts to make it presence felt, during the second half of our lives, we let our values guide our decision-making. If we fail to activate the soul, we will tend to use our beliefs for decision-making throughout the whole of our lives.

At the soul level, we all share the same values because we are all individuated aspects of the same universal energy field; therefore, we desire the same things. At the ego level, we are all brought up in different contexts, therefore, the beliefs we learn about getting our needs met may be different. For this reason, beliefs are always contextual: values are universal. Beliefs separate; values unite.

DNA

Viewed through the lens of 3-D material awareness, deoxyribonucleic acid (DNA) is a molecule that carries the genetic instructions used in the development, functioning and reproduction of living organisms. Viewed through the lens of 4-D energetic awareness DNA is an energetic field of information and instructions that belong in part to the energy field of the species and in part to the energy field of the soul templates of the parents that make a child. In 3-D material awareness, specific parts of DNA molecule are called genes. In 4-D energetic awareness, genes are specific aspects of the energy field of a DNA molecule.

Conventions

Having provided some clarity regarding the terminology I will be using in this book let me now explain some of the conventions and structural approaches I will be using.

Minds and brains

I frequently juxtapose the words "mind" and "brain" together to form the word "mind/brain". I use this form of expression to emphasize that the mind and the brain are not the same. They exist in different realms of reality. The brain is the 3-D material instrument of the 4-D energetic mind that coordinates the functioning of the body. Causation starts in the 4-D energetic mind and is translated into physical action by the 3-D material brain. When I want to emphasize either the material or physical aspect of the mind/brain, I will use the term "brain". When I want to emphasize the energetic decision-making mechanism of the mind/brain, I will use the term "mind". Since everything that is composed of matter has an energy field, I will also from time to time refer to the "mind" as "the energy field of the brain".

Once again, to give emphasis to the different realms of operation of the mind and brain, I will sometimes use the term "body-mind" to refer to the decision-making aspect of the reptilian mind/brain, and I will use the term "emotional mind" to refer to the decision-making aspect of the limbic mind/brain. I will also use the term "rational mind" to refer to the decision-making aspect of the neocortex mind/brain. Normally, when I refer to the ego-mind, I will be referring to the emotional mind and rational mind as a single unit of decision-making to differentiate it from the body-mind and soul-mind.

Stages and levels

We grow in stages of psychological development, and we operate at levels of consciousness. Normally, the level of consciousness you operate from will be the same as the stage of development you have reached. Sometimes, for example, when we are faced with a threat to our survival, safety or security, we will drop to a lower level of consciousness than the one we are currently operating from. This does not mean we are moving to a lower stage of development. It simply means that we are moving to a lower level of consciousness where we are facing some of the same issues we had when we were at that lower stage of development.

Sometimes for the sake of efficiency, I will drop the word "psychological" and simply refer to stages of development as I have just done.

Life span

To give a historical context to the topics I will be discussing, the first time I mention an individual, who is no longer living, I will provide his or her year of birth and death. If I do not provide this information, you can assume that the individual concerned was still living in 2015.

A summary of the important points references and notes

At the end of each chapter, I will provide a brief summary of the key points and a list of references and notes.

A summary of key points

Here are the main points of the Introduction:

1. The discipline of psychology is a relatively recent addition to human knowledge.
2. There are many psychological theories and approaches to the treatment of mental disorders, each one reflecting the particular philosophical orientation of a specific individual or group of individuals.
3. If we trace the divergence of different approaches to psychology back to their philosophical roots we arrive at the concept of dualism—the splitting of the study of human experience into what are regarded as two ontologically separate categories—the study of matter (the body) and the study of mind (the psyche).

4. Before dualism there was monism. Whereas the proponents of dualism maintain that neither mind nor matter can be reduced to each other in any way, the proponents of monism maintain that only one thing is ontologically basic or prior to everything else.
5. What I am attempting to do in this book is define a larger jurisdiction for psychology that reunites the disciplines of knowledge we have split apart, back into a unified whole. At the core of this whole is energy that displays the property of awareness. Energy that displays the property of awareness is called mind. I will argue that the mind energy is the basis of all life, and everything we perceive in our universe is comprised of mind energy.
6. I will also argue that consciousness arose from awareness when aspects of the unified whole separated from the whole. Viewed through the lens of psychology, separation—the splitting off of parts and the limiting of conscious awareness—is known as repression. Repression leads to distortions of reality and mental disorders.
7. When monism evolved into dualism, we split apart the human psyche—the soul (spirituality)—into two parts, body (science) and mind (psychology), and we created the mental disorder or distortion of reality we call three-dimensional material awareness.
8. Viewed through the lens of psychology, healing occurs when what has been repressed is reintegrated into conscious awareness and given a new, more holistic meaning. This is exactly my purpose in defining a larger jurisdiction for psychology. I propose to reunite body and mind with soul. I shall be calling this new awareness, four-dimensional energetic awareness or the awareness of the soul.
9. In a nutshell, this is what this book is about: defining a psychological theory that integrates body, mind and soul.

References and notes

1. Gerald L. Schroeder, *The Hidden Face of God: Science Reveals the Ultimate Truth* (New York: Touchstone), 2001, p. 41.

1

A LARGER JURISDICTION FOR PSYCHOLOGY

We think of ourselves as material beings, whereas in reality, we are energetic beings. We don't have an inner core, a higher self or a soul: We are the inner core; we are the higher self; we are the soul.

My primary inspiration for writing this book was the following statement from the introduction to the second edition of *Toward a Psychology of Being* by Abraham Maslow.

> There is now emerging over the horizon a new conception of human sickness and human health, a psychology that I find so thrilling and so full of wonderful possibilities that I yield to the temptation to present it publicly even before it is checked and confirmed, and before it can be called reliable scientific knowledge.[1]

What Maslow was courageously attempting to do, was to establish the ground rules for a larger jurisdiction for psychology. What I am attempting to do in this book goes further: I am trying to build a theory of human well-being that unites psychology with spirituality and science. I propose to do this by standing on the shoulders of the cutting-edge thinkers who have gone before me to construct a 4-D energetic model of reality that transcends the limitations of our 3-D material model.

The Seven Levels Model

At the heart of the theory I will be putting before you is what I refer to as the Seven Levels Model. There are two aspects to this Model: the Stages of Psychological Development Model and the Levels of Consciousness Model. We grow in stages of psychological development, and we operate at levels of consciousness. Under normal circumstances, the level of consciousness we operate from will be the same as the stage of psychological development we have reached.

The idea for the Seven Levels Model came to me in 1995 when I came across Abraham Maslow's hierarchy of needs. As I studied Maslow's model, I noticed that with some minor changes, his model could be transposed into a model of consciousness.

Changing from needs to consciousness

The first change I made to Maslow's model was to shift the focus from needs to consciousness. It was evident to me that when people have underlying anxieties or subconscious fears about being able to meet their deficiency needs—survival, relationship and self-esteem needs—their subconscious mind stays focussed on finding ways to satisfy those needs.

For example, when a person has a fear-based belief about not having enough of what they need to survive, no matter how much money they earn they will always want more; they will subconsciously stay focused at the survival level of consciousness until they can release the fear-based belief that they don't have enough. The same is true for the relationship and self-esteem levels of consciousness. When you have a fear-based belief about not being loved or not being recognized, your conscious or subconscious awareness will remain focused at the relationship or self-esteem levels of consciousness until you release those fears.

Expanding the concept of self-actualization

The second change I made to Maslow's model was to expand his concept of self-actualization. I wanted to give more definition to our soul's desires. I achieved this goal by integrating aspects of Vedic philosophy with Maslow's hierarchy of needs. According to Vedic philosophy, our minds have the ability to experience seven states of consciousness.

Whereas we all experience the first three states of consciousness—waking, dreaming and sleeping—almost every day of our lives, we experience the higher states of consciousness infrequently. How often we experience the higher states, depends to a large extent, on the evolution of personal consciousness—the degree to which we have learned how to master our deficiency needs and how far we have advanced in mastering our soul's desires.

According to Vedic philosophy, in the fourth state of consciousness, you begin to identify with your soul. You can engage this state of consciousness through mindfulness. Beyond soul consciousness is the fifth state of consciousness, known as cosmic consciousness. In this state of consciousness, you begin to live in a fear-free state of mental and physiological functioning. You can engage this state of consciousness through meditation. In the sixth state of consciousness, known as God consciousness, you begin to realize there are no "others" out there; just like you, everyone you meet is individuated aspect of the universal energy field. When you are charitable to others, you are charitable to yourself. When you criticize others, you are critical of yourself. In the seventh state of consciousness, known as unity consciousness, you become one with all there is.

The higher states of consciousness are transient: they come, and they go. While you are living in ego awareness, you have no control over the frequency of such experiences. They occur through grace. You can increase the frequency of your experiences of higher states of consciousness by letting go of your fears and learning to listen to the voice of your soul. Eventually, you become one with your soul, and you live in a permanent state of grace.

Transformation

The first realization I had after translating the Vedic states of consciousness to levels of consciousness was that soul consciousness corresponds to Maslow's need to "know and understand" and Carl Jung's concept of "individuation". I call this the transformation level of consciousness. At this level of consciousness, you begin to inquire into the true nature of who you are, independent of the social, cultural and environmental framework of existence in which you were raised. You let go of the fear-based beliefs of your parental programming and social conditioning and become responsible and accountable for every aspect of your life; you become the author of your destiny, an independent soul.

The first level of self-actualization

The second realization I had was that cosmic consciousness corresponds to the first level of self-actualization. I call this the internal cohesion level of consciousness. At this level of consciousness, you begin to align your ego motivations with your soul motivations. You find your calling in life; you embrace your soul purpose, and you fully align the beliefs of your ego with the values of your soul.

The second level of self-actualization

The third realization I had was that God consciousness corresponds to the second level of self-actualization. I call this the making a difference level of consciousness. At this level of consciousness, you fully activate your soul's desire for deep connection. You begin to cooperate with others to make a difference in the world. You also develop a sense of knowing that goes beyond logic and reasoning; your intuition begins to guide your decision-making.

The third level of self-actualization

My last realization was that Unity consciousness corresponds to the third level of self-actualization. I call this the service level of consciousness. At this level of consciousness, you fully activate your soul's desire for contribution. You make your gifts, talents and wisdom available to everyone you meet. You embark on a life of selfless service guided by the inspiration of your soul.

Although I realize the correlations I have made between the Vedic states of consciousness and levels of self-actualization may not be precise, they are sufficiently close to provide insights into the underlying spiritual significance of the process of self-actualization.

Relabeling the lower levels of consciousness

The last change I made to Maslow's hierarchy of needs was to combine his physiological survival level and safety level into a single category. I named this combined level "survival consciousness" because it focusses on issues of physical survival and physical health.

I also renamed Maslow's level of love and belonging: I called it the "relationship" level of consciousness and shifted the main focus of this level from belonging, to the reason for our need to belong: the need to establish loving relationships that allow us to feel safe. When you do not feel safe, you cannot trust. If you cannot trust, your relationships will suffer. I did not rename Maslow's self-esteem level.

Whereas the survival level focuses on our physiological needs, the relationship level, and self-esteem levels are focused on our emotional needs. The transformational level focuses on our mental needs, particularly our need to understand who we are and know ourselves more deeply. The three upper levels of consciousness focus on our spiritual needs.

With these three changes—needs to consciousness, expanding the concept of self-actualization and the relabelling of our basic needs—I was able to construct a model of consciousness that corresponds to the evolution of the human ego and the activation of the human soul. The correspondence between the seven levels model and Maslow's hierarchy of needs is shown in Table 1.1.

Table 1.1: From Maslow's hierarchy of needs to Barrett's levels of consciousness.

Maslow's Hierarchy of Needs	Barrett's Levels of Consciousness
Self-actualization needs	7. Service
	6. Making a difference
	5. Internal cohesion
Know and understand needs	4. Transformation
Self-esteem needs	3. Self-esteem
Belonging needs	2. Relationship
Physiological needs	1. Survival

Cultural Transformation Tools

Shortly after developing the Seven Levels of Consciousness Model, I realized that specific values could be attributed to each level of consciousness, and consequently, if you could ascertain the values of an individual, organization, community or nation, you could identify which levels of consciousness they were operating from.

In 1997, I formed a company, the Barrett Values Centre (BVC), and began to use the seven levels model to map the consciousness of leaders, organizations, and communities all over the world. The values measuring system I developed, based on the Seven Levels of Consciousness Model, became known as the Cultural Transformation Tools (CTT). An overview of how to use the model to measure consciousness can be found in my book *The Metrics of Human Consciousness*[2] and a more detailed account of its application to business cultures and leadership coaching can be found in *The Values-Driven Organization: Unleashing Human Potential for Performance and Profit*[3] and *Evolutionary Coaching*.[4]

Over the subsequent years, based on feedback from users, we fine-tuned the measuring system, improving its reliability and validity. Now, almost twenty years later, we have a well-established and globally-recognized set of tools for mapping the values and measuring the consciousness of individuals and all forms of human group structures. To date (Spring 2016), the CTT have been used to measure the consciousness of more than 6,000 organizations, 4,500 leaders and 25 nations.[5]

Around 2007, I began to recognize that in addition to mapping values to levels of consciousness, the Seven Levels Model could also be used as a framework for identifying the stages of psychological development, the step-by-step journey of personal development that is common to every human being. Figure 1.1 shows the correspondence between the Seven Stages of Psychological Development and the Seven Levels of Consciousness Models.

Figure 1.1: Stages of psychological development and levels of consciousness.

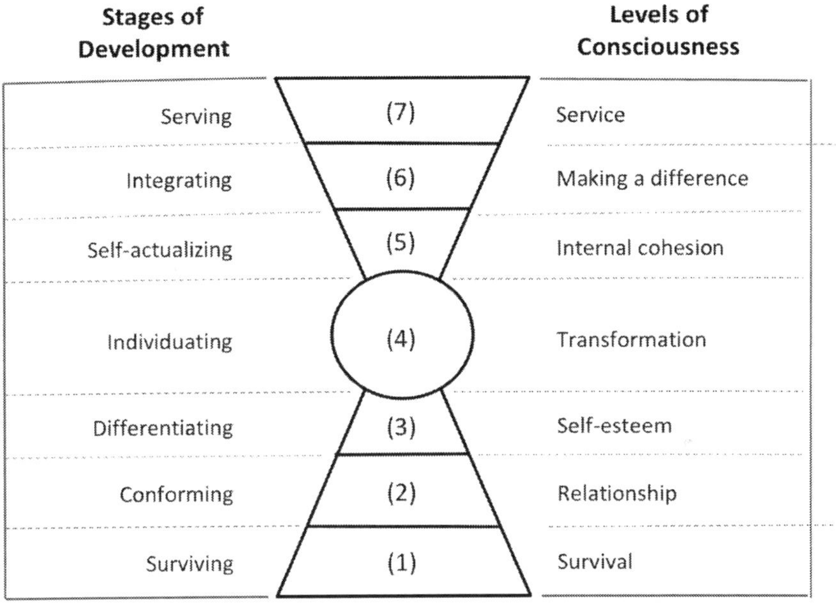

Stages of Development		Levels of Consciousness
Serving	(7)	Service
Integrating	(6)	Making a difference
Self-actualizing	(5)	Internal cohesion
Individuating	(4)	Transformation
Differentiating	(3)	Self-esteem
Conforming	(2)	Relationship
Surviving	(1)	Survival

Deficiency needs and growth needs

Maslow referred to the needs associated with the first three stages of psychological development, as "deficiency" needs, and the needs associated with the last three stages of psychological development, as "growth" or "being" needs. From a psychological perspective, the needs of the first three stage of development correspond to our ego's needs, and the needs of the last three stages of development correspond to our soul's desires. Thus, we can state:

Ego needs = Deficiency needs

and

Growth needs = Being needs = Soul desires

We feel anxious and fearful when we are unable to meet our deficiency needs, but once they are met we no longer pay much attention to them. The joy we experience when we can meet our soul's desires leaves us wanting more. Maslow points out the importance of satisfying our deficiency needs as a foundation for satisfying our growth needs:

> Man's higher nature rests on his lower nature, needing it as a foundation. The best way to develop this higher nature is to fulfil and gratify the lower nature first.[6]

Maslow also makes a direct link between the satisfaction of our needs and health. He states:

> …satisfying our deficiencies avoids illness; growth satisfactions produce positive health.[7]

In other words, when we can satisfy our ego's needs, we stay well, and when we can satisfy our soul's needs, we thrive. Maslow goes on to state:

> …deficit needs are shared by all members of the human species … all people need safety, love and status from their environment … once satiated with these elementary, species-wide necessities … development of individuality can begin … each person proceeds to develop in his own style … development then becomes more determined from within rather than from without … self-actualization is idiosyncratic.[8]

Maslow called the moments we are consciously aware of satisfying our growth needs as "peak" experiences. He describes these experiences in the following way:

> …the powers of a person come together in a particularly efficient and intensely enjoyable way, and in which he is more integrated and less split, more open for experience, more idiosyncratic, more perfectly expressive or spontaneous, or full functioning, more independent of his lower needs, etc.[9]

Here Maslow expresses two important ideas: the idea that self-expression links to the satisfaction of our growth needs; and the idea that aligning our ego motivations with our soul motivations—becoming more integrated and less split—allows us to express ourselves in a particularly efficient and intensely enjoyable way.

We can conclude from these statements that the path to health and well-being involves satisfying our ego's needs and our soul's desires; if we are unable to satisfy the former it will be difficult to satisfy the latter. Without a solid foundation for operating in your physical, social and cultural framework of your existence, you will not be able to focus on satisfying your soul's desires. In other words, satisfying your ego's needs is a necessary foundation for satisfying your soul's desires. When you can satisfy your ego's needs *and* your soul's desires, you will find personal fulfilment and experience a deep sense of well-being.

Understanding spiritual/religious experiences

On this point—the need to focus on the needs of the ego *and* the desires of the soul—Maslow found himself in close alignment with the thinking of the Swiss psychiatrist and psychotherapist, Carl Jung (1875–1961). Maslow and Jung both regarded Freud's theory of the unconscious as being incomplete and unnecessarily negative. They both took exception to Freud's obsession with sexuality as a way of explaining psychological disorders and to his focus on pathology. Maslow summarized the difference between his approach and the Freud's approach in the following way:

> To oversimplify the matter somewhat, it is as if Freud supplied to us the sick half of psychology and we must now fill it out with the healthy half.[10]

In addition to Freud's concept of the personal unconscious, Jung postulated another level of the unconscious, which he referred to as the collective unconscious: a repository of knowledge and information concerning the collective human experience that transcends time and space. For Jung, the conscious integration of the personal and collective unconscious results in a person becoming more whole. He called this process individuation. Jung provides us with a deeper understanding of the term individuation in the following quote:

> The concept of individuation plays a large role in our psychology. In general, it is the process by which individual beings are formed and differentiated; in particular, it is the development of the psychological individual ... as a being distinct from the

general, collective psychology [of the culture]. Individuation, therefore, is a process of differentiation ... having for its goal the development of the individual personality.[11]

Jung considered individuation—the integration of the personal and collective unconscious—to have a spiritual/religious purpose, namely, the fulfilment of our innate potential. In *Modern Man in Search of a Soul* Jung makes this link explicit. He states:

> I have treated many hundreds of patients. Among those in the second half of their life—that is to say over thirty-five—there has not been one whose problem, in the last resort, was not that of finding a religious outlook on life.[12]

Maslow referred to this deeper level of the unconscious as a person's inner nature or the essential core. Like Jung, he considered the recovery of the inner core (the soul) essential to our mental health. Maslow states:

> Each person's inner nature is in part unique to himself and in part species-wide. Since the inner nature is good or neutral rather than bad, it is best to bring it out and to encourage it rather than suppress it.[13]

The idea that we all have an inner core that must be recovered is common to almost all transpersonal theories of psychology. In some of these theories, the ego is referred to as the false self: the mask you wear to get your deficiency needs met. The ego is regarded as an identity you adopt to survive, keep safe and feel secure in the cultural framework of your existence. R. D. Laing (1927–1989), a Scottish psychiatrist who wrote extensively on mental illness, writes about the mask in the following way:

> A man without a mask is indeed very rare. One even doubts the possibility of such a man. Everyone in some measure wears a mask.[14]

We normally define our ego identity by referring to the gender, racial, religious, professional, community and national identities that we assume in the cultural framework of our existence. When I reached my late 30s, I realized that all these identities created layers of separation between me and those with whom I did not share my identities; not only did these identities separate me from others, they also separated me from my soul because at the soul level, we are all connected through the universal energy field.

Since, even at this stage of my life, I was intent on the recovery of my soul, I made a conscious decision to take all forms of separation out of my life. Instead of identifying myself as a white, British, male, Protestant, I decided to become a soul having a human experience and a citizen of the planet. I also decided to embrace my feminine energies and consider myself a member of all religions. With the expanded sense of identity these changes gave me, I was able to pursue my spiritual goals and eliminate the principal layers of separation between me and the rest of humanity.

What I did not realize at the time was that choosing my identity was a significant step in my psychological development. It allowed me to remove the mask of my false self and embrace my true self.

The sooner we learn to let go of the mask of the false self—our ego identity, and embrace who we are—our true self, the sooner we find peace in the world. Marc Gafni, a philosopher and spiritual teacher, writes about the false self and true self in the following way:

> What you need to transcend is your exclusive identification with your separate egoic self. For it is your sense of being a skin-encapsulated ego, that creates the sense of suffocation, fear, and drabness that passes as your life. This fundamental error in identity is the root of virtually all suffering.[15]

Having found your connection to your true self, by letting go of the fears of the false self, we can then move to the next stage of our development, embracing your unique self. Identifying with your unique self allows you to give expression to your innate gifts and talents.

Viktor Frankl (1905–1997), an Austrian neurologist and psychiatrist, describes the task of the unique self in the following way:

> Everyone has his specific vocation or mission in life; everyone must carry out a concrete assignment that demands fulfilment. Therein he cannot be replaced, nor can his life be repeated, thus, everyone's task is unique as his specific opportunity to implement it.[16]

Based on the preceding, when I refer to the ego, I am referring to the false self; when I speak of the soul, I am referring to the true self *plus* the unique self. Thus, we can state:

$$\text{False self} = \text{Ego}$$
$$\text{True self} + \text{Unique self} = \text{Soul}$$

At the level of the true Self, we all share the same values: At the level of the unique self, we all have different skills, gifts, and talents. This, I believe, is what Maslow was referring to when he wrote:

> Each person's inner nature is in part unique to himself and in part species-wide.[17]

The species-wide aspect is our true self; the part that is unique is our unique self.

You begin to let go of your false self and embrace your true self at the individuating stage of psychological development; you begin to embrace your unique self at the self-actualizing stage of development; you give full expression to your unique self at the integrating and serving stages of development.

When you fully embrace your true self and unique self, you become a potent force for change in the world. What you learn about connecting to make a difference at the integrating stage of development provides a foundation for the wisdom you bring to the world at the serving stage of development. At the serving stage, you reach your highest potency: the zenith of your potentiality.

You are now totally connected to your soul, and creativity and synchronicity abound in your life. So long as you listen to your soul's promptings your life will be in a state of flow. You may, from time to time, feel some resistance to your soul's directives, but you must overcome this resistance; you must learn to become the servant of your soul. You must let your soul work through you expressing its unique personality, connecting with others and contributing to the common good.

On several occasions in my 60s, I attempted to resist my soul's impulses but in the end, I always found my soul's arguments persuasive. What I experienced, when I fully committed myself to my soul's promptings, was that providence moved too. The words of explorer and author, William H. Murray summarises my experience precisely.

> A whole stream of events issued from [this] decision, raising in [my] favour all manner of unforeseen incidents, meetings and material assistance, which [I] could have dreamt would have come [my] way.[18]

I have learned not to resist anymore. I have moved from being the "servant of my soul" to "being my soul". I accept my soul's thoughts as my thoughts. I can operate as a soul because I have eliminated fear from my life. However, being human, I still have momentary lapses; I forget who I am and become defensive. One day I am hoping these moments will no longer arise.

As I mentioned earlier, most transpersonal theories of consciousness, recognize the fundamental importance of liberating the inner core. One such theory, known as psychosynthesis, is a movement created and developed by Roberto Assagioli (1888–1974). Assagioli called our inner core, the soul. He also referred to the soul as the spiritual "I" or Higher Self.

Assagioli, like Jung and Maslow, considered the self to have a dual nature: individual (unique self) and universal (true self) at the same time. Assagioli referred to "peak experiences" as experiences of the Higher Unconscious or "Superconscious". In comparing his approach with that of Maslow, Assagioli states:

> He [Maslow] uses the term "being" for the overall range of experiences we call superconscious because one of their characteristics is to give a sense of "fullness of being," a feeling of intensity in existing and living.[19]

Jung, Maslow and Assagioli were not the first to make the link between psychology and religion/spirituality. In the late 1800s and early 1900s, several North American researchers ventured into the arena of the "superconscious". The most well-known is William James (1842–1910), a psychologist-turned-philosopher.

James wrote about the intersection of psychology and religious/spiritual practices in his ground-breaking book, *The Varieties of Religious Experience*, published in 1902. Although he never used the term "peak" experiences, his practical definition of religion is suggestive of this terminology. He states:

> Religion, therefore, as I now ask you arbitrarily to take it, shall mean for us the feelings, acts, and experiences of individual men [or women] in their solitude, so far as they apprehend themselves to stand in relation to whatever they may consider the divine.[20]

In *The Further Reaches of Human Nature*, a book of Maslow's articles published posthumously in 1971, Maslow states:

> What all this means is that so-called spiritual or value-life [meta-motivation], or "higher" life, is on the same continuum (is the same kind or quality of thing) with the life of the flesh or of the body, i.e., the animal life, the material life, the "lower" life. That is, the spiritual life is part of our biological life. It is the "highest" part of it.[21]

I also take this position in this book, but I turn this phrase around: *our biological life is part of our spiritual (energetic) life*. I know this may sound strange, but it is only strange because of the way we have been trained to look at ourselves through the lens of 3-D material awareness and our five physical senses. We think of ourselves as material beings, whereas in reality we are energetic beings. The 3-D material world we live in is contained within a 4-D energetic world. That is why I say our biological life is part of our spiritual life; the material and physical is contained within the energetic.

When you look at the world we live in through the lens of 4-D energetic awareness, it becomes very clear that we are not who we think we are. We don't have an inner core, a higher self or a soul: We are the inner core; we are the higher self; we are the soul.

When we live our lives in alignment with the motivations of our soul, we experience a deep sense of well-being and robust physical health because we are living in a state of psychological and energetic coherence. When we fail to live in psychological and energetic coherence, we experience emotional upsets, mental suffering, stress, and psychosomatic disorders.

It is important to remember that stress is not a derivative of what is going on in your life; it is a derivative of your thoughts about what is going on in your life; about the meaning you give to situations. It is not your work, nor your relationships that are inducing your stress, it is the fear-based beliefs about getting your needs met that create stress.

The same is true for pressure. Stress and pressure are the surface reflections of your internal landscape; of the fear-based beliefs you hold about how to get your survival, safety and security needs met in your current circumstances.[22] Stress and pressure come from within, not from any external source. Your boss may press you to get a job done, but you are the one who converts this demand into pressure and stress. Without your inner fears, there is no pressure and stress, there is only what is.

Like many others modern scientists, Dr. Alan Watkins, an honorary senior lecturer in neuroscience and psychological medicine at Imperial College, London, lays the blame for stress and disease firmly in the psychological arena. In *Coherence: The Secret Science of Brilliant Leadership*[23] he asks the question: "What impacts health and happiness?" He replies to his question:

> Well, it's not probably what you think. There is now a considerable amount of scientific data showing that mismanaged emotion is the cause. Mismanaged emotion is the "superhighway" to disease and distress.[24]

From my perspective, the term "mismanaged emotion" is another way of saying ego-soul misalignment, which in turn is another way of saying your energy field is suffering from energetic instability because you are either unable to get your ego's needs met or you are unable to meet your soul's desires.

You know your energy field is unstable when you feel uneasy, impatient, frustrated, annoyed, anxious, jealous, stressed, depressed, etc. All of the feelings associated with emotional distress are indicators of ego-soul misalignment.

Watkins justifies his assertion that *mismanaged emotions are the superhighway to disease and distress* with pages of facts and figures concerning heart disease, cancer, strokes, and depression.[25] I have summarized his conclusions here:[26]

- There is a mountain of evidence linking prolonged negative emotion to heart disease, cancer, stroke, and depression.
- Emotion is significantly more important to health and happiness than exercise or what you eat.

- Feelings arise from our awareness of emotions. Everyone has emotions. Not everyone is aware of their emotions.
- Emotional mastery is critical to health and happiness, critical thinking, decision-making and clarity of thought.
- Emotional coherence is created by the development of emotional intelligence, emotional literacy, and emotional self-management.

Watkins describes coherence in a similar manner to the way in which Maslow describes a peak experience. Watkins states:

> Coherence is, in essence, the biological underpinning of what elite performers call the flow state … a state of maximum efficiency and super effectiveness, where body and mind are one.[27]

Because biology can be reduced to energy—all cells are composed of molecules, which are composed of atoms, which are composed of electrons, neutrons, and protons, which are composed of elementary particles, which are waves of information in your energy field—I have reconfigured Watkins' statement to read "coherence is the energetic underpinning of the flow state".

The dichotomy between our physical experience and our energetic experience lies at the root of the human fallacy. It is part of what I refer to as the two-world problem. We think we live in a physical world, but in actuality, we live in an energetic world. As I will show in the following chapter, there isn't a two-world problem; it is all a matter of perception.

A summary of key points

Here are the main points of Chapter 1:

1. We grow in stages of psychological development, and we operate at levels of consciousness. Under normal circumstances, the level of consciousness we operate from will be the same as the stage of psychological development we have reached.
2. Maslow referred to the needs associated with the first three stages of psychological development as "deficiency" needs, and the needs

associated with the last three stages of psychological development, as "growth" or "being" needs.

3. We feel anxious and fearful when we are not able to meet our deficiency needs, but once they are met we no longer pay them much attention. The joy we experience when we can meet our growth needs leaves us wanting more.
4. I prefer to call the "needs" of the first three stages of development, ego needs. For me, the terms "ego needs" and "deficiency needs" are equivalent. I also prefer to call the needs of the last three stages of development "soul desires". For me, the terms "growth or being needs" and "soul desires" are equivalent.
5. The path to health and well-being involves satisfying your ego's needs and your soul's desires. If you are unable to satisfy the former, it will be difficult to satisfy the latter.
6. Your false self is the mask you create to get your deficiency needs met during the ego stages of your development.
7. Your true self is the aspect of your soul self that is energetically connected to every other human being, independent of race, religion, nationality or gender.
8. Your unique self is the aspect of your soul that is unique to you: your skills, gifts and talents.
9. We think of ourselves as material beings, whereas in reality we are energetic beings. We don't have an inner core, a higher self or a soul: We are the inner core; we are the higher self; we are the soul.
10. When we live our lives in alignment with the motivations of our soul, we experience a deep sense of well-being and robust physical health because we are living in a state of energetic coherence.

References and notes

1. Abraham Maslow, *Toward a Psychology of Being* (Second Edition) (Van Nostrand Reinhold: New York), 1968, p. 3.
2. Richard Barrett, *The Metrics of Human Consciousness* (London: Fulfilling Books), 2015.
3. Richard Barrett, *The Values-Driven Organization: Unleashing Human Potential for Performance and Profit* (London: Fulfilling Books), 2014.

4. Richard Barrett, *Evolutionary Coaching: A Values-Based Approach to Unleashing Human Potential* (London: Fulfilling Books), 2014.
5. Abraham H. Maslow, *Toward a Psychology of Being* (second edition) (New York: Van Nostrand Reinhold), 1968, p. 173.
6. Ibid., p. 32.
7. Ibid., pp. 33–34.
8. Ibid., p. 97.
9. Ibid., p. 5.
10. Ibid.
11. Carl Jung, *Collected Works*, 6, p. 757.
12. Carl Jung, *Modern Man in Search of a Soul*, 1933, p. 229.
13. Abraham Maslow, *Toward a Psychology of Being* (Second Edition) (New York: Van Nostrand Reinhold), 1968, pp. 4–5.
14. R. D. Laing, *The Divided Self* (London: Penguin Books), 2010, p. 95.
15. Marc Gafni, *Your Unique Self: The Radical Path to Personal Enlightenment* (Tucson: Integral Publishers), 2012, p.17.
16. www.brainyquote.com/quotes/authors/v/viktor_e_frankl.html#W3iAZs5WS1pFl1sM.99
17. Abraham Maslow, *Toward a Psychology of Being* (Second Edition) (New York: Van Nostrand Reinhold), 1968, pp. 4–5.
18. William H. Murray, *The Scottish Himalayan Expedition* (London: Dent), 1951.
19. Roberto Assagioli, *Transpersonal Development: The Dimension Beyond Psychosynthesis* (Findhorn: Smiling Way), 2007, p. 23.
20. William James, *The Varieties of Religious Experience* (New York: Penguin Books) 1982, p. 31.
21. Abraham Maslow, *Toward a Psychology of Being* (Second Edition) (New York: Van Nostrand Reinhold), 1968, p. 97.
22. Andrew Bernstein, *The End of Sress* (London: Piatkus), 2010, p. 12.
23. Dr. Alan Watkins, *Coherence: The Secret Science of Brilliant Leadership* (London: Kogan Page), 2014.
24. Ibid., p. 79.
25. Ibid., pp. 77–139.
26. Ibid., pp. 138–139.
27. Ibid.

2

THE PROBLEM WITH PERCEPTION

Perception is the root of reality. What you believe, is what you perceive. Your perception will become clear when you look through the eyes of your soul.

The question I had in my mind when I started working on this book was a larger version of the question that Abraham Maslow posed at the beginning of *Toward a Psychology of Being*. The question he asked was, "Is there a larger jurisdiction for psychology?" As soon as I started to research this question, I encountered what I call the two-world problem, otherwise known as dualism. This is what Wikipedia has to say about dualism:

> Dualism is closely associated with the philosophy of René Descartes (1596–1650), which holds that the mind is a nonphysical substance. Descartes clearly identified the mind with consciousness and self-awareness and distinguished this from the brain as the seat of intelligence. Hence, he was the first to formulate the mind–body problem in the form in which it exists today.[1]

Dualism maintains a rigid distinction between the realms of mind and matter. Monism maintains there is a single unifying reality from which everything can be explained. Dualism, or the mind-body problem as it is also known in philosophy, is about the relationship between mind and matter, and, in particular, the relationship between consciousness and the brain, where the mind is seen as being synonymous with consciousness, and the brain is seen as being synonymous with matter.

In more recent years, the mind-body problem has become known as the Hard Problem of Consciousness. The hard problem is how to explain phenomenal experiences: Does consciousness arise out of matter (the brain) or does matter arise out of consciousness (the mind)?

It is clear to me that if consciousness arises out of matter, which is the current assumption of science, there cannot be a larger jurisdiction for psychology because mind could not influence matter; thoughts could not influence the physical well-being of our bodies, and there would be no psychosomatic illnesses. If matter arises out of consciousness, or is dependent on consciousness, then there is a larger jurisdiction for psychology because the mind can influence matter.

These words by E. F. Schumacher explain my point:

> In a hierarchic structure, the higher does not merely possess powers that are additional to and exceed those possessed by the lower: It also has power over the lower, the power of organising the lower and using it for its own purposes.[2]

In other words, if consciousness is higher than matter then consciousness has power over matter. Here are a few examples of how consciousness has power over matter.

Sunflowers or in French, "tournesols" (turn to the sun) get their name because the heads of the plant follow the sun. The sunflower is able to track the sun because it can perceive the sun's rays. The sunflower does not have a brain, but it has awareness. This awareness enables the flower to get its energy needs met in a process called photosynthesis. In other words, because the flower follows the sun we can state that awareness (consciousness) has power over matter and the purpose of this awareness, as far as the sunflower is concerned, is maximizing the input of energy so it can survive and grow.

Atoms also possess awareness. For example, the orbiting electrons of an atom of a specific element can differentiate between the orbiting electrons of other elements. When the orbiting electrons of atom A are in proximity to the orbiting electrons of atom B, the atoms bond together to form a new substance; but when the orbiting electrons of atom A are in proximity to the orbiting electrons of atom C, the atoms do not bond. Without awareness, the orbiting electrons of atom A would not be able to differentiate between the electrons of atoms B and C. Therefore, consciousness, in the form of awareness, affects how the building blocks of matter (atoms) organize themselves.

DNA is another example. DNA is a molecule that contains all the instructions for human life. DNA, like all molecules, is comprised of atoms, which in our 3-D world of material awareness are comprised of energetic particles. In our 4-D world, these particles are energetic waves of information (instructions). It is these waves of information, not the material particles that direct our growth and development. Over time, and based on species feedback, the content of the waves of information contained in a DNA molecule change. These changes allow species to evolve. The overall direction that evolution takes is always towards an increase in the possibilities for survival and the evolution of conscious awareness.

Finally, I would like to draw on the work of Bernardo Kastrup, a scientist, and successful entrepreneur. He states:

> ...the function of the brain is to localize consciousness, pinning it to the space-time reference point implied by the physical body. ... When not subject to this localization mechanism, the mind is unbound. ... Therefore, by localizing the mind, the brain filters our consciousness of anything that is not correlated with the body's perspective, like a radio receiver selecting from among a variety of stations.[3]

Even though the human mind/brain is surrounded by frequencies of vibration coming from a larger multi-dimensional energetic continuum, it is constrained in the frequencies it can intercept by the body's five physical senses. Like the dials on a radio receiver, the body's senses can only register a narrow band of frequencies, thereby preventing us from intercepting and interpreting the larger domain of our existence: the 4-D energetic frequencies of the soul and the universal energy field. What we are not aware of is still there, it is just not in our conscious awareness.

Although mystics and shaman have been aware of the unity of the physical and energetic worlds for millennia, it wasn't until the early part of the twentieth century, with the development of the quantum field theory, that scientists began to acknowledge that there was a crack in our 3-D material interpretation of the world. Albert Einstein (1879–1955) was aware of this crack. He fully recognized that we live in a 4-D energetic continuum. He put it this way:

> The non-mathematician is seized by a mysterious shuddering when he hears of four-dimensional things, by a feeling that is not unlike the occult. But there is no more commonplace statement than the world in which we live is a four-dimensional continuum.[4]

Einstein was not alone in this way of thinking. Ervin László, a Hungarian-born philosopher of science, describes the two-world problem in the following way: he calls the observable, manifest, physical 3-D world the M-dimension (M for material or manifest), and he calls the unobservable, energetic 4-D world—the world of the soul—the A-dimension. The A-dimension (Akashic or energetic dimension) is a universal field of information and potentiality that is in constant interaction with the M-dimension.

> ... the A-dimension [energetic] dimension is prior: it is the generative ground of the particles and systems of particles that emerge in the M-dimension [material] dimension.[5]

Max Planck (1858–1947), a theoretical physicist, who was one of the originators of quantum theory, is quoted as saying: "I regard consciousness as fundamental. I regard matter as derivative from consciousness. We cannot get behind consciousness."

Even though we derive our sense of personal reality from focusing our attention on the 3-D material world, what we are observing is just a thin sliver of a much larger energetic world.

One of the links we have to the energetic world is our thoughts. Our thoughts are energetic impulses of positive, neutral or negative intention. Consequently, whatever thoughts you are thinking not only influence the energetic vibration of your energy field (the body-mind) but the energetic vibration of the world around you. When you walk into a place that is being used for spiritual practices, you can literally feel the energetic vibration of love and peace. If you have ever been into the inner sanctum of the Taj Mahal, a beautiful creation to celebrate love, you will recognize what I mean.

Fear-based thoughts make things feel heavy and serious, whereas love-based thoughts make things feel light and cheerful. This is because the energy of fear has a low frequency of vibration and the energy of love has a high frequency vibration. Love energy feels light because it connects (people); fear energy feels heavy because it separates (people), it goes against the natural state of energetic order. We feel "at home" in our soul when we love, and we feel "separate" from our soul when we fear. Feelings are the antennae that allow us to tune into the status of our ego-soul dynamic.

When the fear-based energies of the ego-mind are juxtaposed with the love-based energies of the soul-mind, you feel a sense of instability in your energy field and sensations of discomfort in your body. As you release the fear-based energies of your ego-mind and align with the love-based energies of your soul-mind, the ego-mind and the soul-mind come into energetic alignment, and your body feels vital and healthy. The quote from Maslow I used earlier describes this process:

> ...the powers of a person come together in a particularly efficient and intensely enjoyable way in which he is more integrated and less split.[6]

The key words here are "he is more integrated and less split". In other words, when we raise the frequency of vibration of the ego-mind by releasing our fears, we align with the frequency of the vibration of the soul-mind.

In speaking of the human energy field, John James, a researcher in transpersonal psychology from Australia, describes our situation in the following way:

> Ever since Einstein wrote, "the field is the only reality," we have increasingly come to realize that the universe embodies both these realms [energy and matter], and though they may appear contradictory, they are in fact mutually enfolding [because] everything is both vibration and matter. ...everything is intimately connected through fields of energy. Separation is, therefore, an illusion.[7]

To get a deeper understanding of the relationship between our 3-D physical/material reality and our soul's 4-D energetic reality, I am going to ask you to participate in an exercise.

The five-finger exercise

Take a flat sheet of paper and imagine that there is a small person living on the surface of the paper in what is known as "Flatland". For this person, the world has length and breadth, but no height. In other words, this person operates in a world of two-dimensional awareness (2-D awareness). She cannot perceive height. Now along comes a human being (you) with 3-D awareness (you can perceive height) and you place the fingers of one hand on the paper, on the surface of Flatland. See Figure 2.1.

Figure 2.1: The projection of five fingers into two-dimensional awareness.

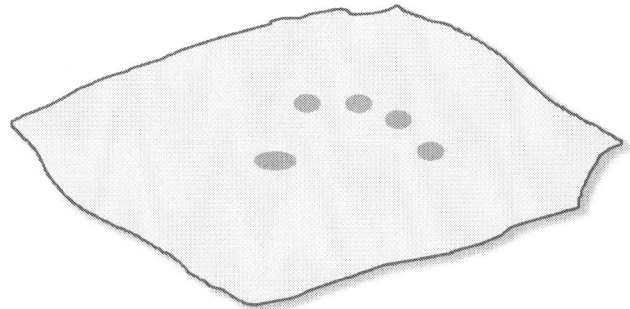

Imagine now that the person living in Flatland is out for a morning stroll. When passing this place yesterday, she noticed nothing unusual. Suddenly, overnight, five circles have appeared (the projection into two-dimensional awareness of your five finger tips). The two-dimensional being is mystified by the appearance of the five circles. She calls her friend, a two-dimensional scientist, and asks her to explain the nature of the five circles. The scientist explores the five circles using her two-dimensional logic.

Her experiments show that the circles can move independently within certain limits, but if she puts a large enough force on one circle eventually it will appear to drag the other circles with it (although the fingers of the hand are separate, they are connected, but in a dimension of awareness that the two-dimensional scientist cannot perceive).

The two-dimensional scientist repeats her experiments. She builds sets of equations to explain the relationship of the circles to each other and before too long she believes she knows everything there is to know about the five circles. She publishes a paper about the circles and calls a meeting of the Academy of Two-Dimensional Scientists to show them her discovery. The two-dimensional scientists repeat the experiments and get very similar results. Everyone in the two-dimensional world believes they know all there is to know about the five circles.

Viewed from the perspective of 3-D awareness, we know that these are not five circles. They are five connected fingers that form part of a living organism. The two-dimensional beings are completely unaware of this larger picture. They believe the five circles are separate, but also linked in some manner which they cannot perceive. They have equations to explain these linkages. Their equations are symbolic: they do not convey the full reality of the connection that exists at the third-dimension of consciousness. The two-dimensional scientists are tuned into the frequencies of two-dimensional awareness and cannot pick up the frequencies of 3-D awareness.

This is exactly the situation we find ourselves in with regard to the fourth dimension of awareness. We have countless experiences that appear unconnected, but, in reality, are linked. They are linked in the fourth dimension of consciousness. Some of these experiences we can explain with our 3-D logic; this is the domain of science, and some we cannot explain. We have a range of names we can use for the experiences we cannot explain. Depending on the context, we can call them paranormal, magical, miraculous, spiritual or synchronistic.

These words are disguises for our ignorance. Because we rely on our 3-D awareness, we cannot perceive the linkages that exist in the higher dimensions of consciousness where these experiences originate. The reason they are beyond our comprehension is that our minds are focused on the partial information we receive from our five physical senses. Our physical senses are only tuned in to interpreting what is happening in our 3-D material reality. As long as we identify with our physical body and its senses, we will be unaware of what is happening in our 4-D energetic reality.

One of the most important connections we have to the higher dimensions of reality are our emotions and feelings, the shifts in the energy field of the ego-mind and soul-mind that occur when we get our needs met or fail to get our needs met. As you pursue your psychological development, you find yourself connecting with your soul's 4-D energetic reality through your intuition and inspiration.

The comb analogy

There is another way of explaining the two-world problem. Take out a comb and cover up the top half. What you see are the unconnected teeth of the comb. You see the separation. When you uncover the top half of the comb, you see that the teeth are joined at a higher level. You see connectedness; you see unity. Without the higher-level connection, the comb would fall apart and would not fulfil a useful purpose.

As human beings, this is how we are. What we perceive through our 3-D awareness are separate human beings (the teeth of the comb). When we raise our awareness to the "fourth-dimension" of consciousness, we can begin to understand and feel the connection to other souls; we begin to appreciate the unity.

Just as it is difficult to understand the meaning and purpose of the separate teeth until we are aware that they belong to a comb, so too it is difficult for us to understand our meaning and purpose until we become aware of who we are and our connection to other souls. We are not separate; we are connected through our energy fields in the fourth-dimension of consciousness. We are all individuated aspects of the same universal energy field.

Newtonian mechanics versus quantum mechanics

Based on this understanding, it quickly becomes obvious that if we rely solely on our 3-D awareness to explain our reality, we will not have a complete idea of who we are or the world in which we live.

Just like the two-dimensional scientists who believed they knew all there was to know about the five circles, until about a century ago our 3-D scientists believed they knew all there was to know about our material world. Everything could be explained by Newtonian mechanics.

In 1900, Lord Kelvin (1824–1907), a British mathematical physicist and engineer, summed up the state of science in the following statement:

"There is nothing new to be discovered in physics now. All that remains is more and more precise measurement."

Twenty-five years later, quantum field theory began to emerge onto the scientific stage. Our 3-D scientists had to face up to the fact that there was a crack in 3-D material reality. They discovered that there was a macro world of objects (made up of particles) that we find in our 3-D material world, and a micro world of energy (waves of information) that we find in our 4-D energetic world.

What we discovered through quantum theory was all that was necessary to bridge these two worlds was an observer. When a person is present, the energy waves of potentiality collapse into a specific outcome that aligns with the beliefs of the observer.

The reason we are so mesmerized with Newtonian (classical) mechanics is that it accurately describes the movement of objects and systems susceptible to our 3-D human perception: objects that are larger than a molecule and smaller than a planet, at temperatures close to those that living organisms can survive in, and going at speeds significantly less than the speed of light. When these boundary conditions are violated, and we move into the micro world of atomic particles, classical mechanics no longer holds sway. This is where quantum mechanics takes over. Physicists were able to connect the causal energy of the mind with our 3-D material reality. Everything in the universe has an energetic dimension including every aspect of our physical bodies. Even the brain and our physical senses that we use to interpret our reality are energetic in nature.

> [If you focussed] on the structure of the atom, you would see nothing; you would observe a physical void. The atom has no physical structure, we have no physical structure; Atoms are made out of invisible energy, not tangible matter.[8]

Niels Bohr (1885–1962), one of the originators of quantum theory, puts it like this: "Everything we call real is made of things that cannot be regarded as real." What is "real" is not what we see, hear, smell, taste or touch; it is what we feel. Everything we see, hear, smell, taste or touch is a 3-D material representation of an energy field. Our emotions and our feelings are our connection to that energetic world. What we feel are energy shifts: energy if motion. This is why feeling is so important to managing our ego-soul dynamics. We cannot know what is happening in our energy field if we are not in touch with our feelings. Whenever we block our feelings, we cut ourselves off from the world of our soul and our true reality.

What we can conclude from the five-finger exercise is that materiality is not a property of the world; it is a property of our senses. What we observe in our 3-D world is energy in the form of matter.

Edward O. Wilson, Professor Emeritus at Harvard University and one of the world's pre-eminent biologists and naturalists, also points out the limitations of our physical senses. He states:

> Vision is based in Homo sapiens on an almost infinitesimal sliver of energy.[9]

Wilson concludes:

> …we are aware of only minute slivers of space-time and even less of the energy fields, in which we exist.[10]

Plato's cave

Another way of thinking about our limited 3-D perspective is described by the story of Plato's cave. In this allegory, Plato describes the reality of a group of prisoners who have spent all their lives in a cave chained up, and facing a blank wall. These prisoners watch shadows projected on the wall from things passing in front of a fire behind them, and they give names to these shadows. The shadows and the names they give to them represent their reality.

Plato uses this story to explain that philosophers are like prisoners who escape from the cave and come to understand that the shadows on the wall are symbols of another reality. We can regard the shadows on the wall as representing as our 3-D perception; only when we leave the cave do we discover our 4-D perception. From this higher level of awareness, we can now understand more clearly the true meaning of the shadows we saw in our 3-D awareness.

In other words, as long as we identify with our body and make use of its physical senses to interpret our reality we are like the prisoners in the cave. What we can see, hear, smell, taste and feel are only the objects and sounds that vibrate at frequencies that our senses can detect. The rest of our energetic world goes unnoticed. The only way we can resolve the two-world problem is to stop identifying with the ego's material world and start identifying with the soul's energetic world.

This shift in perception, from material awareness to energetic awareness, brings a new perspective to our understanding of the meaning of health; one that aligns more closely with Eastern traditions.

Beyond death

Finally, to help illustrate in a more pragmatic way the unseen connections we have to the 4-D energetic world of souls, I would like to recount two stories.

In 2008, my mother moved into a nursing home. She was 98 years old. The only reason she moved into the home was because of troubles with her knees; she found it difficult climbing the stairs in her house. Otherwise, she was in good health. Shortly after she moved into the nursing home, I left America and moved to England so I could be close to her. I moved into my mother's house.

Just after she reached the age of 99, my mother caught pneumonia and almost died in hospital. She survived and went back to the nursing home. She was now bedridden and unable to take care of herself. Her health gradually deteriorated over the next ten months.

One morning, around six o'clock, a few days after my mother's 100th birthday, I had a remarkable dream. I dreamt about a female form suddenly appearing and hugging me. My dream was so vivid, quite unlike any other dream I have ever had before, or since. A little later, around seven-thirty, just after I had finished my breakfast, the phone rang. It was the warden from the home where my mother was living. She told me my mother had died. I realized then that my "dream" was my mother's soul visiting me.

Within 24 hours a deep sense of joy descended on me. It lasted for about two weeks. Although I can't prove it, I believe the joy I was feeling was my mother's joy at being released from her body. Normally, one is overtaken by grief when a loved one dies. That is not what I felt. My mother had wanted to leave her body for several months. She kept on saying to me, "Why can't I die like my sisters?" They had all died suddenly and had not suffered.

My mother had been profoundly deaf for much of her life and always wore a hearing aid. A few weeks later, I gathered all my mother's clothes together and took them to a charity shop near the home where she had been staying. I was not familiar with this charity shop; I had noticed it when I had gone to the local council office to collect my mother's death certificate. When I asked the assistant which charity they collected for she answered "for the deaf and hard of hearing". I will leave you to draw your conclusions on what guided me to that shop.

While I was writing this book, I came across another story that caught my attention. It concerns Michael Shermer, a well-respected man in his community. Somewhat ironically, as you will appreciate after you have read his story, he was the founding publisher of Skeptic magazine and Presidential Fellow at Chapman University in the USA. Here is his story in his words:

> Often I am asked whether I have ever encountered something that I could not explain … anomalous and mystifying events that suggest the existence of the paranormal or supernatural. My answer is: yes, now I have.
>
> The event took place on June 25, 2014. On that day I married Jennifer Graf, from Köln, Germany. She had been raised by her mom. Her grandfather, Walter, was the closest father figure she had growing up, but he died when she was 16. In shipping her belongings to my home before the wedding, most of the boxes were damaged and several precious heirlooms lost. His 1978 Philips transistor radio arrived safely, so I set out to bring it back to life after decades of muteness. I put in new batteries and opened it up to see if there were any loose connections to solder. I even tried "percussive maintenance", said to work on such devices—smacking it sharply against a hard surface. Silence! We gave up and put it at the back of a desk drawer in our bedroom.
>
> Three months later, after affixing the necessary signatures to our marriage license at the Beverly Hills courthouse, we returned home, and in the presence of my family said our vows and exchanged rings. Jennifer was feeling lonely. She wished her grandfather were there to give her away. She whispered that she wanted to say something to me alone, so we excused ourselves and went to the back of the house where we could hear music playing in the bedroom. We don't have a music system there,

so we searched for laptops and iPhones and even opened the back door to check if the neighbours were playing music. We followed the sound to the printer on the desk, wondering—absurdly—if this combined printer/scanner/fax machine also included a radio. Nope.

At that moment Jennifer shot me a look I haven't seen since the supernatural thriller *The Exorcist* startled audiences. "That can't be what I think it is, can it?" she said. She opened the desk drawer and pulled out her grandfather's transistor radio, out of which a romantic love song wafted. We sat in stunned silence for minutes. "My grandfather is here with us", Jennifer said, tearfully. "I'm not alone."

Shortly thereafter we returned to our guests with the radio playing as I recounted the story. My daughter, Devin, who came out of her bedroom just before the ceremony began, added, "I heard the music coming from your room just as you were about to start". The odd thing is that we were there getting ready just minutes before that time, and there was no music.

Later that night we fell asleep to the sound of classical music emanating from Walter's radio. Fittingly, it stopped working the next day and has remained silent ever since.[11]

Only when we realize that the material world we live in is contained within the 4-D energetic world of the soul can we appreciate that events such as those I have just described are meaningful interventions from a higher dimension of consciousness. They appear to be purposeful communications designed to send us a loving message: a message of connection.

A summary of key points

Here are the main points of Chapter 2:

1. Even though the human mind/brain is surrounded by frequencies of vibration coming from a larger multi-dimensional energetic continuum, it is constrained in the frequencies it can intercept through the body's five physical senses.
2. One of the most important connections we have to the higher dimensions of reality are our emotions and feelings, the shifts in

the energy field of the ego-mind and soul-mind that occur when we get our needs met or fail to get our needs met.
3. We cannot know what is happening in the soul's energy field if we are not in touch with our feelings. Whenever we block our feelings, we cut ourselves off from the world of our soul and our true reality.
4. When the fear-based energies of the ego-mind are juxtaposed with the love-based energies of the soul-mind, you feel a sense of instability in your energy field and sensations of discomfort in your body.
5. As you release the fear-based energies of your ego-mind and align with the love-based energies of your soul-mind, the ego-mind, and the soul-mind come into energetic alignment.
6. We are aware of only minute slivers of space-time and even less of the energy fields, in which we exist.
7. Physical forms and materiality are properties of 3-D awareness, not properties of the reality we live in.
8. The shift in perception, from material awareness to energetic awareness, brings a new perspective to our understanding of the meaning of health; one that aligns more closely with Eastern traditions.

References and notes

1. *Wikipedia: The Free Encyclopaedia*. Wikimedia Foundation, Inc. 22 July 2004. Web. 10 August. 2004.
2. E. F. Schumacher, *A Guide for the Perplexed* (London: Random House), 1995, p. 35.
3. Bernardo Kastrup, *Why Materialism is Baloney* (Winchester: Iff Books), 2014, p. 40.
4. R. W. Clarke, *Einstein the Life and Times* (New York: World Publishing), 1971, p. 159.
5. Ervin László, *The Self-actualizing Cosmos: The Akasha Revolution in Science and Human Consciousness* (Rochester: Inner Traditions), 2014.
6. Abraham H. Maslow, *Toward a Psychology of Being* (second edition) (New York: Van Nostrand Reinhold), 1968, p. 97.
7. John James, *The Great Field*, 2007, p. 22.

8. Arjun Walia, *Nothing is Solid, Everything is Energy*—Scientists Explain The World of Quantum Physics, Collective Evolution, September 27, 2014.
9. E. O. Wilson, *The Meaning of Human Existence* (New York: Liveright Publishing), 2014, p. 48.
10. Ibid., p. 166.
11. www.scientificamerican.com/article/anomalous-events-that-can-shake-one-s-skepticism-to-the-core.

3

THE FILTERING OF AWARENESS

We think we live in a three-dimensional material world, whereas we actually live in a multi-dimensional energetic world. The reason we are unaware of this is that we have filtered it out. Further progress in the evolution of human consciousness requires us to stop filtering our awareness and start expanding our awareness.

In the last chapter, I discussed how our senses create our 3-D material reality by filtering out most of what is happening in our 4-D energetic world. In this chapter, I want to explore the concept of personal and collective filtering in more detail, in particular, I want to explore how filtering relates to consciousness and the impacts that filtering has on our sense of identity and our life in general. These impacts can be positive and negative.

Positive aspects of filtering

There are many positive benefits associated with filtering. Here are four of them:

Acts of creativity

Filtering allows us to concentrate on what we are *doing* by filtering out any extraneous noise or distractions, especially when we are involved in creative acts or doing something that demands our full attention. Filtering also allows you to focus your mind on an intention or a goal, and in so doing, helps you to achieve what you want in life.

Subconscious awareness

Filtering allows you to be fully present with your *thinking* while your subconscious takes care of any routine tasks you may be doing. Many people experience this type of filtering when they drive long-distances on their own. They focus on their thoughts and allow their subconscious mind to do the driving. If anything unusual occurs, they know they can rely on their subconscious to alert them to danger.

Mindfulness

Filtering also allows you to experience mindfulness. Mindfulness involves being the observer of your internal conscious experience. You enter into mindfulness by focusing on your breathing: when you are sufficiently relaxed, you can observe your thoughts. You do not engage with your thoughts; you remain detached from them. During this process, you become your own self-witness.

Mindfulness and meditation are very similar. Although they involve the same process, the intention is different. In mindfulness, the intention is to observe your thoughts; in meditation the intention is to move beyond your thoughts so you can experience pure awareness, a place of pure being.

Cultural filtering

Filtering can also occur at the cultural level in all forms of group structures: organizations, nations and religious groups. Whenever you identify with a specific culture, you filter out of your awareness everything that is not regarded as important by that culture, and you bring into your awareness everything that is important to that culture. This is why organizations create visions and missions and adopt a set of values. The vision, mission and values of an organization are intended to keep employees focused on the organization's goals and motivations.

In all these cases we use filtering to either concentrate on what is important to us or manifest our intentions. We filter out what is extraneous to our purpose.

Negative aspects of filtering

There are many negative aspects associated with filtering. Here are three of them:

Rumination

Rumination involves filtering out of your awareness any thought that could be regarded as positive. You ruminate when you compulsively focus your attention on the symptoms of your distress: on your failures to meet your needs. You focus on the cause of your distress, rather than the solutions to your distress. You let your anger or fear guide your conscious awareness. This can lead you into an energetic downward spiral that usually ends in depression.

Repression

Repression involves suppressing your emotions and filtering out of your conscious mind any negative feelings or thoughts associated with situations where you failed to get your needs met. The energy associated with these painful feelings and thoughts is repressed to the subconscious mind. Repression has both positive and not so positive aspects.

The upside of repression is that it allows your conscious awareness to go on functioning—you can concentrate on meeting your current needs or desires—taking care of your deficiency needs and your soul's desires. The downside of repression is that the energetic instability associated with the emotions, feelings and thoughts you have repressed do not go away. They create energetic instability in your subconscious mind.

Later, when situations arise that trigger the memory of these experiences, the emotions, feelings and thoughts come flooding back into your conscious awareness, disturbing your equilibrium. Your consciousness becomes overwhelmed, and you can no longer make rational decisions. In such a state, you may do things that you later regret.

The personal and collective shadow

The shadow aspects of your personality are the "dark" parts that you have filtered out of your of conscious awareness. Your shadow contains the emotions, feelings and thoughts that you do not want to own; the things you are not proud of; all the aspects of your personality that you do not want others to see and do not reflect the values of your soul. You hide them away because you want to be liked and respected by others. The reason you want to be liked is so you can feel loved and safe; the reason you want to be respected is so you can feel recognized and secure.

Even though they are repressed, the shadow aspects of your personality don't go away. When the emotions, feelings and thoughts of your shadow are triggered into conscious awareness, you can deal with them in two ways: if you accept your complicity in creating the pain associated with your past failings, you become overwhelmed with guilt or shame; if you deny your complicity in creating the pain associated with your past failings, you get angry and project the pain you are feeling onto other people in the form of criticism. Everything that irritates you about others is an indication of an issue you have not yet mastered yourself.

When we judge and criticize others, we bring to light what is in our shadow—we make our pain visible in a way that is acceptable to the ego. When we put others down, we are trying to raise ourselves up; the ego is trying to feel better about its failings.

We not only do this individually, we also do it collectively. Every human group structure with a history will almost certainly have a shadow. There will be an aspect of the group's collective past about which the group is ashamed. As with individuals, the shame arises from a failure to measure up to the values of the soul. Although, the shadow aspects of a group's history are seldom talked about, they sill influence the group's decision-making.

Three conclusions about filtering

There are three main conclusions I draw from this brief overview of filtering:

Filtering is primarily a survival mechanism. It allows you to stay focused on what is happening in your framework of existence so you can assure your personal survival, safety and security.

Filtering is synonymous with separation and affects our identity. Whatever you filter out of your conscious awareness is what you separate yourself from. Whatever you allow into your conscious awareness is what you identify with.

The more you filter out of your conscious awareness, the more isolated you become; the more you allow into your conscious awareness, the more connected you become. Therefore, when you identify with your 3-D physical body, rather than your 4-D energetic body, you separate yourself from your soul. Your soul, who you are, is always present in the background, but as long as you identify with your ego and its material reality, you will be unaware of your soul and your energetic reality.

Filtering dysfunctions

There are two main types of filtering dysfunction: one that involves too much filtering, for example, obsessive compulsive disorder (OCD) and one that involves too little filtering, for example, attention deficit hyperactivity disorder (ADHD). Both are associated with fear.

Obsessive compulsive disorder (OCD)

OCD is an obsession with an urge to fulfil a need. When the need takes on significant importance, it becomes a compulsion. If the need is not met, we become extremely anxious. We filter out of our awareness all our other needs until we can satisfy the compulsion. OCD symptoms can range from mild to severe and typically start during early adulthood. They usually involve fears we develop during the conforming and differentiating stages of psychological development concerning our unmet safety or security needs. OCD symptoms can be reduced by bringing the fear associated with an unmet need into conscious awareness and learning how to stay with the fear for longer and longer periods of time without giving into the compulsion.

Attention deficit hyperactivity disorder (ADHD)

As far as filtering is concerned, ADHD is the opposite of OCD. Instead of being focused on one thing, our minds are continually distracted by many things. People suffering ADHD are prone to inattentiveness, hyperactivity and impulsiveness.

ADHD tends to occur in young children. I believe this is because ADHD is rooted in the experiences we have during the surviving stage of development, in particular, any struggles we had in getting our needs met while we were in the womb. I come to this assumption because the incidence of ADHD symptoms tends to be most common in children born prematurely, children having a low birth weight, and children whose mothers smoked, imbued alcohol or were involved in drug abuse.

The struggles and painful experiences we have in the womb lead the reptilian mind/brain of the developing foetus to develop a psychological imprint (belief) that the world is not safe. The baby is born hypervigilant, always scanning incoming information for what is changing and what could compromise its ability to meet its needs.

Having discussed the positive and negative aspects of filtering and the dysfunctions associated with too much and too little filtering, I now want to move onto some bigger questions about filtering: the evolutionary context of filtering. How and why did filtering begin, and how is filtering related to our 3-D material experience of reality?

The emergence of filtering

According to modern science, everything that exists in our universe originated from a "big bang"[1] that occurred about fourteen billion years ago.

> The big bang produced, from nothing, a universe composed of photons, energy-packed radiations, unimaginably hot and compressed beyond description, a soup of energy, nearly homogenous throughout. The universe was born as an undifferentiated unity.[2]

After the big bang, as far as our 3-D scientists are concerned, it was all about evolution: the evolution of energy into matter, matter into living organisms, and living organisms into creatures; one of those creatures being ourselves, the species known as *Homo sapiens*. This is the story we have created to explain our 3-D reality because it fits with the physical evidence of our senses, similar to the stories that the 2-D scientists created in Flatland in Chapter 2.

When I say everything in our 3-D material universe had its origins around fourteen billion years ago, I mean everything, including not only the tangible world of atoms, cells and creatures but also the intangible world of emotions, feelings, thoughts and beliefs. Indeed, evolution would not have happened if the tangible faculties of meaning-making—our five physical senses and brains—had not evolved in parallel with the intangible faculties of meaning-making—our minds.

If the big bang theory is correct, then it follows that the physical world emerged from the energetic world. Not only did energy precede matter, we know, thanks to Einstein, that energy and matter are intimately related ($E=mc^2$). What we actually observe through our 3-D physical senses are energy fields that we interpret as matter.

Following Einstein's insight, that energy and matter are related, French physicist, Louis de Broglie (1892–1987), introduced the idea that all matter has wave properties, and different types of matter have their own energetic frequency of vibration, their own energy signature. He first demonstrated this in 1927 and won a Nobel Prize for this discovery in 1929.

Physicist, Gerald Schroeder, writing around the year 2000, states:

> Seventy years of experiments have sustained both Einstein's and de Broglie's claims. Absurd though these principles seem to the human mind, this wisdom has made possible transistors, and lasers and cellular phones.[3]

We appear to live in two worlds. In one, everything is wave-like—the energy dimension; a world we cannot observe with our physical senses. In the other, everything is particle-like—the material dimension; a world we can observe with our physical senses. The energy dimension is the reality of the soul, and the material dimension is our filtered perception of the reality of the soul. One we call 4-D awareness and the other we call the 3-D awareness. Viewed through the lens of 4-D awareness we can call our 3-D reality a form of illusion. It is an illusion because it is based on incomplete information.

The barrier between 3-D reality and 4-D reality is not real; it is a function of our perception and therefore, is permeable. It becomes more permeable as you expand your consciousness by progressively mastering the higher stages of psychological development and identifying with your soul. In other words, the expansion of our consciousness leads to a greater awareness of our 4-D reality.

The most direct way we have of experiencing 4-D awareness is through the sensations experienced in the body and the feelings experienced in the mind. The source of these sensations and feelings are changes in the energetic vibrations in the energy field of our body-mind, ego-mind and soul-mind. Other examples of 4-D awareness are:

- Clairvoyance: the ability to perceive things or events in the future.
- Clairsentience: the ability to read the feelings of others.
- Clairaudience: the ability to hear voices of non-sentient beings.
- Clair cognizance: the ability to receive knowing insights.

These abilities represent cracks in our ego's 3-D awareness through which we can experience 4-D awareness.

Pure awareness

Having established that the starting point for everything in our 3-D world was an undifferentiated multi-dimensional energetic field, let us now progress down the staircase of filtering that leads from the big bang to 3-D material reality.

Immediately after the big bang, the only thing that existed was the universal energy field. There was no filtering. There was nothing outside the universal energy field and nothing inside the field that could be regarded as separate. The field was all there was. Everything was part of the field. There was nothing for the universal energy field to be conscious of except itself. Therefore, we can regard the universal energy field as a field of pure self-awareness.

The one-mind

In our 3-D reality, we have come to recognize that awareness and mind are synonymous. In other words, awareness is a fundamental property of mind. There can be no awareness without mind, and there can be no mind without awareness. Since the universal energy field is a field of pure awareness, we can refer to this field as the one-mind.

Pioneering physicist, Sir James Jeans (1877–1946) expresses a similar thought. He writes:

> The stream of knowledge is heading toward a non-mechanical reality; the universe begins to look more like a great thought than like a great machine. Mind no longer appears to be an accidental intruder into the realm of matter; we ought to hail it as the creator and governor of the realm of matter. Get over it, and accept the inarguable conclusion. The universe is immaterial-mental and spiritual.[4]

Viewed through a monotheistic perspective, we could equate the one-mind with God, and we can equate the energy field of the one-mind with Spirit. In other words, Spirit is the all-embracing energy field of God that enlivens everything in the universe. The essence of this spirit is love. The term "inspiration" is an insight from soul consciousness given with love. When we feel inspired, we are enlivened by the energy of love: we are in-spirit.

Conscious awareness

Just as awareness and mind are synonymous, so are awareness and consciousness. Wherever there is a mind, there is awareness *and* consciousness. In a field of pure awareness, consciousness may be present, but there is no reason for it to be active: conscious becomes active only when there is a purpose for it to be active. What makes consciousness active is separation. Anything that separates itself from its context (environment) must become conscious in order to manage its separation. Consciousness is not just a consequence of separation; it is a pre-condition for separation.

To maintain separation, there has to be a boundary between what an entity recognizes as "self" and "not self". In other words, there has to be recognition of what is internal and what is external; there has to be a sense of identity. Without a sense of identity, it is difficult to establish a boundary between "self" and "not self".

If an entity cannot establish an identity—a boundary between self and not self—it cannot separate and emerge from its background. This is what individuating is all about: you either emerge from the culture you are embedded in and find your true identity or you stay embedded in the culture. Some people refer to cultural identity as tribal identity because it links to the group of people with whom we share our ethnic characteristics.

We can conclude that mind, awareness, consciousness *and* identity are not just necessary requirements for separation they are also necessary requirements for survival. We can also conclude that the primary purpose of conscious is to keep an entity in a state of (energetic) internal stability and external equilibrium so the entity can maintain its separation and its identity.

Based on this, we can define consciousness as *awareness with a purpose*, and the purpose of consciousness is to manage an entity's energetic stability. If an entity cannot manage its internal stability and external equilibrium—if it cannot stay alive—it will return to the context from which it originally separated. First it emerges and then it returns: it unfolds, and then it enfolds.

Localization

As soon as entities separated themselves from the universal energy field and established an identity (a boundary between self and not self) the consciousness of these entities activated. Their consciousness activated so they could stay separate and survive—they had to be aware of what was happening in their local environment. To be aware of and stay focused on what was important for their survival in their local environment, they had to filter out of their awareness anything that was not important—anything that was not threatening and not changing. With a sense of identity came filtering and localisation.

The progression of filtering

The progression of the filtering of awareness (increasing levels of separation) from the one-mind all the way down to a soul experiencing 3-D awareness in a physical body is shown in Figure 3.1.

Figure 3.1: Filtering from the one-mind to the body-mind.

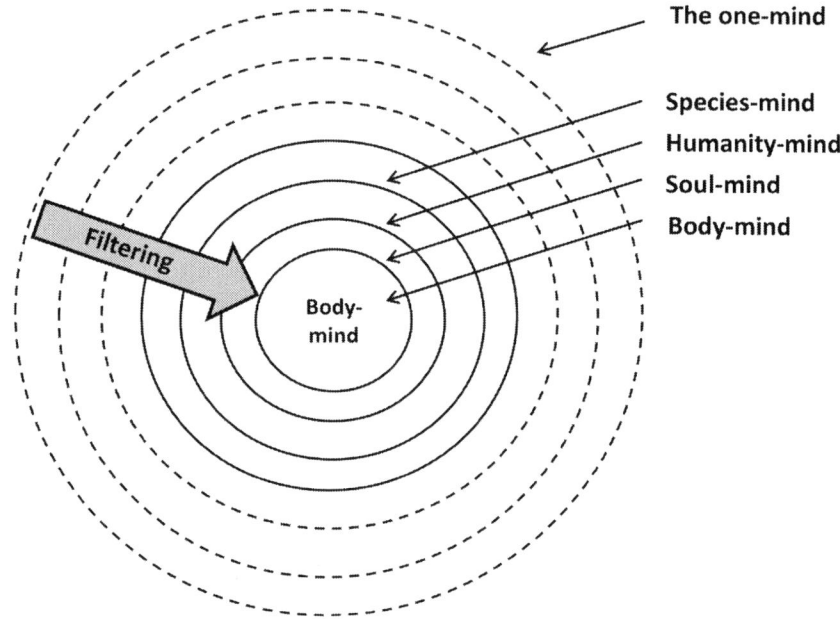

There are many stages of filtering involved in getting from the one-mind (universal energy field) to the energy field of the individual human soul. The last three stages involve the filtering out of the species mind from the mind of humanity, the filtering out of the mind of humanity from the 4-D soul-mind, and the filtering out of the 4-D soul-mind from the 3-D human mind. One could say that the 4-D soul-mind represents the subconscious of the 3-D human mind and the 5-D mind of humanity represents the unconscious of the 3-D human mind, and so on. String theory suggests there are eleven such dimensions. These minds, with all the other larger more expansive minds are always present; we are simply not aware of them because we have filtered them out of our awareness.

This idea is at the root of almost all religions: God is always present, we are simply not aware of it, him, her.

Most of this book is focused on the last stage of the filtering process, the filtering that occurs between 4-D consciousness and 3-D conscious. My focus is on the relationship between the soul, operating with 4-D awareness and the individual human being, operating with 3-D awareness. I am not focusing very much on the relationship between the universal energy field (the one-mind) and the soul-mind. I am filtering most of that out.

The journey into 3-D awareness

The soul's journey into 3-D awareness begins when the soul incarnates into a human body; when it takes possession of the energy field created through the process of conception. As the embryo and then the foetus grows and develops, the soul's 3-D material awareness increases. The soul is aided in this process by the creation of the body-mind (the reptilian mind/brain).

The first experiences the soul has of 3-D material existence are the sensations experienced by the body-mind. Some of these experiences are positive—life enhancing (the body-mind's needs are met) and some are negative—life depleting (the body-mind's needs are not met). The soul experiences life-enhancing experiences as love energy and life depleting experiences as fear energy. The soul continues to experience life-enhancing (love) and life-depleting (fear) experiences through the birth process and the first two years of life as a baby. When the embryo's, foetus's and baby's needs are met, the soul experiences the energy of love. When the needs are not met, the soul experiences the energies of anger and fear.

Around the age of two, when the soul's 3-D awareness has developed to the point that it begins to experience separation, it realizes there are other people in the world. It is no longer living in a world of oneness. At this point, the pain (energetic instability) associated with the negative sensations of the body-mind and the experience of separation, cause the soul to protect itself by creating a buffer we call the ego. I will explain this process in more detail later.

The ego-mind develops in three stages: It learns how to survive with the help of the body–mind (the reptilian mind/brain); it learns how to stay safe with the aid of the emotional mind (the limbic mind/brain), and it learns how to keep secure with the aid of the rational mind (the neocortex mind/brain).

Only after the ego-mind has learned how to maintain its internal stability and external equilibrium in its physical, societal and cultural framework of existence does the soul-mind venture into 3-D awareness again. The ego-mind must let go of its fears before the soul-mind can be reactivated. The activation of the soul-mind occurs in three stages: the self-actualization stage, the integrating stage and the serving stage. The whole of this process is described by the Seven Stages of Psychological Development. Each stage of development requires an expansion in conscious awareness.

For consciousness to expand there must be a decrease in separation and an increase in the sense of identity. Filtering, in the form of repression, prevents expansion. Whatever has been repressed by the ego must be reintegrated into conscious awareness before the soul can complete its journey.

The process of consciousness expansion is shown in Figure 3.2. We expand our conscious awareness by gradually learning to master the needs associated with each stage of development. The numbers in this figure refer to the Seven Stages of Psychological Development.

Figure 3.2: The expansion of conscious awareness.

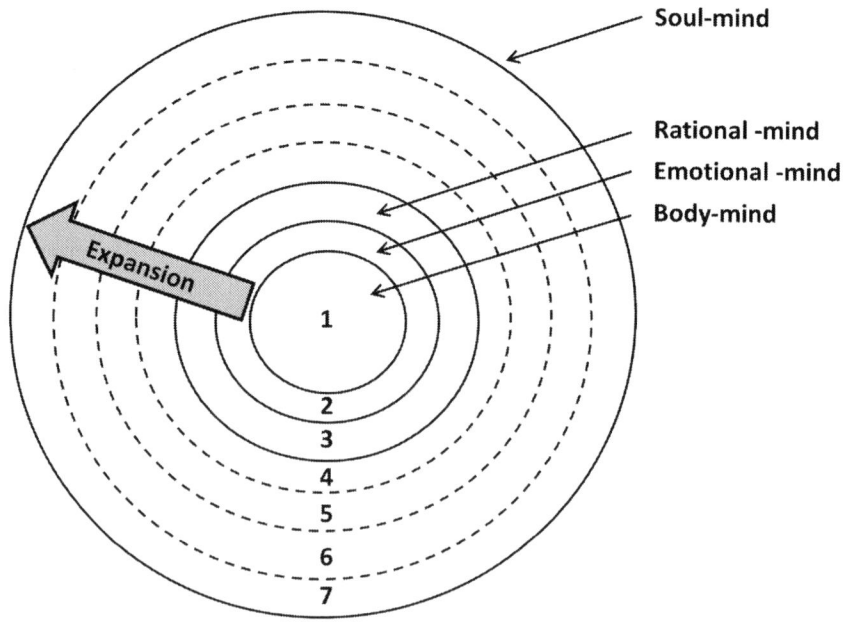

In broad terms we can say that the body-mind corresponds to the surviving stage of development (1), the emotional mind corresponds to the conforming stage of development (2), and the rational mind corresponds to the differentiating stage of development (3). The emotional mind with the rational mind represents the ego-mind. At the fourth stage of development (4), the ego reintegrates into its conscious awareness what has been repressed.

If we are unable, for whatever reason, to reintegrate what has been repressed or we are unable to disembed ourselves our cultural framework of existence, our ego-mind will stay dominant for the rest of our lives and the soul-mind will not be reactivated. What prevents the awareness of the soul-mind from emerging is the ego's energy of fear. The energy of fear has a low frequency of vibration whereas the energy of love has a high frequency of vibration.

The difference between ego awareness and soul awareness

To complete this chapter, I think it is important to describe the differences that exist between the ego's perception of reality and the soul's perception of reality.

Viewed from the perspective of the ego, the fundamental properties of the material dimension of reality are time, space and matter. By conjoining time and space, we create the illusion of separation; by conjoining time and matter, we create the illusion of death and decay; by conjoining space and matter, we create the illusion of physical forms and mass. Together, taken as a whole, all of these concepts align with the classical 3-D physical interpretation of reality explained by Newtonian mechanics and the First and Second Laws of Thermodynamics.

Viewed from the perspective of the soul, the fundamental properties of the energetic dimension are timelessness, omnipresence and energy. Because the soul has no awareness of time or space to give the illusion of separation, the soul experiences a sense of oneness and connectedness. Because the soul has no awareness of time and matter to give the illusion of death and decay, it experiences a state of being (present moment awareness). Because the soul has no awareness of space and matter to give the illusion of form and mass, the soul experiences shifts in energetic vibrations. Together, taken as a whole, all of these concepts align with the quantum mechanical interpretation of reality, which is explained by Quantum theory.

In the world of the soul everything is wave-like with different frequencies of vibration—the energy dimension; in the world of the ego, everything is particle-like with different densities of matter—the material dimension.

Table 3.1 compares the fundamental properties of ego and soul awareness and Table 3.2 shows the manner in which the ego experiences its material reality and the manner in which the soul experiences its energetic reality.

Table 3.1: Properties of the ego's and soul's awareness.

Properties of ego awareness	Properties of soul awareness
Time	Timelessness
Space	Omnipresence
Matter	Energy

Table 3.2: The ego's and soul's experience of reality.

The ego's experience of reality	The soul's experience of reality
Death and decay	Being
Separation	Connection
Limitation	Possibility
Lack	Abundance
FEAR	LOVE

In the material dimension of reality, the ego lives in a world limited by time and matter. Therefore, it believes in death and decay. Because it believes in death and decay, it experiences separation. Because it experiences separation, it believes in limitation. Because it believes in limitation, it experiences lack. Because it experiences lack, it believes it has needs. Because it believes it has needs, it experiences anger when its needs are not met and fear if it believes its needs might not be met.

In the energetic dimension of reality, there is no time or space. Because there is no time and space, the soul lives in a constant state of being and connection. Because it lives in constant state of being and connection, it experiences oneness and is not aware of separation. Because it has no awareness of separation, it does not experience limitation. It lives in a world of possibility and abundance. Every thought of the soul is an act of creativity. It instantaneously creates through its thoughts whatever it needs. Because it has no needs, it has no fears, and its primary experience of its world is unconditional love.

The first law of thermodynamics confirms the eternal nature of the soul. The first law states that energy cannot be created or destroyed, but it can change from one form into another, hence, the soul can go on forever unless it chooses to shift into a different energy form.

The second law of thermodynamics confirms the destabilizing effect that the fears of the ego have on the energy field of the soul. The second law states, that whenever energy is transformed from one form into another, the amount of disorder and instability (entropy) in a system increases. Low entropy is an indication of order and stability, and high entropy is an indication of disorder and instability. When entropy is high, the amount of energy available for doing the work of maintaining internal stability and external equilibrium decreases.

In its natural state the energy field of the soul is comprised only of love energy: it lives in a world of order and equilibrium. Whenever the energy field of the soul experiences the ego's energy of fear, the level of entropy— the level of disorder and instability—in the soul's energy field increases. In other words, when we let the fears of the ego influence our thoughts, the level of energetic instability in the soul's energy field increases and the amount of love energy available for "doing useful work" decreases. From the soul's perspective, the energy associated with the emotion of anger, which the ego experiences when its needs are not met, and the energy associated with the emotion of fear which the ego experiences when its needs might not be met is experienced by the soul as a lack of love.

Unmet needs = Anger/fear = Lack of love

Having identified the source of energetic stability in the soul's energy field as the ego's anger and fear, let us hold this idea in our minds as we explore the motivations of the ego and the motivations of the soul in more detail.

A summary of key points

Here are the main points of Chapter 3:

1. Filtering has positive and negative aspects.
2. Filtering is primarily a survival mechanism. It allows you to stay focused on what is happening in your framework of existence so you can insure your personal survival, safety and security.
3. Filtering is synonymous with separation and affects our identity. Whatever you filter out of your conscious awareness is what you separate from. Whatever you allow into your conscious awareness is what you identify with. The more you filter out of your conscious awareness, the more isolated you become; the more you allow into your conscious awareness, the more connected you become.
4. Everything that exists—in the tangible world of cells and creatures and the intangible world of emotions and feelings—originated from the big bang.
5. We appear to live in two worlds. In one, everything is wave-like—the energy dimension; a world we cannot observe with our physical senses. In the other, everything is particle-like—the material dimension; a world we can observe with our physical senses.
6. The energy dimension is the reality of the soul, and the material dimension is our symbolic filtered perception of the reality of the soul. One we call 4-D awareness and the other we call the 3-D awareness.
7. For self-awareness to be present, there must be a mind because awareness is a property of mind. We can refer to the universal energy field as the one-mind.
8. Anything that separates itself from its context must become conscious to manage its separation. Consciousness is not a consequence of separation; it is a pre-condition for separation.

9. We can define consciousness as awareness with a purpose, and the purpose of consciousness is to manage the internal stability and external equilibrium of the entity that possesses the consciousness so it can maintain its separation from its context.
10. The soul's journey into 3-D awareness begins when the soul incarnates into a human body. When it takes possession of the energy field created through the process of conception. As the embryo and then the foetus grows and develops, the soul's 3-D material awareness increases.
11. Around the age of two, the soul's 3-D awareness has developed to the point that it begins to experience separation. It is no longer living in a world of oneness. At this point the pain (energetic instability) associated with the negative sensations of the body-mind and the experience of separation cause the soul to protect itself by creating a buffer we call the ego.
12. Only after the ego-mind has learned how to maintain its internal stability and external equilibrium in its physical, social and cultural framework of existence does the soul-mind venture into 3-D awareness again.

References and notes

1. The big bang is the prevailing scientific model of how the universe developed. According to this theory, the universe we live in is estimated to have begun 13.798 billion years ago.
2. Gerald L. Schroeder, *The Hidden Face of God: Science Reveals the Ultimate Truth* (New York: Touchstone), 2001, p. 41.
3. Ibid., p. 27.
4. R. C. Henry, *The Mental Universe*; Nature 436: 29, 2005.

4

THE MOTIVATIONS OF THE EGO AND THE SOUL

Every decision we make in life is either motivated by the ego or motivated by the soul. There are no exceptions to this rule. The reason we make decisions is to get our needs met.

Now that we have a clear idea of the realities of the ego—the world of 3-D material forms, and the realities of the soul—the world of 4-D energy fields, we can reach a deeper understanding of the drivers and motivations of the ego and the drivers and motivations of the soul. We can also develop a deeper understanding what it means to recreate the soul's 4-D reality in 3-D awareness.

Motivations of the ego

Since the ego believes it is dependent on the body for its existence, its primary motivation is physical survival. The ego also has two secondary motivations: physical and emotional safety and physical and emotional security. Physical safety means keeping the body safe from harm, and emotional safety means feeling accepted and loved in your family/social environment. Physical security means keeping the body safe from harm in your community/cultural environment, and emotional security means feeling recognized and respected in your community/cultural environment.

The Motivations of the Ego and the Soul

First we learn how to survive in our body, and then we learn how to keep safe in our family/social environment, and finally we learn how to feel secure in our community/cultural environment. The need to satisfy each of these motivations aligns with the surviving, conforming and differentiating stages of psychological development, respectively (see Table 4.1).

Table 4.1: The motivations of the ego.

Differentiating	Physical and emotional security
↑	↑
Conforming	Physical and emotional safety
↑	↑
Surviving	Physical and emotional survival

The degree to which you can fulfil your ego's survival, safety and security needs is the degree to which you will experience love in your life. Love brings health, happiness and contentment during your childhood, teenage and young adult years. When you can master your ego's needs, energetically, you feel a sense of internal stability.

The degree to which you are unable to fulfil your ego's survival, safety and security needs is the degree to which you experience anger and fear in your life. Fear brings anxiety and anger brings sadness during your childhood, teenage and young adult years. When you are engaged in a constant struggle to satisfy your ego's survival, safety and security needs, the fear and anger you feel create energetic instability in your body-mind.

The impacts that love and fear have on your life during the ego stages of development are shown in Figure 4.1

Figure 4.1: The impact of love and fear on ego development.

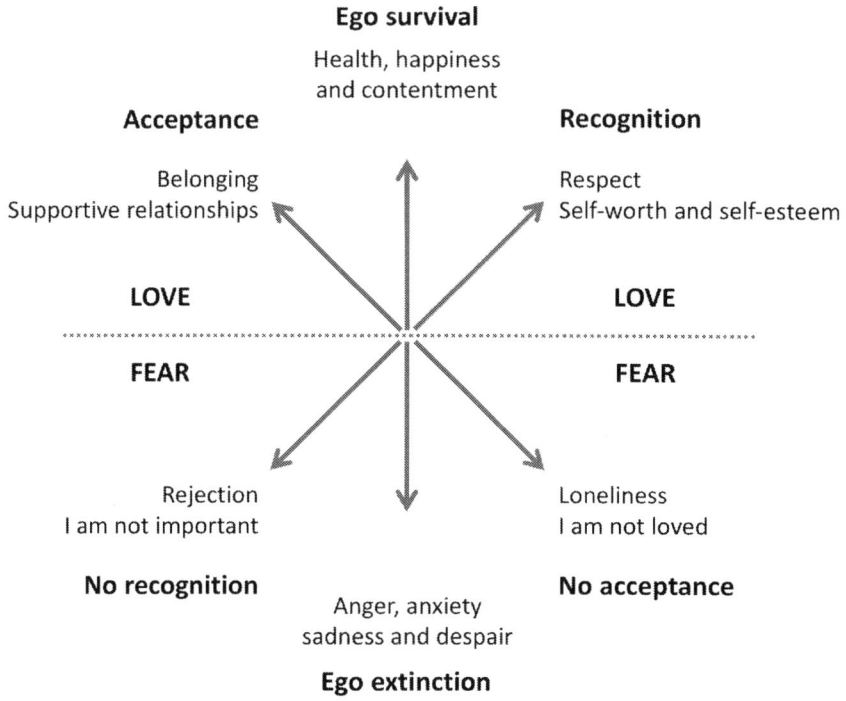

When you don't feel accepted, you feel lonely and you grow up feeling unloved. You don't feel that you belong, and consequently, you don't feel supported by others and don't feel safe. When you don't feel recognized, you feel rejected and you grow up feeling unimportant. You don't feel respected, and consequently, you have a low sense of self-worth and don't feel secure.

Motivations of the soul

The primary motivation of the soul is self-expression. Self-expression means allowing the passion and creativity of the soul to flow through your being. The soul also has two secondary motivations: connecting and contributing. We connect when we form unconditional loving relationships

The Motivations of the Ego and the Soul

and live a values-driven life. We contribute when we use our skills, gifts and talents to support the well-being of others and live a purpose-driven life.

Recreating the soul's 4-D reality in 3-D awareness means learning how to express who you are, learning how to connect through unconditional love, and learning how to contribute to the well-being of the people you meet. The need to satisfy these motivations aligns with the self-actualizing, integrating and serving stages of psychological development, respectively (see Table 4.2).

Table 4.2: The motivations of the soul.

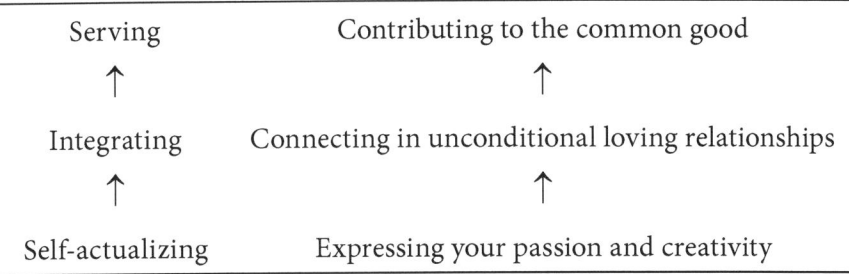

Your success in leading a purpose-driven life depends to a great extent on your ability to lead a values-driven life. At the soul level, we all share the same values. When you learn to live by these values, you resonate with other people and can connect. If you do not resonate with other people, you cannot connect, and will not be able to contribute to their well-being.

The degree to which you can fulfil your soul's self-expression, connection and contribution desires is the degree to which you experience well-being, fulfilment and joy in your adult and senior years. When you can master your soul's desires, energetically, you feel a sense of internal stability.

The degree to which you are unable to fulfil your soul's self-expression, connection and contribution desires is the degree to which you experience sadness, depression and poor health during your adult and senior years. When you are unable to master your soul's desires, energetically, you feel a sense of internal instability.

The impact that satisfying or not satisfying your soul's desires has on your life is shown in Figure 4.2.

Figure 4.2: The impact that meeting your soul's desires has on your life.

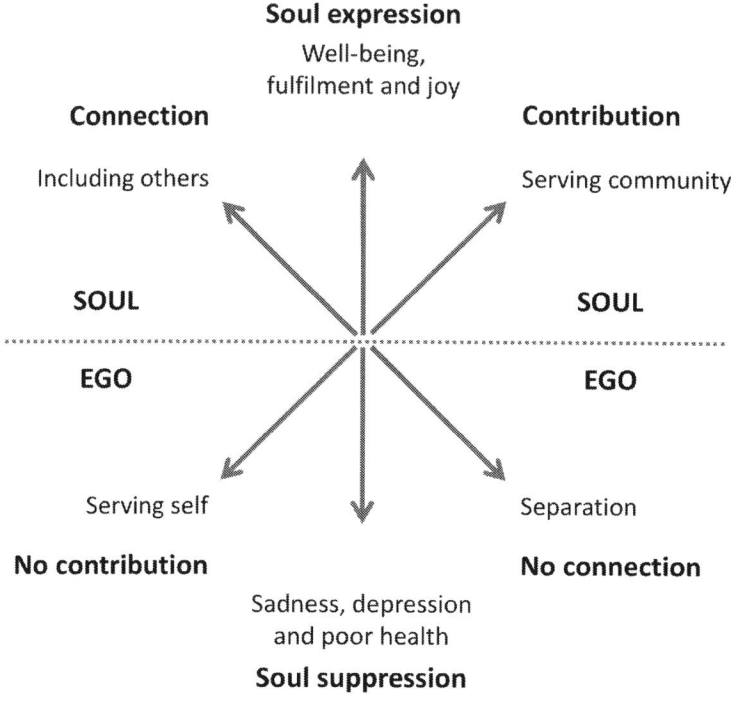

When you compare Figures 4.1 and 4.2, it becomes obvious that the fulfilment of the soul's motivations is inextricably linked to the fulfilment of the ego's motivations.

If the ego struggles to satisfy its survival needs, the soul will find it difficult to satisfy its self-expression needs: survival needs always take precedence over self-expression needs. If the ego struggles to satisfy its safety needs, the soul will find it difficult to satisfy its desire for connection: when you don't feel loved, it is difficult to love others. If the ego struggles to satisfy its security needs, the soul will find it difficult to satisfy its desire for contribution: when you don't feel recognized in your community, it is difficult to make a contribution.

Or as Maslow would have put it, you have to master your deficiency needs before you can fulfil your growth needs.

Well-being theory

It is somewhat obvious that fulfilling your ego's and soul's motivations has a lot to do with well-being. If you cannot satisfy your ego's needs, you cannot satisfy your soul's desires, and if you cannot satisfy your soul's desires you cannot find fulfilment. For this reason, I believe the current theories that support the well-being movement, which succeeded the happiness movement, are flawed.

They are flawed for two reasons: they fail to recognize the primacy of the satisfaction of the needs of the ego in the early part our lives, and they fail to recognize the primacy of the satisfaction of the desires of the soul in the latter part of our lives. In other words, the current well-being movement fails to give attention to the impact that stage-related psychological development has on what makes us happy and how we find joy in our lives. Our happiness in life is dependent on being able to master the ego stages of development—satisfy our ego's needs, and our joy is dependent on being able to master the soul stages of development—satisfy our soul's desires.

I am not the only one to have noticed flaws in the happiness and well-being movements. David Harper, a Reader in clinical psychology at the University of East London writing in the *Guardian* newspaper also views these movements with suspicion. He makes, what I believe are some valid points. His first point is that insisting that happiness is an internal construct is not helpful when confronted with people who have experienced significant child abuse. They are not happy, because, through no fault of their own, their childhood experiences taught them that getting their needs met is a constant struggle.[1] Harper also points that creating the conditions that bring happiness are sometimes out of our hands. He states:

> Evidence shows that a major contribution to serious emotional distress is income inequality—the growing gap between the richest and poorest people in society. To increase happiness, we need firm action on inequality.[2]

The lacunae in the theories that support the happiness and well-being movements to my mind are hardly surprising because most happiness and well-being research is carried out in universities, where, as I have already indicated, the soul is persona non grata, and the significance of stage related development is not well understood and integrated.

Corroboration

Finally, I would like to provide some evidence to corroborate my statements about the importance of self-expression, connection and contribution to the experience of well-being and fulfilment in the latter part of our lives. I will be drawing on several resources, but mainly on the results of the Harvard Grant study reported in George Vaillant's *Triumphs of Experience*.[3]

As part of his research Vaillant developed what he referred to as, a Decathlon of Flourishing[4]: ten factors that he used to evaluate life success. These are reproduced in Annex 2. Vaillant found that the capacity that most contributed to these ten factors was the capacity for intimate relationships.[5]

This finding aligns with my contention that the satisfaction of the soul's desire for connection is one of the primary predictors of well-being. The importance of connection is further reinforced by Vaillant's research on the relationship between happiness and love:

> There are two pillars of happiness revealed by the seventy-five-year-old Grant Study. One is love. The other is finding a way of coping with life that does not push love away.[6]
>
> ...love early in life facilitates not only love later on but also the other trappings of success, such as prestige and even high income. It also encourages the development of coping styles that facilitate intimacy, as opposed to ones that discourage it. The majority of the men who flourished found love before thirty and that was why they flourished.[7]

Vaillant concludes:

> The seventy-five years and twenty million dollars expended on the Grant Study points, at least, to me, to a straightforward conclusion: "Happiness is love. Full stop." ... Love conquers all.[8]

Vaillant is not the only person to recognize the fundamental importance of loving relationships in our lives. Dr. Arthur Janov, the author of *The*

Biology of Love, agrees with Vaillant. Speaking of the importance of love in our early lives, he states:

> ...love ultimately determines how we think, feel, perceive and act as adults. It determines what illnesses we fall prey to later in life. It is no exaggeration to say that very early lack of love already sets the limits on how long we will live and how happy we will be.[9]

Dr. Barbara L. Fredrickson, Director of the Positive Emotions and Psychophysiology Laboratory at the University of North Carolina at Chapel Hill, calls love the "supreme emotion".[10] She states:

> ...[love] is perhaps the most essential emotional experience for thriving and healing.[11] Your body was designed to harness this power—to live off it.[12] Love is far more ubiquitous than you ever thought possible for the simple fact that love is connection.[13]
>
> Love is the momentary upwelling of three tightly interwoven events: first, a sharing of one or more positive emotions between you and another; second, a synchrony between your and other person's biochemistry and behaviors; and third, a reflected motive to invest in each other's well-being that brings mutual care.[14] My shorthand for this trio is positivity resonance.[15]

For me, and I suspect most other people, the idea of positive "resonance" provides a link to the energetic world. Resonance occurs as a result of an energy system increasing its amplitude of vibration in response to another system that is vibrating at a similar frequency. When you feel this sense of alignment with another person, you not only experience love, you experience connection. When you feel this sense of alignment within yourself—when you love yourself—your ego will fall into alignment with your soul. People who do not love themselves, and deny their self-expression, fall sick.

As far as contribution and self-expression through creativity is concerned, Vaillant's review of the results of the Terman study of women (see Preface) shows a significant link between generativity—manifesting care for the development of those younger than yourself—and creativity. Vailland defines creativity as "putting into the world what was not there before".

> The most creative women supported and cared for those younger than themselves and showed selfless concern for the well-being of others. In midlife the creative women were more likely to have had activities outside the home; at 60 they were more likely to express joy in living.[16]
>
> Among the 20 most creative women were nine who achieved their greatest public success after the age of 60.[17]

When Vaillant turned his attention to the men of the Grant Study he found similar results, but the distinctions were not as marked between the most creative and the least creative. He concludes:

> Like creativity in the Terman women, creativity in the College men [Grant Study] was associated with successful aging.[18] To summarize, creativity was positively correlated with generativity, sublimation, and altruism.[19]

Creativity is one of the key components of self-actualization. When we tap into our soul's purpose, creativity and a passion for our work abound.

Other research confirms that having a sense of purpose in life leads to reduced odds of suffering a stroke. A stroke occurs when the flow of blood to the brain is blocked. The research team carried out autopsies on 453 older adults who were enrolled in the Rush Memory and Aging Project. All of the participants underwent annual physical and psychological evaluations, including a standard assessment of purpose in life. Purpose in life was judged on a five-point scale with higher scores indicating a greater purpose. At autopsy, 154 of the deceased were found to have macroscopic infarctions (areas of stroke damage visible to the naked eye).

The researchers found that with every one-point increase in the score measuring purpose, the likelihood of having one or more macroscopic infarctions decreased by about 50 per cent. Those with a strong sense of life purpose were 44 per cent less likely to have suffered the kind of major brain tissue damage that drives up the risk of age-related dementia and disability. This link persisted even after adjusting for contributing factors such as obesity, smoking, diabetes, blood pressure and lack of exercise.

The lead author, Lei Yu, a statistician at Rush Alzheimer's Disease Centre and Assistant Professor of Neurological Sciences with Rush University told *Reuters News Agency*:

> We and others have shown that purpose in life is protective against multiple adverse health outcomes in older age. Importantly, purpose in life may be improved through changes in behaviours or participation in activities like volunteerism, among other things.[20]

It turns out that having a sense of purpose in life is a key component of psychological well-being. When you have a sense of purpose, your life has meaning and you are driven forward by your need to make a difference. According to the study:

> Older people with a greater sense of purpose are less likely to develop adverse health outcomes, including early mortality, decline in physical function, frailty, disability, Alzheimer's disease and clinical stroke.[21]

If the ability to connect and contribute later in life reduces the onset and occurrence of physical and mental disabilities, we would expect that those who have mastered these skills would live longer lives.

The results of extensive research into longevity are in agreement with this hypothesis. In his book entitled, *The Blue Zones*,[22] Dan Buettner reports on the research he and his team carried out into longevity.

> To identify the secrets of longevity, our team of demographers, medical scientists, and journalists went straight to the best sources. We travelled to the Blue Zones—five of the healthiest corners of the globe—where a remarkably high percentage of the longest-living people manage to avoid many of the diseases that kill Americans. These are places where people enjoy a three times better chance of reaching 100 than we do.[23]

Buettner describes the results of his research in what he refers to as "9 lessons for living longer." I have divided his nine lessons into three groupings: physical lessons, connection lessons and contribution lessons.

Among the physical lessons, we find regular exercise, reduced intake of food, a mainly vegetarian diet, a small daily dose of alcohol, and a stress-free slow-pace of life. Among the connection lessons, we find making family a priority and social connectedness. Among the contribution lessons, we find life purpose and affiliation to a strong faith community. Buettner concludes:

> ...the world's longevity all-stars not only live longer, but they also tend to live better. They have strong connections with family and friends. They're active. They wake up in the morning knowing that they have a purpose, and the world, in turn, reacts to them in a way that propels them along. An overwhelming majority of them still enjoy life. And [not surprisingly] there's not a grump in the bunch.[24]

Having established the importance of self-expression, connection and contribution to living a long, healthy and enjoyable life, let us now look at the key factors that prevent us from enjoying our elder years. Let us once again draw upon Harvard Grant study:

> ...it is the quality of a child's total experience, not any particular trauma or any particular relationship, that exerts the clearest influence on adult psychopathology.[25]

This finding—that the experiences of childhood play a significant role in adult development—is also supported by recent work carried out by Lord Richard Layard and his colleagues at the London School of Economics (LSE). The LSE research indicates that a child's emotional health is far more important to their satisfaction levels as an adult than other factors, such as, whether they achieve academic success when young, or wealth when older.[26]

A failure to nurture the emotional development of our children during the first twenty years of their lives—during the time they are focused on learning how to satisfy their survival, safety and security needs—significantly impacts their ability to master the higher stages of psychological development.

A longitudinal study in Minnesota involving 243 people born into poverty reaches the same conclusion. Dr. Lee Raby, who led the study, states:

> The study suggests that children's experiences with parents during the first few years of life have a unique role in promoting social and academic functioning—not merely during the first two decades of life, but also during adulthood.[27]

The study found that sensitive caregiving in the first three years of life can predict academic achievement and social competence all the way into adulthood. Parents who are sensitive caregivers tend to respond to their child's signals promptly and appropriately. When this happens the child feels love.

One of the world's former leading child psychologists, Alice Miller (1923–2010), goes much further in linking parental caregiving or the lack of it, to adult development. In her book, *The Body Never Lies: The Lingering Effects of Hurtful Parenting*,[28] she makes a strong link between childhood trauma and adult physical and mental illness. According to Miller, illness arises in:

> ...the conflict between the things we feel—the things our bodies register—and the things we think we ought to feel so as to comply with moral norms and standards we have internalized at an early age.[29]

When our need for physical safety forces us to hide or deny our real feelings—when we feel the need to conform—the energy associated with these feelings does not go away. It lies dormant in our bodies (our energy field) yearning for release. Miller explains:

> When children are born, what they need most from their parents is love, by which I mean affection, attention, care, protection, kindness and the willingness to communicate. If these are gratified, the bodies of these children will retain the good memory of such caring affection all their lives, and later, as adults, they will be able to pass on the same kind of love to their children. The more children are deprived of love and negated or maltreated in the name of [good] "upbringing" the more those children, on reaching adulthood, will look to their parents (or other people substituting for them) to supply all the things that those same parents failed to provide when they were needed most.[30]

When, as adults, we fail to find what our parents did not provide, sadness, depression and physical illness result. The only way back to health, Miller states, is to find someone, a psychotherapist or enlightened witness, with whom we can share our untold story. Someone who is willing to listen and acknowledge the repressed feelings and hurts of our childhood; someone who cares for us in a non-judgemental way with whom we can unburden the pain, guilt and shame of our suppressed emotions.

In support of her theory, Miller cites the results of research carried out in San Diego in the 1990s:

> ...a total of 17,000 people, with an average age of fifty-seven, [were asked] what their childhood was like and what illnesses they had suffered in the course of their lives. The study revealed that the incidence of severe illness was many times higher in people who had been abused it their childhood than in people who had grown up free of such abuse and had never been exposed to beatings meted out for their own good.[31]

Those who had not been exposed to abuse and beatings had had no illness to speak of in their later lives.

Miller illustrates the impact that abusive or neglectful parenting can have on our lives by referring to the childhood experiences of such well-known writers as Fyodor Dostoevsky, Anton Chekov, Franz Kafka, Friedrich Nietzsche, Friedrich von Schiller, Virginia Wolf, Arthur Rimbaud, Yukio Mishima, Marcel Proust and James Joyce.[32]

All of these writers and playwrights suffered greatly with physical or mental illness and eventually took their lives. None of them lived beyond the age of sixty; half of them died in their mid-40s. Of particular interest to our current inquiry are the lives of Friedrich von Schiller, Arthur Rimbaud and Yukio Mishima, who all died before the age of forty-six. In all three cases, in addition to the abuse they received when they were children, their creative talents were actively suppressed by one or other of their parents.

I do not think it is a coincidence that these three people died at the point in their lives when they would normally be entering the self-actualization stage of their psychological development.

To live out their soul's purpose through self-expression would have meant severing ties with their parents by going against their wishes. For them, this stage of psychological development was too painful and fearful to contemplate. Choosing self-actualization would have meant severing their relationship with their parents on whom they depended for the satisfaction of their unmet need for love. They chose to end their lives rather than face this conflict and pursue their soul's destiny.

Dr. Arthur Janov takes this argument further. Based on more than three decades of experience he concludes that:

> ...the first weeks and months of life, pre-social womb-life, change our brains. Nothing in adult life can radically alter what happened to us as infants and even before birth. If a trauma or lack of love happened to us during a critical [early period in our lives], nothing in adult life can change it because the changes that took place at the time were imprinted in the neurobiological system permanently.[33]
>
> Simply put, unexpressed feelings can drive us "crazy," or at least, make us agitated and uncomfortable.[34]

Don't be discouraged, he adds, "there are solutions". Janov's solutions align with Miller's approach: bringing unexpressed feelings into conscious awareness, re-experiencing them and giving them a new meaning.

Having confirmed through the research cited that the satisfaction of the ego's needs and soul's desires are of fundamental importance to human well-being, and that our early life experiences significantly impact our ability to thrive later on life, let's now explore the Seven Stages of Psychological Development in greater detail.

A summary of key points

Here are the main points of Chapter 4:

1. The ego's primary motivation is staying alive. In addition, the ego has two secondary motivations: safety and security.
2. The primary motivation of the soul is self-expression. In addition, the soul has two secondary motivations: connecting and contributing.
3. Connecting involves leading a values-driven life: adopting the values that are shared by everyone at the soul level.
4. Contributing involves leading a purpose-driven life: using your gifts, talents and creativity to support those who are in need.
5. You cannot live a purpose-driven life until you have learned to live a values-driven life.

6. The ability to connect and contribute later in life reduces the onset and occurrence of physical and mental disabilities.
7. Sensitive caregiving in the first three years of life can predict academic achievement and social competence all the way into adulthood. Parents who are sensitive caregivers tend to respond to their child's signals promptly and appropriately.
8. When our need for physical safety forces us to hide or deny our real feelings—when we feel the need to conform—the energy associated with these feelings does not go away. It lies dormant in our bodies (our energy field) yearning for release.
9. When, as adults, we fail to find what our parents did not provide, depression and physical illness result.
10. Without a basic understanding of the stages of psychological development and the ego's needs and the soul's desires, you cannot reach a full understanding of human well-being.

References and notes

1. www.theguardian.com/society/2012/feb/21/sad-truth-action-for-happiness-movement
2. Ibid.
3. George E. Vaillant, *Triumphs of Experience* (Boston: First Harvard University Press), 2012.
4. Ibid., p. 30.
5. Ibid., p. 40.
6. Ibid., p. 50.
7. Ibid., p. 52.
8. Ibid.
9. Dr. Arthur Janov, *The Biology of Love* (New York: Prometheus Books), 2000, p. 19.
10. Barbara Fredrikson, *Love 2.0* (New York: Hudson Street Press), 2013, p. 10.
11. Ibid., p. 10.
12. Ibid., p. 18.
13. Ibid., p. 17.
14. Ibid.
15. Ibid.

16. George E. Vaillant, *The Wisdom of the Ego* (Boston: Harvard University Press), 1993, p. 219.
17. Ibid.,
18. Ibid., p. 223.
19. Ibid., p. 224.
20. www.theglobeandmail.com/life/health-and-fitness/health/high-sense-of-purpose-in-life-tied-to-lower-stroke-risk/article23860486/
21. Ibid.
22. Dan Buettner, *The Blue Zones* (Second Edition) (Washington, D. C., National Geographic), 2012.
23. Ibid., pp. 4–5.
24. Ibid., p. 52.
25. George E. Vaillant, *Triumphs of Experience* (Boston: First Harvard University Press), 2012, p. 52.
26. Lord Richard Layard et al., *What Predicts a Successful Life? A Life-Course Model of Well-Being*, IZA DP No. 7682.
27. Lee Raby et al., *Child Development, The Enduring Predictive Significance of Early Maternal Sensitivity: Social and Academic Competence through Age 32 years*. First published online 17 December 2014.
28. Alice Miller, *The Body Never Lies: The Lingering Effects of Hurtful Parenting* (New York: W. W. Norton & Company), 2006.
29. Ibid., p. 19.
30. Ibid., p. 21.
31. Ibid., p. 29.
32. Ibid., pp. 43–81.
33. Dr. Arthur Janov, *The Biology of Love* (Amherst, Prometheus Books), 2000, p. 17.
34. Ibid., p. 20.

5

THE STAGES OF PSYCHOLOGICAL DEVELOPMENT

When you have a map of the territory, it makes your journey a lot easier. When you know what you need to feel happy, now and in the future, you can move forward with confidence. When you know what your soul desires, you can find fulfilment.

There are many models of psychological development, each of them describes the process of human development in slightly different ways.[1,2] The Seven Stages of Psychological Development Model differs from most other models in one important way. It looks at individual development through the lens of the *ego-soul dynamic*: the growth and development of the ego, the alignment of the ego with the soul, and the activation of the soul consciousness.

The first three stages of development involve establishing the ego as a viable, independent entity in its physical, social and cultural framework of existence. The fourth stage of development involves aligning the motivations of your ego with the motivations of your soul. The last three stages of development involve activating your soul's consciousness. The Seven Stages of Psychological Development and the three evolutionary stages of the ego-soul dynamic are shown in Figure 5.1.

Figure 5.1: The Seven Stages of Psychological Development and three evolutionary stages of the ego-soul dynamic.

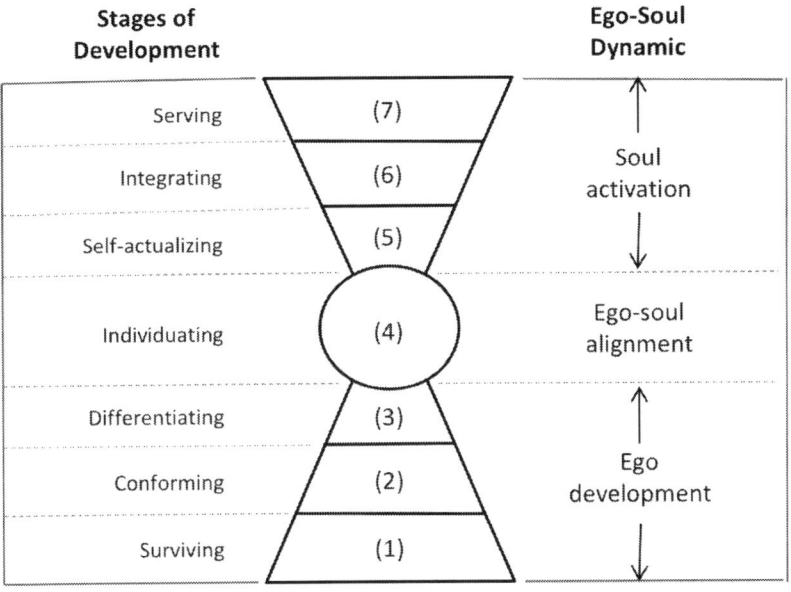

Ego development

Between the moment, we are born and the time we reach physical and mental maturity, around 20–25 years old, we pass through three stages of psychological development: surviving, conforming and differentiating. What we are learning during these stages of psychological development is how to satisfy our deficiency needs—our survival, safety and security needs—in the physical, social and cultural framework of our existence. If for any reason, you are unable to satisfy your deficiency needs you will feel anxious and fearful.

How well you were able to master your deficiency needs will, to a large extent, depend on the parental programming and cultural conditioning you experienced during your infant, childhood and teenage years. If you grew up in a safe physical environment and a loving and respectful social and cultural environment, without experiencing any traumatic experiences, you will find it relatively easy to master your deficiency needs. If, you grew up in a challenging physical, social and cultural environment where you had to struggle, and often failed, to get your deficiency needs met, you will find it difficult to master your deficiency needs.

Ego-soul alignment

The process of ego-soul alignment begins at the individuating stage of psychological development. What you are attempting to do at this stage of development is to let go of the fears of your ego that keep you dependent on your social and cultural frameworks of existence to satisfy your deficiency needs. The goal at this stage of development is to become a viable independent human being—to find freedom and autonomy in your life by disembedding yourself from your tribe—from the social and cultural context of your dependency. You do this by letting go of the fears you learned during the first three stages of development about satisfying your deficiency needs and by becoming responsible and accountable for every aspect of your life.

Unlike the ego stages of psychological development, the individuating stage of development is not thrust upon you by the biological and societal exigencies of growing up: it is driven by the evolutionary impulse of your soul willing itself to become fully present in 3-D material awareness.

The individuating stage can be quite challenging for a number of reasons. First, it involves facing and overcoming your fears. Second, it involves becoming responsible and accountable for every aspect of your life. Third, it involves embracing your soul nature, the values that support soul consciousness. This may mean distancing yourself from your family of origin, your cultural heritage and your religious affiliation.

For various reasons, some of which are out of our control, most people find it difficult to individuate. They remain "stuck" in the self-esteem, relationship and survival levels of consciousness (not the stages of development but the levels of consciousness) because the physical, social or cultural conditions in which they live actively discourage them from embracing their true nature, finding their voice and expressing themselves.

Soul activation

The last three stages of psychological development represent various stages of soul activation. If you have been relatively successful in mastering the individuating stage of development, you will begin to feel the pull of the self-actualizing stage of development in your early 40s. This is the stage of development where you begin to embrace your true nature and your inborn, soul-given gifts and talents. This is also normally the stage where you begin to uncover your soul's purpose, the activities that give your life meaning.

Uncovering your soul's purpose can be challenging, especially if the career you chose in your teens or 20s does not align with your gifts and talents. I know first-hand what it means to give up a successful career to follow your soul purpose. It was scary but it also felt unavoidable: it was something I had to do. Now, some twenty-five years later, I am in awe of the benefits and the joy that choosing to follow my soul's purpose has brought to my life.

The next stage of soul activation—the integrating stage of development, which usually occurs in your 50s—involves connecting with others in unconditional loving relationships so you can use your gifts and talents to make a difference in the world. The hard work of understanding who you are, and embracing your soul purpose is past. Your challenge now, is to develop your empathy skills so you can connect and collaborate with others and thereby use your collective gifts and talents to make a difference in people's lives. If you cannot reach out and connect with others, you will be unable to fulfil your purpose.

The last stage of soul activation—the serving stage of development, which usually occurs in your 60s—involves living a life of self-less service focused on future generations and the good of humanity. Having learned how to connect, what you are now tasked with doing is making a contribution to the common good. To fulfil this requirement, you will need to develop your compassion, to embrace the deepest aspects of your soul's intelligence and wisdom to help those who are suffering, disadvantaged or are less well off than yourself. At the integrating stage you make use of your empathy skills to connect; at the serving stage, you use of your compassion skills to contribute.

The seven stages of psychological development are shown in Table 5.1. The first column identifies the stages of psychological development; the second column indicates the approximate age ranges when each stage of development starts to become important; the third column describes the developmental tasks associated with each stage of development; the fourth column identifies the motivations and needs associated with each stage of development; the fifth column lists the primary internal and external focus of development at each stage of development.

The age ranges given are approximate but appear to apply to well-educated people of all races, religions and cultures. Those who are less well-educated, are poor or who live in authoritarian regimes may find it challenging to move beyond the differentiating stage of development. They will be too focused on meeting their deficiency needs or too fearful of the repercussions they might experience by giving voice to their soul's values and expressing their soul's purpose.

It is important to note that there are some significant differences between the first three stages of psychological development, which occur in our infant, childhood and teenage years, and the last four stages, which occur after we have reached adulthood.

The first three stages of development occur during a period when our physical brains and our minds are growing and developing; during a period of rapid emergent learning about how to establish ourselves in the physical, parental, and cultural frameworks of our existence. Furthermore, the first three stages of development are thrust upon us by the circumstances of growing up: from being a baby, through childhood and adolescence, to becoming a young adult. Not only do we have no choice in this matter, we are completely unaware of the fact that we are transitioning through the first three stages of psychological development.

As far as adult development is concerned, we can choose to individuate or not, and we can choose to self-actualize or not. If we make both of these choices, then the remaining stages of psychological development will naturally flow when we reach our 50s and 60s. Our ability to master the soul activation stages of our development is fundamentally dependent on our ability to master the ego development stages. We have to learn to meet our ego's deficiency needs before we can learn to satisfy our soul's growth desires.

The stages of psychological development

Table 5.1: The tasks, motivations and developmental focus associated with each stage of psychological development.

Stages of psychological development	Age range	Developmental task	Motivation	Developmental focus	
				Internal	External
Serving	60+ years	Alleviating suffering and caring for the well-being of humanity and the planet.	Satisfying your need for self-less service.	Compassion	Contribution
Integrating	50–59 years	Connecting with others in unconditional loving relationships.	Satisfying your need to make a difference.	Empathy	Connection
Self-actualizing	40–49 years	Expressing your true nature by embracing your soul's values and purpose.	Satisfying your need to find meaning and purpose.	Authenticity	Self-expression
Individuating	25–39 years	Discovering your true identity by letting go of your dependence on others.	Satisfying your need for freedom and autonomy.	Responsibility	Accountability
Differentiating	8–24 years	Establishing yourself in a community by displaying your gifts, skills and talents.	Satisfying your need for respect and recognition.	Security	Achievement
Conforming	2–7 years	Feeling safe and protected by staying close to your kin and your family.	Satisfying your need for love, and belonging.	Safety	Harmony
Surviving	Birth to 2 years	Staying alive and physically healthy by getting your survival needs met.	Satisfying your need for physiological survival.	Health	Survival

Having briefly explored the structure of our ego-soul dynamic and how it relates to the Seven Stages of Psychological Development, let us now examine what is involved in mastering each stage of psychological development.

Surviving (0–2 years)

The quest for survival starts before the human baby is born; it begins in the womb. From the moment the reptilian mind/brain becomes functional, around the end of the first trimester of gestation, the primary focus of the mind of the foetus is survival.

Because of its species programming, the foetus, and later the baby, instinctively knows how to regulate its body's internal functioning, how to suckle once it is born and how to signal to its mother that it has unmet physiological needs. At this stage of development, the baby is completely dependent for its survival on its mother or other primary caregivers.

The first thing the baby has to learn, as soon as it is born, is to interact with the world around it so it can get its survival needs met. If the infant finds this task difficult or challenging because its parents or caregivers are not vigilant, or if it is abused or left alone or abandoned for long periods of time, the infant may form subconscious beliefs that the world is an unsafe place and that it is not loved. Thereafter, throughout his or her life, this person will seek to control their environment to assure their needs get met. Such a person will be cautious and vigilant and have a tendency to micro-manage whatever is happening in their world.

If, the infant's parents or caregivers are attentive to its needs and are watchful and responsive to signs of distress, then the child will grow up with the feeling that the world is a safe place and people can be trusted.

Feeling competent, and confident about taking care of yourself is an essential prerequisite for mastering the self-actualization stage of development later in life.

Conforming (2–7 years)

Towards the end of the surviving stage of development, the child becomes mobile and learns to communicate. This is the time when the limbic mind/

brain, also known as the emotional mind, becomes dominant. The focus of the limbic mind/brain is on physical and emotional safety—keeping the body safe from harm, and satisfying its need for love and belonging. Thus begins the conforming stage of development.

At first, the child rebels: it wants what it wants when it wants it. It has not yet learned that the people it depends on for its survival and safety also have needs. To get its needs met, the child learns to follow the rules laid down by its parents. It learns that life is more pleasant and enjoyable, less threatening and less difficult, if it can live in a state of harmony with its caregivers and siblings.

Conforming—obeying the rules—has benefits: it allows the child to meet its physical and emotional safety needs. Participating in family rituals are also important at this stage of development because they contribute to the child's feeling of belonging and safety. If the parents make the child's adherence to rules conditional on the child getting its desires met, or the child is coerced into behaving in specific ways, the child will learn that love is conditional.

If, because of poor parenting or lack of attention, the child feels unloved, unimportant, not accepted and not protected or it doesn't feel a sense of belonging, the child may develop the subconscious belief that it is unlovable. When you do not get your safety needs met at a young age, they do not go away; they are imprinted in the subconscious memory of your emotional mind. You become needy, always searching for love.

If the child's parents or caregivers are attentive to the child's needs; if it is raised in a caring, loving environment, where its feels safe and protected, then the child will grow up with the desire and willingness to form committed relationships when it reaches adulthood.

Learning to feel safe, comfortable and loving in the presence of strangers is an essential prerequisite for mastering the integrating stage of development later in life. If you don't feel safe with others, you will find it difficult to reach out and connect.

Differentiating (8–24 years)

Around the age of 7 or 8, the neocortex mind/brain becomes functional. The focus of the neocortex mind/brain, also known as the rational mind, is on physical and emotional security. Thus begins the differentiating stage of psychological development.

At this stage of development, the child is beginning to explore the world outside of the home. Whereas parental and sibling relations were of significant importance to satisfy the child's safety needs when the locus of its life was the parental home, relations with peers and authority figures such as teachers, now take on added importance.

Once a child enters a community outside the home it can no longer rely on its parents for its personal safety. It must take responsibility for its self-protection by belonging to a group, community or gang. This means building friendships, fitting in, and being respected by members of the group. Taking on dares, can become a rite of passage for membership of some groups in the teenager's or young adult's world. This may lead young people "off the straight and narrow". They may do things they know to be wrong simply to belong to a group where they can feel recognized and secure.

Feeling respected and recognized by parents or members of a group, enables us to establish a feeling of self-worth; feeling accepted and acknowledged, gives us a sense of belonging and security. The gifts, skills and talents that allow us to feel recognized become important to us. We focus on them because they are our passport to security.

The types of gifts or talents we develop, depend to a large extent on the type of community we belong to. These could include beauty, intelligence, strength, sporting ability, musical ability, fearlessness, etc. Developing our strengths—the things that bring us recognition—allow us to establish ourselves in a community. If, however, we want to become the group leader, we need to stand out from the crowd. We may need to prove our superiority or defend ourselves from those who also want to lead the group.

What is important at this stage of development is exploring your talents and getting positive feedback and appreciation for your efforts. If your efforts are not appreciated by those who are important to you, particularly your parents and teachers, you will stop trying, and may begin to develop a low sense of self-esteem. If instead of having your efforts appreciated, you are constantly reminded of your failures, you will grow up lacking in confidence, with a low sense of self-worth, and the belief that you are not good enough.

When you do not get your security needs met in your childhood or teenage years, they do not go away; they remain in your subconscious mind. Later in life you may become highly competitive or seek status or power so you can be acknowledged as someone important or someone to be feared.

If you do not get the approval and feedback you need from your parents, you may seek out groups, gangs or communities where you feel accepted and valued; where your gifts, skills or talents are recognized. This may create conflict in your life at home because you may get caught between two value systems: the values of your parents, and the values of the group with which you identify. If this situation is not handled sensitively by your parents, your home life will become difficult and may become intolerable. You will rebel.

From a parental perspective, guiding rather than controlling, allowing rather than preventing, encouraging rather than denigrating and trusting rather than doubting, gives teenagers the space to safely explore who they are and find their sense of identity in the larger world outside the family home.

Feeling physically and emotionally secure in your community—being respected and recognized by others—is an essential prerequisite for mastering the serving stage of development later in life. If you don't feel secure in your community, you will not be able to contribute.

Individuating (25–39 years)

Around your mid-20s you begin to feel a new impulse: you want to explore who you really are. You want freedom, and the feeling of independence. To do this, you must let go of your parental programming and cultural conditioning and find your own way in life.

If you can transition through the first three stages of development without experiencing any significant trauma or without developing too many subconscious fears, you will find it relatively easy to establish yourself as a viable independent adult in the social and cultural framework of your existence.

So long as you can find opportunities to earn a living that allow you to explore your freedom, and work that gives you autonomy, everything will be fine. If you cannot find work that allows you to be independent of your parents, you will feel demoralized or dispirited.

The task at the individuating stage of development is to find your authentic self. You are finished with being dependent; you are seeking independence. You are no longer looking for the validation of others to feel good about yourself. You want to be responsible and accountable for every aspect of your life; you want to embrace and express your values. Without realizing it, you are disembedding yourself from your parental and cultural background, and beginning to align the motivations of your ego with the motivations of your soul.

The individuating stage of development usually begins in earnest in your mid-20s and continues through your 30s—after you have left your parental home and established yourself in the outside world.

This shift from dependence to independence can be one of the most difficult stages of human development to master because it brings us face to face with our survival, safety and security fears. Many find it difficult to extract themselves from the influence of their parents; others, such as those who live in authoritarian or repressive regimes, may be afraid to express themselves because they know they can be locked up or lose their life for speaking their truth or for being homosexual.

If you were fortunate enough to have been brought up by self-actualized parents; to have lived in a community or culture where freedom and independence are celebrated, where higher education was easily available, where men and women are treated equally, and where you are encouraged from a young age to express your needs and think for yourself, you will find it relatively easy to move through the individuating stage of psychological development.

If the contrary is true, if you were brought up by authoritarian parents, if you do not live in a democratic regime, if you are discriminated against because of your gender, sexual preferences, religion or race, and you developed fears about not being able to meet your deficiency needs, you are likely to have difficulties moving through the individuating stage of development. Struggling to survive, and seeking the safety and security you did not get when you were young can keep you anchored in the lower levels of consciousness all of your life.

Self-actualizing (40–49 years)

When you reach your 40s, sometimes a little earlier and sometimes a little later, your soul begins to make its presence felt in your life. If you have mastered your deficiency needs and successfully moved through the individuating stage of development, you will start to search for meaning and purpose in your life; you will be looking for a vocation or calling that allows you to fully express your authentic self. Welcome to the self-actualizing stage of development.

For most people, finding their vocation or calling usually begins with a feeling of unease or boredom about their job, profession or chosen career—with the work they thought would enable them to feel secure by providing them with a good income and prospects for advancement leading to increased wealth, status or power. Uncovering your soul's purpose not only brings vitality to your life, it also sparks your creativity. You will become more intuitive and spend more time in a state of flow; being totally present to what you are doing, and feeling committed and passionate about your work.

Mastering the self-actualizing stage of development can be challenging, especially if your vocation or calling offers less security than the job, profession or career you trained for earlier in your life. You may feel scared or uncomfortable embarking in a new direction that does not pay the rent or finance your children's education but does bring meaning and purpose to your life.

Some people find their vocation early, others discover it much later; some spend their whole lives searching. Uncovering and embracing your soul's purpose is vitally important because it is the key to living a fulfilling life.

Your ability to manage your survival needs will significantly influence your ability to make progress at the self-actualizing stage of development. Knowing you can take care of yourself gives you the confidence you need to explore your self-expression. If you are afraid that you might not be able to survive doing what you love to do, you may deny your soul expression. This will lead to suffering later in life.

Integrating (50–59 years)

If you learned how to master your deficiency needs and were successful in traversing the individuating and self-actualizing stages of development, when you reach your 50s, you will want to embrace your soul's purpose by making a difference in the world. To do this you will need to connect with others; to form caring relationships with those you want to help and those you want to collaborate with to leverage your impact in the world. Welcome to the integrating stage of psychological development.

Connecting with others who share your passion and purpose and connecting with those who will be the beneficiaries of your gifts and talents are essential components of this stage of development. The skills you learned at the conforming stage of development about building safe relationships will become extremely important at this stage of development. To connect with and support others, you will need to tap into your empathy skills. You will need to feel what others are feeling if you are truly going to help them.

At this stage of development, you must be able to recognize your limitations, cooperate with others, assume a larger sense of identity and shift from being independent to being interdependent.

Some people get so wrapped up in themselves and their calling at the self-actualizing stage that they are unable to make this shift. They get lost in their own creativity, focusing only on their contribution, rather than the larger contribution they could make if they connected with others. There is nothing wrong with this approach; however, in normal circumstances, learning to work with others in service to the common good is more likely to bring a sense of fulfilment to your life than working on your own.

How well you mastered the conforming stage of development will significantly influence your progress through the integrating stage of development. Knowing you can handle your relationship needs—knowing you are lovable—gives you the confidence to create unconditional loving relationships with others.

Serving (60+ years)

The last stage of development follows naturally from the integrating stage. I call this the serving stage of development. This stage of development usually begins to occur in your early 60s, sometimes a little earlier, sometimes a little later. The focus of this stage of development is on self-less service to the community you identify with. It is about making a contribution. It does not matter how big or small your contribution is, what is important is knowing that your life has a purpose. Alleviating suffering, caring for the disadvantaged and building a better society are some of the activities you may want to explore at this stage of your life.

At you enter the serving stage of development, you will find yourself becoming more introspective and reflective—looking for ways to deepen your sense of connection to your soul and the deeper levels of your being—connecting to whatever you consider divine. You may become a keeper of wisdom, an elder of the community or a person to whom younger people turn for guidance or mentoring.

As you make progress with this stage of development, you will uncover new levels of compassion in your life. You will experience a deep sense of meaning and feelings of fulfilment and well-being that you never experienced before. You will begin to see how connected we all are; how, by serving others, you are serving your larger self. At this level of consciousness, giving becomes the same as receiving.

How well you mastered the differentiating stage of development will significantly influence your progress through the serving stage of development. Having a healthy sense of self-esteem will give you the confidence to go out into your community and make your gifts, skills and talents available to those who need them.

A summary of key points

Here are the main points of Chapter 5:

1. The Seven Stages of Psychological Development Model differs from most other models in one important way. It looks at development through the lens of the ego-soul dynamic: the growth and development of the ego, the alignment of the ego with the soul, and the activation of the soul consciousness.
2. The first three stages of development are about the development of the ego—learning how to satisfy your survival, safety and security needs.
3. The process of ego-soul alignment begins at the individuating stage of psychological development.
4. The last three stages of psychological development are about soul activation—uncovering your soul's purpose, connecting with others in unconditional loving relationships, and living a life of self-less service focused on the common good.

5. The task at the surviving stage of development is to learn how to stay alive and physically healthy by getting your survival needs met.
6. The task at the conforming stage of development is to learn how to feel safe and protected by staying close to your kin and your family.
7. The task of the differentiating stage of development is to learn how to establish yourself in a community by displaying your gifts, skills and talents.
8. The task at the individuating stage of development is to learn who you are by letting go of your dependence on others to satisfy your needs.
9. The task at the self-actualizing stage of development is to learn how to express your true nature by embracing your soul's values and purpose.
10. The task at the integrating stage of development is to learn how to connect with others in unconditional loving relationships.
11. The task at the serving stage of development is to learn how to alleviate suffering and care for the well-being of humanity and the planet.

References and notes

1. For a list of development models, see Ken Wilber, *Integral Psychology: Consciousness, Spirit, Psychology, Therapy* (Boston: Shambhala Publications), 2000, and Dr. Alan Watkins, *Coherence: The Secret Science of Brilliant Leadership* (London: Kogan Page), 2014.
2. You can also find a discussion of six models of maturation in George E. Vaillant, *Triumphs of Experience*, (Boston: First Harvard University Press), 2012, pp. 114–189.

6

Notes on the Stages of Psychological Development

Understanding your value priorities enables you to work out where you are on your journey of psychological development and what is motivating you. Your primary motivations and values will reflect the needs of the stage of development you have reached..

Having described the Seven Stages of Psychological Development and the developmental tasks associated with each stage, I would like to make some additional comments about the stages of psychological development model. The topics I want to cover are:

- The ordering of the stages of development.
- The seven levels of consciousness.
- Primary and secondary motivations.
- Values priorities.
- The evolution of creativity.
- Identity and maturing.
- Engaging your soul as self-witness.

Ordering of stages

The Seven Stages of Psychological Development occur in consecutive order. Each stage of development provides a foundation for the subsequent stage.

You cannot jump stages, but from time to time, you may experience higher *states* of consciousness, especially after you have reached the individuating stage.

For most people, it takes a full lifetime—at least 60–70 years—to pass through the Seven Stages of Psychological Development, because each stage is linked to the seasons of our lives. Occasionally you may come across a person who is on accelerated growth path. If you complete the journey, you can look forward to joy, good health and a feeling of well-being in the latter years of your life.

Your ability to master the higher stages of development can be significantly impaired by the difficulties you have in mastering the first three stages of development. Repeated painful experiences of not getting your needs met when you are young get "hard-wired" into your mind because this is a time of rapid emergent learning when the synapses in your brain are forming.

Synapses are "electrical" connections that correspond to the beliefs in your mind. The links made by your synapses are like causal linkages that enable you to interpret your experiences by giving them meaning. The meaning you give them is based on the strongest synaptic connections.

Consequently, when you constantly fail to get your needs met at an early age, you form limiting beliefs that haunt you for the rest of your life. You must build new positive beliefs and new synaptic connections if you want to change your life.

Levels of consciousness

We grow in stages of psychological development, and we operate at levels of consciousness. The level of consciousness we operate from will normally reflect the concerns of the stage of psychological development we have reached. If at any moment in time an issue arises that reflects the concerns of an earlier stage of development, you will revert to that level of consciousness.

For example, if you are at the individuating stage of development, and you suddenly lose your job and run out of money, you will immediately shift from the transformation level of consciousness to the survival level of consciousness.

No matter what stage of development you are at, an unmet deficiency need will always cause you to shift to the level of consciousness that reflects that need. If you have any limiting beliefs about your ability to meet your deficiency needs, you could find yourself being triggered into a lower level of consciousness quite frequently, sometimes to the extent that it impairs your ability to focus on mastering the stage of development you are at.

Fears or anxieties about meeting our deficiency needs must be addressed because without the ability to master these needs we cannot master the later stages of development. We must master our survival needs to master the self-actualizing stage of development; we must master our relationship needs to master the integrating stage of development; we must master our self-esteem needs to master the serving stage of development.

Table 6.1 shows the relationship between the Seven Stages of Psychological Development and the Seven Levels of Consciousness. Alongside each level of consciousness, I have indicated the concerns and issues—unmet ego needs or unmet soul desires—that cause us to shift from the level of consciousness of the stage of development we are at, to a lower level of consciousness.

Table 6.1: Concerns and issues associated with each level of consciousness.

Stage of development	Level of consciousness	Concerns and issues
Serving	Service	Isolation and lack of ability to contribute
Integrating	Making a difference	Loneliness and lack of ability to connect
Self-actualizing	Internal cohesion	Life purpose and lack of meaning
Individuating	Transformation	Freedom and lack of autonomy
Differentiating	Self-esteem	Self-worth, recognition and lack of respect
Conforming	Relationships	Relationships, conflicts and lack of harmony
Surviving	Survival	Health, finances and threat to life

To contribute, we must be able to connect. To connect, we must be able to express what is important to us. To express what is important to us, we must have freedom. To have freedom we must feel secure. To feel secure, we must feel safe in our relationships. To feel safe in our relationships, we must be able to survive. Without an ability to survive, we cannot meet any of our needs.

Table 6.2 shows some of the main feelings and the thoughts we have that reflect the concerns and issues associated with each level of consciousness. These feelings frequently lead to depression and can lead to suicide, particularly when you feel you don't belong, you feel trapped or your feel your life has no meaning. I will explore the topic of suicide at different stages of development in Chapter 14.

Table 6.2: Feelings and thoughts associated with a lack of mastery of levels of consciousness.

Level of consciousness	Feelings and thoughts associated concerns and issues
Service	I feel I have nothing to offer my community.
Making a difference	I feel I have nothing in common with the people around me.
Internal cohesion	I feel my life has no meaning.
Transformation	I feel trapped and there is no way out.
Self-esteem	I feel I am not enough. I feel like I do not belong.
Relationships	I feel I am not loved enough. I do not feel accepted.
Survival	I feel I do not have enough to survive. I feel vulnerable.

Primary and secondary motivations

At any moment in time, your primary motivation will be to satisfy the needs of your current stage of psychological development. If you have any needs from the earlier stages of your development that remain unsatisfied or limiting beliefs associated with not getting your deficiency needs met, these will be your secondary motivations.

No matter what stage of development you have reached when a situation arises that reminds you of one of your unsatisfied needs, your secondary motivations will take precedence over your primary motivation.[1] This happens because our fears, either our present moment fears or the fears we formed when we were young about not being able to get our needs met, always hijack our conscious. This in-built mechanism is extremely useful for survival, but can considerably hinder our psychological development later on in life.

Most people are not conscious of their primary or secondary motivations. The only criteria they have for making choices and decisions in their lives is what makes them feel good in the moment. What makes them feel good in the moment is the satisfaction of their current needs and any unmet needs they have still have from the past.

This is why it is extremely useful if you are in one of the caring or coaching professions to understand the seven levels of psychological development. By identifying the primary motivation of your clients and their most important secondary motivations, you will be able to help them reach a deeper understanding of what is important to them in their lives at the current moment in time.

In my book, *Evolutionary Coaching*, you will find exercises and tools to help you identify a person's primary motivation—the stage of psychological development they are at, and clarify their most important secondary motivations—the stages of psychological development they have passed through where they still have unmet needs.[2]

Value priorities

Each stage of psychological development has its own motivations, tasks and needs, and therefore its own values. The Italian psychiatrist Roberto Assagioli makes the following observation about the link between values and stages of development:

> The existence of different levels of being having different values is an evident and undeniable manifestation of the great law of evolution, as it progresses from simple and crude stages to more refined and highly organized ones.[3]

Whatever is important to us in our lives at any given moment—what we need—is what we value. Consequently, what we value at one stage of development can change or shift priority when we move to a higher stage of development. Figures 6.1 and 6.2 provide examples of how value priorities change as we grow older.

Figure 6.1 shows the proportion of people in the UK in different age ranges that chose friendship as one of their top ten value priorities. Figure 6.2 shows similar data for the value of honesty. What we observe from these two figures is that friendship decreases quite rapidly as a value priority from our teenage years to our mid-30s and then levels off. Honesty tends to increase in priority until we reach our 60s and then declines slightly. Two of the conclusions we can draw from this data are that friendship is more important when we are young and single and a lower priority when we get married and have children and that honesty appears to have increasing utility as we get older, but begins to have a lower priority when we reach old age.

Figure 6.1: Proportion of people in the UK choosing the value of friendship as one of their top ten value priorities.

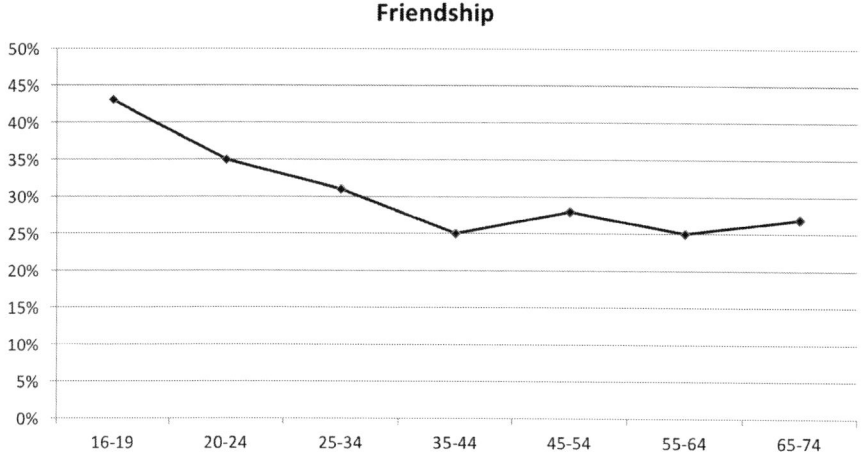

Figure 6.2: Proportion of people in the UK choosing the value of honesty as one of their top ten value priorities.

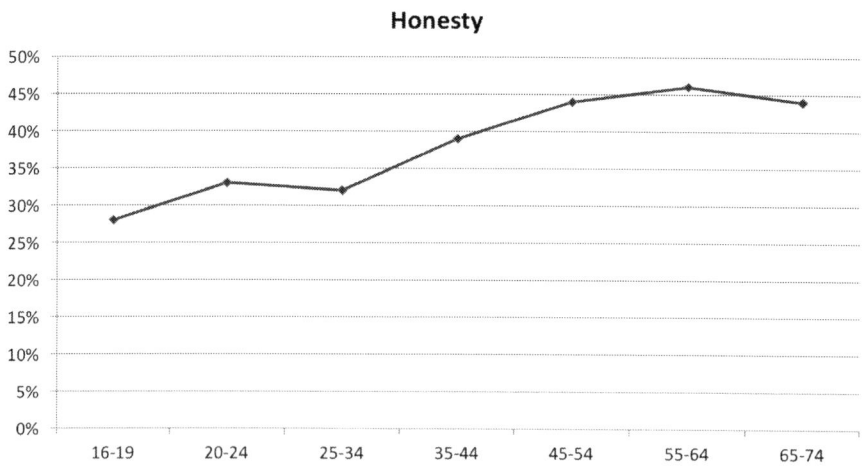

The changing nature of our value priorities is a reflection of two things: the shift in the tasks associated with each of the stages of psychological development; and the shift in our life circumstances. Generally speaking, our values are more focused on our needs during the early stages of development and more focused on the needs of others in the later stages of development.

Experiencing the shift in value priorities means that when you reach the later stages of your development, you are in a better position to understand the needs, motivations and challenges of those who are younger than yourself. Conversely, someone in the early stages of development will have difficulties understanding the needs, motivations and challenges of those who are older than them.

This is why it is important, as soon as you can in your life, to stop blaming your parents for whatever they did to you and try to understand what was going on in their lives. See their lives through their eyes, not yours. What challenges did *they* have when *they* were young? What needs did *they* have that went unmet? What made them the way they are, and how might this have affected their relationship to you? We all have the unreasonable assumption that our parents should have been perfect, but the truth is that every family is dysfunctional to some degree. Growing up without forming some subconscious or unconscious fear-based beliefs is impossible. Parenting without letting your subconscious and unconscious fears influence your children to some degree is equally impossible.

Evolution of creativity

One of the most significant benefits of choosing to explore the latter stages of your psychological development is the re-engagement you have with your creativity.

A landmark study by George Land, reported in *Break-point and Beyond*,[4] explored the changing level of creativity of a cohort of young children as they grew up to become young adults. Sixteen hundred children in the US were involved.

Land gave the children tests to assess their level of creative divergent thinking. The first set of eight tests was given between the ages of three and five, the second set between the ages of eight and ten, and a third set between the ages of thirteen and fifteen. The results were striking (see Figure 6.3).

Figure 6.3: The percentage of people with genius level creativity by age.

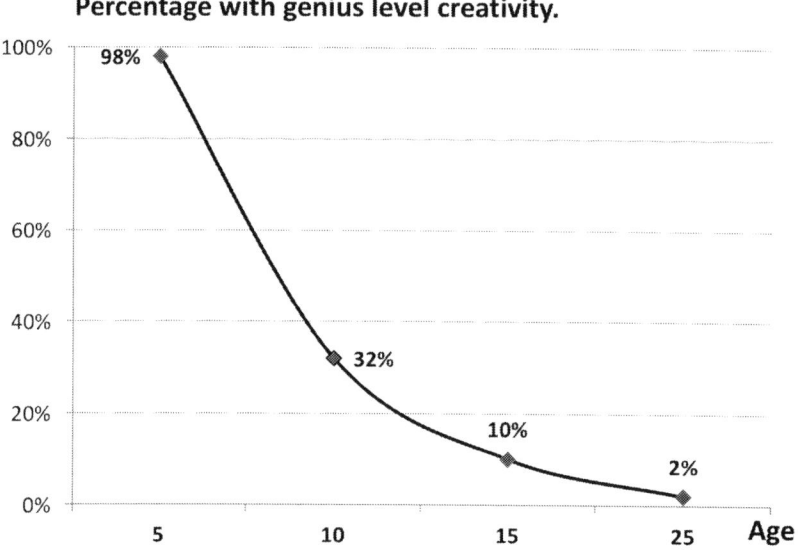

Land found that 98 per cent of the children in the three to five age group had genius level creativity, but only 32 per cent had genius level creativity five years later. Five years later, only 10 per cent had genius level creativity. Two-hundred thousand adults over the age of 25 had the same tests, and only 2 per cent had genius level creativity.

The principle question that this research poses is what happened to our creativity? Land concludes:

> …the socialization process restricts the natural creativity of our thinking potential by automatically assigning value judgments such as good, bad, right, wrong, proper, improper, ugly, beautiful.[5]

I believe it is not the socialization experience that blocks our creativity, it is the abandonment of our soul. What we do during the first 24 years of our lives is sacrifice the soul's desire for self-expression to meet the ego's needs for survival, safety and security. As the ego grows and develops, we abandon our connection to our soul. By the time we reach our 20s we have practically lost contact with our soul and its creativity. Only if you choose to individuate and explore the later stages of your psychological development, can you reconnect with your soul and its creativity.

In summarizing the results of the Grant and Terman studies, George Vaillant points out the positive correlation that exists between creativity and successful ageing. Although we may lose contact with our creativity in the first half or our lives, we can reconnect with it in the second half of our lives. I can certainly attest to this fact. At age 71, I have never been more creative. Why? Because I have never been more in touch with my soul.

Amit Goswami, a Professor of theoretical physics, reaches a similar conclusion about the difficulties that the well-developed ego has in accessing creativity:

> Creativity consists of making discontinuous quantum leaps into a non-local domain of pure potentiality that is not accessible to the thinking ego.[6]

In a study of college students, people who reported feeling happy and active were more likely to be doing something creative at the time. Paul Silvia of the University of North Carolina-Greensboro, who led the research team, writes in the journal *Psychology of Aesthetics, Creativity, and the Arts*.

> Engaging in creative pursuits allows people to explore their identities, form new relationships, cultivate competence and reflect critically on the world. In turn, the new knowledge, self-insight, and relationships serve as sources of strength and resilience.[7]

This leads me to the question: "What is the link between soul consciousness and creativity?" The answer is relatively simple. The soul creates everything it needs in the energy field of the fourth-dimension of consciousness through its thoughts. What it thinks, is the reality it creates. For the soul, thought *is* creativity. It lives in the world of its creation. This is also true for the ego. However, the problem with the ego is that it limits its creative potential through its beliefs. Instead of living in a field of possibilities, the ego lives in a field of limitations.

I will never forget learning this lesson when I was 17 years old. I was an only child, and my parents were relatively poor. They were good, hard working people but struggled at times to pay the bills. When I was 17, my father died, leaving my mother and I with hardly any savings. My mother was a stay-at-home mum and hadn't worked for more than twenty years. My father's one wish was that I go to university: no one in our family had ever been to university. My father had turned down that option when he was young to care for his widowed mother. I think he had always regretted that decision.

My mother took me aside a couple of months after my father's death and said, "We have to find a way to live. If you can get a grant to go to university, I will find a way to look after myself so you can fulfil your father's dream".

That is what happened. I got a grant from the education authority to cover the cost of my education, and my mother became a cleaner at the local Methodist Chapel. We somehow got by for the next five years. Then, when I started work, I quickly saved up my income to pay off my mother's mortgage and we lived "happily ever after".

My point is that my mother did not let the fears for her future get in the way of my future. She did not close down my options. She lived in a world of possibilities. She could have asked me to go straight to work after I had finished school at eighteen and earn enough money so we could both survive. I remember that we discussed that option, but instead of letting her fears guide her decision-making, she stayed open to other possibilities.

Identity and maturing

When we look at the stages of psychological development through the lens of the ego-soul evolutionary dynamic, we see some interesting shifts. We start our lives in soul consciousness; we shift into ego consciousness, and if we are successful in our maturing—if we can master the stages of psychological development—we finish our lives in soul consciousness. If we are not successful in our maturing—if we get stuck in the early stages of development—we finish our lives in ego consciousness.

The normal developmental journey from soul to ego consciousness and back to soul consciousness is shown in Figure 6.4. We begin our "descent" into ego consciousness soon after we are born. The soul becomes less dominant in our lives as we pass through our infant years. By the time we reach the differentiating stage of development, the ego is now in charge, and the soul has taken a back seat. We begin the "ascent" back into soul consciousness after we have passed through the individuating stage of development. If we complete this stage of development, by aligning the motivations of our ego with the motivations of our soul, and we find our soul's purpose, then we ascend back into soul consciousness.

Figure 6.4: Normal developmental process.

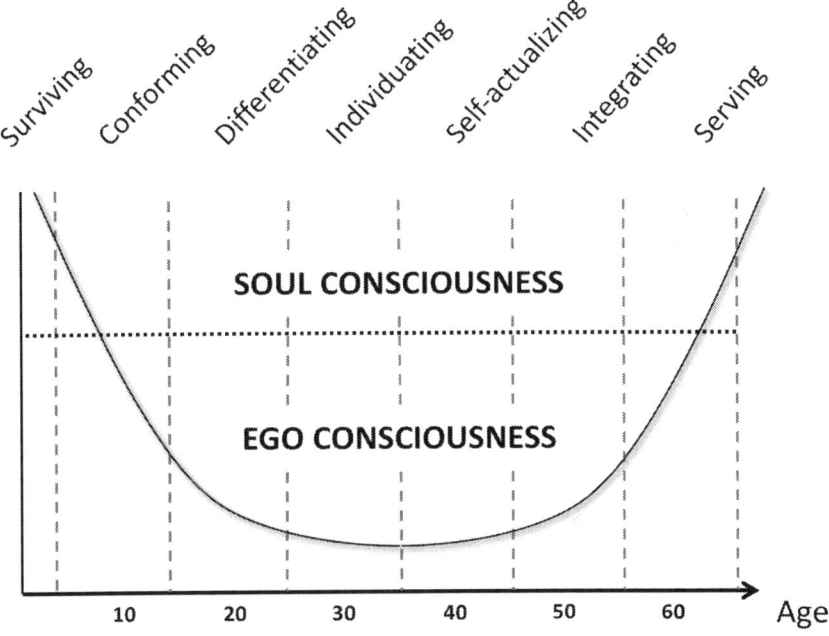

If you have the good fortune to live in a liberal democracy, have been brought up by self-actualized parents, and received an education that fostered your self-expression, and do not have any significant survival, safety or security needs in your life, you will not descend so deeply into ego consciousness. Figure 6.5 show what this looks like. You still pass through all the stages of psychological development, but your ego consciousness will be less dominant. Your soul consciousness will be more apparent, and you will begin to feel your soul impulses more strongly as you move through the individuating and self-actualizing stages of psychological development. This means your ascent into soul consciousness will be easier and more fluid.

Figure 6.5: Accelerated developmental process.

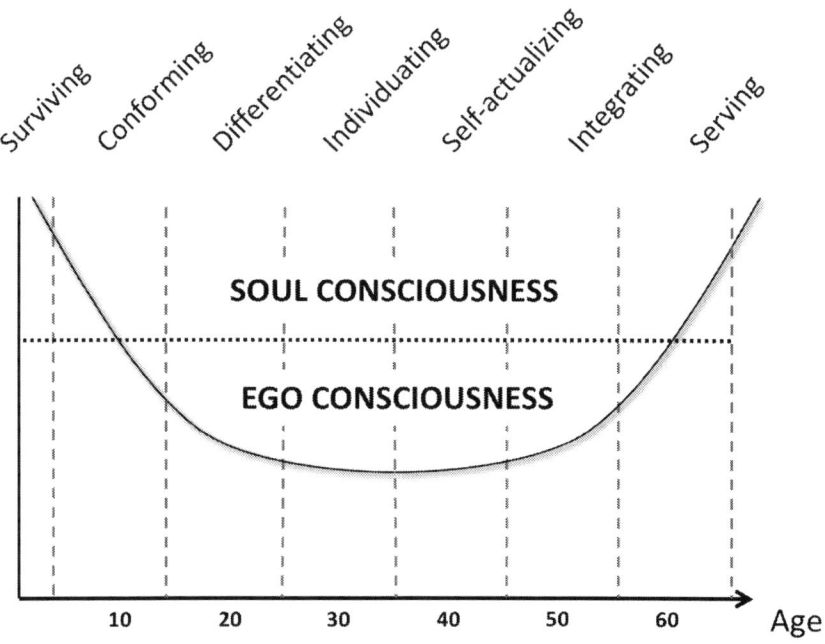

I believe these stages of development—starting off in soul consciousness and moving into ego consciousness—align with the work of Robert Kegan, a Professor at the Harvard School of Education. He describes the first stage of our life journey in the following manner:

> Most psychoanalytic psychologies share a common conception of the newborn's state. They consider the newborn to live in an objectless world, a world in which everything sensed is taken to be an extension of the infant, where out of sight (or touch, or taste or hearing or smell) can mean out of existence.[8]
> The transformation in the first eighteen months of life—giving birth to object relations—is only the first instance of that basic evolutionary activity...[9]

Keegan's description of the first two years of life sounds like the world of the soul—a complete sense of connection without separation—undifferentiated wholeness at the personal level.

According to Kegan, during this stage of development, we are learning to be in a body. We are involved in disembedding ourselves from our reflexes and recognizing objects: we move from being our reflexes, to having reflexes; we move from an expansive sense of self to a restricted sense of self; we begin to recognize the limitations of being in a material body rather than an energetic field. The new self can coordinate reflexes and recognize objects. I believe this is the beginning of the birth of the ego. For me this represents the first stage of the filtering out of soul consciousness. The soul does not know separation; it only knows connection.

At Kegan's second stage, the self becomes a set of needs. The child becomes aware that it can consciously manipulate objects and relationships to get its needs met. Gradually, we become aware that we are not our needs, but that we have needs. We can objectify our needs. We split off our needs from the process that generated the need. We objectify the need, but the process by which the need arose is relegated to our subconscious. For me, this represents the second stage of the filtering out of soul consciousness, because at the soul level we have no needs.

At this stage, the child is aware of other people but not aware that they also have needs. This leads into the third stage when the child reaches the understanding that it shares its world with other people. It leaves what I refer to as the surviving stage of development and enters the conforming stage of development. It is during this stage that the ego becomes dominant.

Kegan describes it this way:

> I no longer am my needs (no longer the imperial I); rather I have them. In having them I can now coordinate, or integrate, one need system with another, and in so doing, I bring into being that need-mediating reality which we refer to when we speak of mutuality.[10]

Because we can recognize that others also have needs, this stage of development gives rise to a sense of conscience and the potential for guilt and shame. Guilt is about recognizing that you have done something wrong: you have broken the rules that have been impressed on you by others. You have let people down. Shame internalizes the guilt by saying there is something wrong with me. For me, this represents the third stage of the filtering out of soul consciousness, because you internalize the sense of separation.

At Kegan's fourth stage of development, we begin to establish self-dependence. We move from "I am my relationships" to "I have relationships". There is now someone who is coordinating or reflecting on mutuality. At this stage, we split off the relationship from the process that generated the need for the relationship. We objectify the relationship, but the process by which it arose gets split off into our subconscious.

At this stage of development, I become more focused on my peers and up to a point, can choose the groups with which I affiliate. I also begin to understand that you don't have to like me (I don't need to fit in as much as I did at the previous stage because I am less dependent, more independent), but within the groups I affiliate with, it is important you respect me. You have to see me as an individual in my own right. This is the stage of development I refer to as the differentiating stage.

At Kegan's fifth stage of development, which I refer to as the individuating stage of development, we recognize that everyone we encounter is an individual like us. The self is no longer embedded in its physical body, in its needs, in its relationships or in the groups with which it affiliates. It is raw, individual, free and emergent, full of potential for self-expression. Having let go of what we are not, we are now in a position to connect with who we are; to feel and follow the impulses of the soul.

Kegan speaks of his fifth stage of development in the following manner:

> [The fifth stage gives you the] capacity to ... join others as individuals—people who are known ... as value-originating, system-generating, history-making individuals. The community is for the first time a "universal" one, in that all persons, by virtue of their being persons, are eligible for membership. The group which this self knows as "its own" is not a pseudo species, but the species.[11]

Kegan's developmental process which involves constant disembedding is similar to the approach pioneered by Roberto Assagioli. He calls it disidentification. According to Assagioli, once disidentification is complete then self-identification can begin. In other words, once we have let go of the mask of the ego and its identification with the body and the family and culture in which we are embedded, we can embrace our soul identity and our energetic reality. We had to embed ourselves in our social and cultural existence to learn how to survive, stay safe and feel secure—to meet the

Notes on the Stages of Psychological Development

soul's desire to be present in 3-D material reality—but once that has been achieved we are free to re-identify with the soul.

Engaging your soul as self-witness

Kegan states that at the fifth stage of development we can:

> ...hear and seek out information which might cause the self to alter its behaviour, or share in a negative judgement of that behaviour.[12]
>
> At stage 4, one's feelings [and emotions] seem often to be regarded as a kind of recurring administrative problem, which the successful ego-administrator resolves without damage to the smooth functioning of the "organization". When the self is located not in the institutional but the coordinating of the institutional, the interior life gets "freed up" ... [this] results in the capacity of the new self to move back and forth between psychic systems within in itself... emotional conflict seems to become recognizable and tolerable to the "self".[13]

I believe the shift from being part of the "institutional" to being the coordinator of the institutional is the shift from identification with the ego to identification with the soul. Instead of subjectively experiencing the ego, we can now objectify the ego. Instead of looking at the world through the ego, we can look at a world that includes the ego.

We have now reached the stage where we become self-reflective, and the soul becomes the witness of the ego. Engaging your self-witness can be achieved through the practice of mindfulness. Only when we can look at our lives through the lens of the self-witness are we able to objectify our subjective experiences. When we look at our emotions and thoughts, rather than through them, we can make conscious choices about what we think and how we want to feel.

Once you have learned to become your own self-witness, you can objectify your ego's thinking and emotions. By objectifying your ego's thinking and emotions, you can use your cognitive abilities to explore them. You can find out where your fears came from and how they arose. Once you have understood your fears and brought them into conscious awareness, they no longer have power over you. This is one of the fundamental skills involved in personal mastery.

Millennials

In recent years, I have noticed the early onset of the individuation stage of psychological development among a group of people known as the millennials. These are children who were born after 1982, live in liberal democracies, and have been raised by well-educated, wealthy parents where they did not encounter any difficulties in learning how to satisfy their deficiency needs. Research on Millennials in the US suggests:

> Millennials are unlike any other generation in living memory. They are more numerous, more affluent, better educated and more ethnically diverse. They are beginning to manifest a wide array of positive social habits that older Americans no longer associate with youth, including a new focus on teamwork, achievement, modesty and good conduct.[14]

They are optimists: they are happy, content and positive. They are cooperative team players. They accept authority. They trust and feel close to their parents. They are smarter than most people think. They believe in the future and see themselves living at the cutting-edge of society.

In my mind, the millennials display all the characteristics that I would associate with being brought up by individuated and self-actualized parents; parents who have mastered most of their fears and have found occupations that align with their gifts and talents.

The young people we call millennials have been loved and cherished, treated fairly and generously, and have been encouraged from an early age to express themselves. In other words, they feel secure in themselves; they have relatively few fears about satisfying their survival, safety and security needs, and many of them are ready and willing to explore their growth needs.

Despite the early onset of the individuation stage of development among millennials, we cannot yet draw the conclusion that they are on an accelerated path of development. I would rather say they are on an easier or more fluid path of development.

I make this remark for two reasons: first, this group have not struggled to get their needs met and therefore, have fewer fear-based beliefs to overcome; second, they are growing up with a peer group that has a more expansive world view. Annex 3 provides a detailed account of the evolution of world views and the impact that world views have on our psychological development.

Let us not forget, in speaking of millennials that they are mostly found in affluent democratic nations that have been politically stable for several decades. These are nations that support their populations in meeting their deficiency needs and encourage freedom of thought and freedom of speech. People in these countries are free to explore who they are and satisfy their growth needs.

A summary of key points

Here are the main points of Chapter 6:

1. The Seven Stages of Psychological Development occur in consecutive order. Each stage of development provides a foundation for the subsequent stage.
2. Your ability to master the latter stages of development can be significantly impaired by the experiences you have during the first three stages of development.
3. At any moment in time, your primary motivation will be to satisfy the needs of your current stage of psychological development.
4. If you have any unmet needs from the earlier stages of your development, these will be your secondary motivations.
5. Each stage of psychological development has its own motivations, tasks and needs, and therefore, its own values.
6. Whatever is important to us in our lives at any given moment—what we need—is what we value.
7. One of the most significant benefits of choosing to explore the later stages of psychological development is the re-engagement you have with your creativity.
8. We start our lives in soul consciousness; we shift into ego consciousness, and if we are successful in our maturing—if we

can complete the latter stages of psychological development—we finish our lives in soul consciousness.
9. Only when we can look at our lives through the lens of the self-witness are we able to objectify our subjective experiences.
10. Millennials display the characteristics that are associated with being brought up by individuated and self-actualized parents.

References and notes

1. For details on identifying people's primary and secondary motivations, please consult Richard Barrett, *Evolutionary Coaching: A Values-Based Approach for Unleashing Human Potential* (London: Fulfilling Books), 2014.
2. Richard Barrett, *Evolutionary Coaching: A Values-Based Approach to Unleashing Human Potential* (London: Fulfilling Books), 2014.
3. Roberto Assagioli, *The Act of Will* (New York: Penguin Books), 1973, p. 98.
4. George Land and Beth Jarman, *Break-point and Beyond* (New York: Harper Business), 1992.
5. Ibid., p. 153.
6. Amit Goswami, *Quantum Creativity* (New York: Hay House), 2014, p. 32.
7. http://www.psmag.com/books-and-culture/forget-tortured-artist-stereotype-creativity-breeds-happiness-74813
8. Robert Kegan, *The Evolving Self: Problem and Process in Human Development* (Boston: Harvard University Press), 1982, p. 78.
9. Ibid., p. 79.
10. Ibid., p. 104.
11. Ibid.
12. Ibid., p. 105.
13. Ibid.
14. Neil Howe and William Straus, *Millennials Rising: The Next Great Generation* (New York: Vintage Books), 2000, p. 4.

7

UNDERSTANDING NEEDS AND DESIRES

> *All you need to know about yourself is that the search to satisfy your ego's needs and your soul's desires is the engine of your psychological development. When you can meet your soul's desires, you become a co-creator in the evolution of human consciousness.*

Almost every hour of every day, every person on the planet is focused on the same thing: getting their needs met. Even when we are serving others in helping them to get needs met, we may still be attempting to satisfy our need to make a difference or be of service. There are hardly any activities we undertake that do not involve in some way trying to satisfy our ego's needs or our soul's desires.

Having recognized in the previous chapter the importance that satisfying our ego's needs and soul's desires plays in the stages of psychological development, I think it is now timely and important to define what needs and desires are and what they are not.

In his book, *Towards a Psychology of Being*, Abraham Maslow asks the question: "How does growth happen?" He answers in the following way:

> The single holistic principle that binds together the multiplicity of human motives is the tendency for a new and higher need to emerge as a lower need fulfils itself by being sufficiently gratified.[1]

What Maslow is saying is that what motivates our psychological development is the stage by stage gratification of our needs. When we have learned how to gratify the needs at one stage of psychological development, new, higher order needs automatically emerge that are associated with the next stage.

Human beings have four basic types of needs: physiological needs—the needs of the body; emotional needs—the needs of the ego; spiritual needs—the desires of the soul; and mental needs. What I believe is meant by "mental" needs is the need to understand what is happening to us and around us so that we can identify threats that might prevent us from meeting our survival, safety and security needs, as well as opportunities that could support us in satisfying our ego's needs and our soul's desires.

To my way of thinking, "understanding" is equivalent to meaning-making. Viewed from this perspective, meaning-making is not so much a need, but a fundamental construct of consciousness. Without meaning-making, evolution would never have happened, and human beings would not have learned how to survive.

People sometimes refer to our mental needs as intellectual needs. I do not believe we have intellectual needs; some people, and certainly not everyone, have intellectual curiosity. They want to know for the sake of knowing.

At the surviving stage of psychological development, our mind is primarily focused on satisfying our physiological *survival* needs. At the conforming stage of development, our mind is primarily focused on our physical and emotional *safety* needs. At the differentiating stage of development, our mind is primarily focused on our physical and emotional security needs. At the self-actualizing, integrating and serving stages of psychological development, our soul-mind is focused on our so-called spiritual needs, which I prefer to refer to as soul desires. The ego's desire for meaning, making a difference and being of service, correspond to the soul's desires for self-expression, connection and contribution.

In this context, the word "meaning" has a specific connotation: It means a sense of alignment. When the motivations of the ego are in alignment with the motivations of the soul, you will feel your life has meaning. The process of alignment begins at the individuating stage of development when you develop an understanding of who you are separate from the cultural context in which you live and with which you identify. Alignment continues at the self-actualizing stage of development when you discover and activate your soul-self.

Although finding meaning is important to the ego, it is not important to the soul. The soul already knows why it decided to incarnate. What the soul is looking for is to express this purpose in the material world of 3-D awareness. The ego is unaware of the soul's purpose and must, therefore, discover it. Only when the ego discovers the soul's purpose and takes action to manifest it in 3-D consciousness, can the ego fulfil its desire for meaning and the soul fulfil its desire for purpose.

Defining needs

At this point, I think it is important that we get more specific about what a need is and what it is not. I define needs as either a deficiency sensations experienced by the body or a feeling deficiencies experienced by the ego.

Deficiency sensations

The body has deficiency sensations. Although we say we feel hungry, or we feel thirsty, what we are experiencing is a deficiency sensation. We say we *feel* thirsty, or we *feel* hungry because the ego identifies with the body. Whenever we identify with the body, we interpret bodily sensations as feelings.

I think it is important to recognize that the sensations of the body are not feelings because they are not generated by the emotional mind; they are generated by the body-mind. This is why they are sensations.

Deficiency sensations occur when something that is essential for the maintenance of the internal stability (biological functioning) of the body is lacking. This is why satisfying a deficiency sensation is a physiological survival need. Deficiency sensations arise from the body-mind—the unconscious of the ego-mind—and only capture our conscious attention when they cause us discomfort. You know you need to eat when you have the sensation of hunger. You know you need to defecate when your bowels feel uncomfortable.

3-D material deficiency sensations are signs of 4-D energetic instability. Hunger is a signal from the body-mind that its energetic resources have been depleted, and this depletion is causing the body to experience difficulties in functioning. The same is true for all other bodily deficiency sensations.

Feeling deficiencies

The ego has feeling deficiencies. When we say we want/need to be loved, we are expressing the need to experience the feeling we call love—we want connection. Similarly, when we say we want/need respect, what we are saying is, we want to experience the feeling we call respect—we want to feel valued.

When we say we need love, or we need respect, it is because the meaning we have given to a situation we are experiencing causes us to feel that either love or respect is absent. Love and respect may or may not be absent; they may just be showing up in a form we do not recognize.

In other words, feeling deficiencies occur when the ego *believes* that something essential for the maintenance of its internal stability; safety or security, is lacking. It may not be lacking, but the ego believes it is lacking. This can happen in the present moment or when a present moment experience triggers the memory of a feeling deficiency that we experienced in the past. What is being triggered is a childhood memory of an unmet need that has not yet been resolved in your mind. We project the emotion and feelings associated with that unmet need onto the present situation.

Feeling deficiencies are a direct signal from your energy field that either love energy is not present, or your ego believes that love energy is missing. If love energy was present or you believed love energy were present, then you would not have feeling deficiencies. Love energy "cures" all feeling deficiencies.

Defining requirements

I think it is also important to differentiate between a need and a requirement. I say this because I often say to people I have no needs, meaning that all my needs are taken care of by my soul before I know I have them. However, the response I usually get is that of course you have needs. Everyone needs oxygen, or they will die. For me, oxygen is a requirement, not a need. Let me explain.

Whereas a requirement is something that is necessary, a need is something that is lacking. We say we need oxygen to survive, but rarely, if ever, are we in a situation where we don't have oxygen. That's why oxygen is a requirement. A requirement only becomes a need when what is required is not available or is believed to be lacking. For example, a supply of oxygen becomes a need when we go mountaineering or fly in a light aircraft above 3,000 metres. Unless we are used to living at high altitudes, we wouldn't dream of mountaineering or flying without oxygen because we would not *feel* safe.

Similarly, food, like oxygen is a requirement that is necessary to sustain life. However, food only becomes a need when food is not available or is believed to be lacking. Food and oxygen are known as physiological needs because they are necessary to sustain the life of the body. Other examples of physiological needs are water and warmth. When these are lacking, they are needs; when they are not lacking, they are requirements. All our physiological needs are requirements until we don't have them available. Only then do they become needs.

Defining wants

Another confusion we often make is between a want and a need. A want is not a need. A want is an object, action or situation we believe will enable us to get a need met—alleviate a deficiency sensation or feeling deficiency. When I say I want food, I am responding to a deficiency sensation. When I say I want love, I am responding to a feeling deficiency.

When I use the term "want", there is an implication that I believe that I will be able to get a need met when I get what I want. What we are effectively saying when we are dealing with "wants" is: if I get this (object), if you do that (action) or if this (situation) happens then my need will be met. In other words, a "want" is a wish for something that we believe will satisfy a need. We are using the object, action or situation as a substitute for a deficiency sensation or a feeling deficiency.

False needs and real needs

If what we want satisfies a deficiency sensation we can say that the want is a need, and it is a *real need*. If what we want (an object, action or situation) is intended to satisfy a feeling deficiency that arises from our failure to master our deficiency needs, what we want is a *false need*. Soon after we have got over the excitement (relief) of getting a false need met, we will want more.

Defining desires

Desires are not needs because a desire is not a yearning for something that is lacking; it is a longing for something that is as yet nascent or unexplored. It is a yearning for the "materialisation" of potential.

Whereas the ego gets anxious if its deficiency needs are not met, the soul does not get anxious if its desires are not met. When we can satisfy the soul's desires for self-expression, connection and contribution, the soul feels a sense of fulfilment and the ego feels a sense of meaning.

Definition of a need

Based on this we can define a need as:

> A real or imagined lack of something that is essential for maintaining the body's physiological (biological) stability or the ego's emotional stability.

A need is the ego's or the body's response to the soul's desire to be present in 3-D awareness. It is what the ego consciously and subconsciously believes is necessary for the soul to fulfil its purpose. It is what the body knows it has to do to keep the soul's incarnation intention alive.

You know you have an unmet need whenever you experience fear, anxiety, anger, frustration, impatience or any other form of emotional upset. The emotion of fear and its derivatives are signs that you either have a belief that something is lacking or a belief that something you have that is important to the satisfaction of your needs may be taken away.

What I am saying, when I believe I have a need is: "My life conditions are not perfect because I am currently experiencing a deficiency sensation or a feeling deficiency. I lack something that I believe is necessary to satisfy my soul's desire to be present in 3-D material awareness."

When you can convince yourself that nothing is lacking from your life—when you consider your life is perfect the way it is, when you are grateful for what you have and consider what you have to be sufficient—you are not just living in soul consciousness, you are living in a state of grace.

Love is all we need

The reason our souls don't have needs is that in their natural energetic environment of 4-D consciousness they instantaneously create the energy form of whatever they wish for through their thoughts. That's how the energetic world works: your energetic reality is created through the thoughts you hold in your mind. Consequently, our souls lack for nothing and never experience needs; they live in a state of abundance and connection. This is the energetic state we call love.

Love is the energy that supplies all our needs. If we have love, we have no other needs. When we allow love to flow out into the world through us, all our needs get met because love flows back to us through the "automatic" provision of the things we need to fulfil our soul's purpose.

The Beatles got it—they understood. They sang about it:

> There's nothing you can do that can't be done…
> No one you can save that can't be saved
> Nothing you can do but you can learn how to be you in time
> It's easy
>
> All you need is love
> All you need is love
> All you need is love, love
> Love is all you need[2]

I believe there are two key phrases here: "… you can learn to be you in time" and "love is all you need". When you learn to be who you are—a soul operating from 4-D consciousness in a 3-D material world, everything you need to fulfill your soul's purpose "magically" appears. Even the needs you did not know you had are met. When you live in this state, "there is nothing you can do that can't be done".

Implications

The implication of living in a world where your thoughts and beliefs create your energetic reality, where your thoughts and beliefs attract material outcomes, is not as far-fetched as the rational mind would have you believe.

Let me give you two examples: one linking thoughts and beliefs to material outcomes—the placebo effect—and one linking subconscious thoughts and beliefs to emotional outcomes. Both of these examples illustrate the quantum reality, that believing is experiencing.

Material outcomes

Whatever we believe, is the outcome we attract. That is why pessimists and optimists are equally successful in creating their realities. These statements align with quantum theory, which suggests that everything exists in all its possibilities in the quantum energy field, and it is the belief of the observer that collapses the field into a specific outcome that aligns with the observer's beliefs.

Nowhere is the positive belief phenomenon more obvious than in the practice of medicine. Countless studies have highlighted the importance of the placebo effect, sometimes called the placebo response. The placebo response is often used to test new drugs. One group of patients with a particular ailment are given a new drug, and another group with the same ailment are administered an inert substance, such as sugar, distilled water or a saline solution. Both groups are told they can expect the medication they have been given to improve their condition.

What is surprising to those who believe in 3-D material cause and effect, is that a significant number of people who are given the placebo recover from their ailment. The placebo response was first reported in 1955, in a paper by anaesthesiologist Henry K. Beecher (1904–1976).[3] Beecher concluded that across the 26 studies that he analysed, an average of 32 percent of patients responded to the placebo. These results suggested that there is a psycho-energetic effect in believing that the drug you are taking will give you the outcome that you have been told it will give.

Amazingly, sham (placebo) surgery also produces similar results. A Baylor School of Medicine study, published in 2002 in the *New England Journal of Medicine* describes a study that split sufferers of osteoarthritis of the knee into three groups. Two groups were operated on using proven, but different, clinical techniques. The third group went through the same surgery protocols, but once in the hands of the surgeon they only received an incision, then the incision was closed up. All groups went through the same rehabilitation process. The researchers were shocked by the results.

The outcomes of those who had placebo surgery were the same as those who had real surgery, and the improvements in the placebo group were just the same after one year as they were after two years. The conclusion of this study states:

> In this controlled trial involving patients with osteoarthritis of the knee, the outcomes after arthroscopic lavage or arthroscopic débridement were no better than those after a placebo procedure.[4]

Another article,[5] published in 2002 by Professor Irvine Kirsch in the American Psychological Association, entitled, *The Emperor's New Drugs*, made even more shocking discoveries. He found that 80 per cent of the effect of antidepressants, as measured in clinical trials, could be attributed to the placebo effect.

I could fill the rest of this book describing other studies about the impact of the placebo effect, but I won't. If you need more proof, please research the topic. The online article referenced in the following quotes is a good place to start.

Harvard researchers have found that:

> ...placebo treatments—interventions with no active drug ingredients—can stimulate real physiological responses, from changes in heart rate and blood pressure to chemical activity in the brain, in cases involving pain, depression, anxiety, fatigue, and even some symptoms of Parkinson's.[6]
>
> ...the methods of placebo administration are as important as the administration itself ... patient's perceptions matter and the ways physicians frame perceptions can have significant effects on their patients' health.[7]

When Harvard researcher's told a group of Irritable Bowel Syndrome sufferers they were going to be given fake, inert drugs (delivered in bottles labelled "placebo pills") and also told that placebos often have healing effects, they were shocked when these people showed real improvement.

What these studies show is that we can change our biology through our beliefs. We can express this statement in the following manner: Consciousness takes in information; beliefs turn that information into meaning; the meaning that is given delivers an outcome which aligns the belief. This applies to both the emotional world and the material world.

Consciousness → Information → Belief → Meaning → Outcome

If we want to be more precise, we can say beliefs convert waves of energetic information into meaning and the meaning that is given causes the potentiality that aligns with the belief to manifest at the emotional or material level of existence.

In the energetic quantum world, everything exists in all its potentialities. The belief of the observer "collapses" the wave of information containing all potentialities into the outcome that aligns with the belief.

This statement can be stated in the following way:

Consciousness → Information → Belief → Energy change → Matter change

The stronger the belief, the more energy there is behind the belief, the stronger the psycho-energetic causation will be and the stronger and more instantaneous the material outcome will be.

Because consciousness is associated with three psychic entities—the body-mind, the emotional mind and the rational mind—we can write causality statements for beliefs held in each of these three minds:

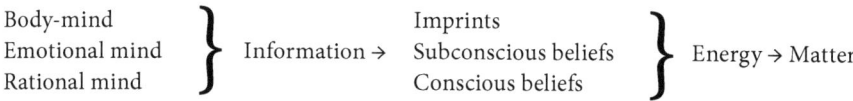

Each form of consciousness takes the same information from the external world, creates meaning and manipulates energy to affect change in matter. In each case, the operator on the energy—the meaning influencer that manipulates the energy—is different.

In the case of the body-mind, the operators are imprints: the learned "beliefs" of the reptilian mind. In the case of the emotional and rational mind, the operator is beliefs: learned subconscious or conscious assumptions. In the case of the rational mind, there is an additional operator we can consider: intentions. Setting an intention, and infusing it with the energy of belief in the outcome, is a powerful way of creating reality. Intentions can be conscious, for example, when they are used to set a vision for the future or used in a prayer for healing, and they can be unconscious, when they are direct interventions from the soul as in the spontaneous remission of disease.

When the operators are love-based (positive), they create energetic stability; they have a beneficial effect on the human energy field and the body. When the operators are fear-based (negative), they create energetic instability; they have an injurious effect on the human energy field and the body because they block the life-enhancing energy of love.

Emotional outcomes

If we can accept that positive beliefs create life-enhancing outcomes, it is not too difficult to accept that limiting (negative) beliefs create life-suppressing outcomes.

What is a limiting belief, and where do limiting beliefs come from?

Limiting beliefs (and imprints) are formed when our needs are not met or when we struggle to meet our needs, particularly during the periods when our reptilian mind/brain, limbic mind/brain and rational mind/brain are growing and developing. Repeated attempts to meet our needs which result in failure create limiting beliefs. The three most significant limiting beliefs we can learn are:

- I do not have enough of what I need to survive.
- I am not loved enough to feel safe or I am not lovable enough.
- I am not enough to feel secure, or I am not important enough.

When circumstances are such that during our early lives we fail to get our needs met, we form limiting beliefs. The limiting beliefs thus formed continue to operate throughout the rest of our lives attracting negative outcomes. Whatever we believe, consciously or subconsciously, attracts the reality we experience.

When your needs are not met, or you believe they may not be met, you will have negative emotions—anger or fear—and you will have negative feelings. Feelings are the conscious awareness of emotions. Feelings represent shifts in our energy field. When we hide, deny or suppress our feelings, the energy associated with our emotions and feelings cannot dissipate. The negative energy of anger and fear stay in your energy field causing energetic instability.

Just as when you deny your hunger, the energetic imbalance that is creating the hunger sensations does not go away when you deny your need for love, the energetic imbalance that is creating this feeling deficiency does not go away. Just as you can only satisfy your deficiency sensation when you allow yourself to express your need for food, you can only satisfy your feeling deficiency when you allow yourself to express your need for love.

Similarly, if you are suppressing your anger about not getting your needs met, a failure to express that anger will create energetic instability in your energy field. Unexpressed anger towards someone creates energetic separation; the opposite of love. For this reason, anger is the most injurious emotion. It leads to depression—the sadness of the soul about not being able to connect—and eventually heart disease. The heart is the centre of love. Whatever blocks love, blocks the heart. Cholesterol is not the issue in heart attacks; the issue is unexpressed anger. In the following chapters, I will show that unexpressed emotions are the cause of all our mental and physical disorders.

A summary of key points

Here are the main points of Chapter 7:

1. Almost every hour of every day, every person on the planet is focused on the same thing: getting their needs met.
2. What motivates our psychological development is the stage by stage gratification of our needs.
3. When we have learned how to gratify the needs at one stage of development, new, higher order needs automatically emerge that are associated with the next stage of development.
4. There are two types of needs: deficiency sensations and feeling deficiencies. The body has deficiency sensations. The ego has feeling deficiencies.
5. The term "need" is often used when we mean "requirement". Whereas a requirement is something that is necessary, a need is something that is lacking.

6. A want is not a need. A want is an object, action or situation we believe will enable us to get a need met, alleviate a deficiency sensation or feeling deficiency.
7. A desire is a longing for something that is as yet nascent or unexplored. It is a yearning for the "materialization" of potential.
8. A need is a real or imagined lack of something that is essential for maintaining the body's physiological (biological) stability or the ego's emotional stability.
9. Love is the energy that supplies all our needs. When we allow love to flow out into the world through us, all our needs get met because love flows back to us through the "automatic" provision of everything we need to fulfil our soul's purpose.
10. Whatever we believe, is the outcome we attract.
11. The stronger the belief, the stronger the psycho-energetic causation will be, and the stronger and more instantaneous the material outcome will be.
12. Unexpressed emotions are the cause of all our mental and physical disorders.

References and notes

1. Abraham Maslow, *Towards a Psychology of Being* (New York: Van Nostrand), 1968, p. 56.
2. Songwriters: John Lennon and Paul McCartney published by Lyrics © Sony/ATV Music Publishing LLC.
3. H. K. Beecher, *The Powerful Placebo*, Journal of the American Medical Association, Vol.159, No. 17, (24 December 1955).
4. J. Bruce Moseley et al., *A Controlled Trial of Arthroscopic Surgery for Osteoarthritis of the Knee*, New England Journal of Medicine, July 11, 2002, 347: 81–88.
5. Kirsh, Moore, Scoboria, and Nicholls, *The Emperor's New Drugs: An analysis of antidepressant medication data submitted to the US Food and Drug Administration*, Prevention and Treatment, July 2002, 5 (1).
6. http://harvardmagazine.com/2013/01/the-placebo-phenomen
7. Ibid.

8

A THEORY OF EMOTIONS AND FEELINGS

Understanding your emotions, how they arise and their impact on your energy field is fundamental to understanding how your psychology affects your physiology. Mismanaged emotions are the quickest route to mental and physical disorders.

Having explored what our needs and desires are, and what they are not, I now propose to explore the link between needs, desires, emotions and feelings. I am focusing on these topics because emotions are the source of our life-enhancing energy and our life-depleting energy: They are the source of sickness and health, and sadness and well-being. We experience positive, life-enhancing emotions when we get our needs met, and we experience negative, life-depleting emotions when we don't get our needs met. Emotions are the entry point to understanding the ego-soul dynamics that occur in our energy field.

Emotions can arise in two ways; by the triggering of the memory of a positive or negative experience or by creating positive or negative scenarios in our mind. When we ruminate on negative scenarios and outcomes, we generate fear-based life-depleting emotions. When we visualize positive scenarios and outcomes, we generate love-based life-enhancing emotions. Love-based emotions have a healing effect because they bring our ego's energy field into alignment with our soul's energy field, and our soul's energy field into alignment with the universal energy field.

Theories of emotion are grouped into three main categories: physiological, neurological and cognitive. Physiological theories suggest that responses within the body are responsible for emotions. Neurological theories propose that activity within the brain leads to emotional responses. Cognitive theories argue that thoughts and other mental activities play an essential role in the formation of emotions. The theory postulated in this book falls into the latter category. It starts from the premise that all emotions are linked to the satisfaction or non-satisfaction of our needs.

In his book, *Emotions and Life*,[1] Robert Plutchik lists sixteen emotional theories. Fear is listed as an emotion in all sixteen theories and anger is listed in fourteen. In the two theories that do not list anger, rage is included. When we bottle up our anger by not expressing it, we eventually reach a point where a seemingly innocuous situation can cause our emotional pressure cooker to explode: this is what we call rage. Sadness is listed as an emotion in eight theories. Joy is listed in seven theories; disgust in six; surprise in five; happiness in four, and love in three.

Emotions versus feelings

Before I describe my theory of emotions, I believe it is important that we come to an understanding of the difference between emotions and feelings.

Antonio Damasio, in *The Feeling of What Happens*,[2] states that:

> ...the term "emotion" should be reserved to designate the collection of responses, many of which are publicly observable ... and the term "feeling" should be reserved for the private, mental experience of an emotion.[3]

Emotions and feelings are part of the same functional continuum.[4] Your feelings are your conscious connection to shifts in your energy field. We only become aware of an emotion after we experience a positive or negative feeling. Emotions are visible, feelings are not. It is difficult to hide your emotions. It is relatively easy to hide your feelings. Emotions start in the subconscious or unconscious mind and are felt in the energy field of the body. The mind gives context to an emotion by creating a feeling. The emotion of fear can lead to terror, insecurity or worry and a range of other feelings; it depends on the type of situation that has triggered the emotion of fear.

Emotions

My theory of emotions starts from the premise that all emotions are a reflection of energy shifts: a sudden increase or decrease in the amplitude of vibration of our energy field caused by the body's or the ego's reaction to changes in their external environment. A positive energy shift enhances the stability of the human energy field, thereby supporting the health of the body. A negative energy shift diminishes the stability of the human energy field thereby inhibiting the health of the body.

Emotions do not arise from an actual change in circumstance; they arise from the meaning we give to a change in circumstance. Two people can experience the same change in circumstance; one may experience the emotion of fear, and the other may experience the emotion of happiness.

Positive (healthy) energy shifts occur when the ego can meet its deficiency needs and the ego's actions or behaviours enable the soul to meet its desires. Negative (unhealthy) energy shifts occur when the body and ego are unable to meet their deficiency sensations or feeling deficiencies or when the ego believes it may not be able to meet its feeling deficiencies in the immediate or not too distant future. Negative energy shifts also occur when the actions and behaviours of the ego prevent the soul from fulfilling its desires.

In other words, all emotions are related to our ability to either meet or not meet the needs of the body or the ego or the desires of the soul within the context of the framework of our individual human existence.

This leads me to postulate that the number of emotions we can experience is six: meeting or not meeting the needs of the ego and the desires of the soul account for four emotions (happiness and anger, and joy and sadness), and the ego believing it may not be able to get its needs met (anxiety), and the body sensing it may not be able to get its needs met (fear), accounts for the other two.

Happiness, anxiety and anger are emotions of the ego-mind; joy and sadness are emotions of the soul-mind; fear is an emotion of the body-mind.

The emotions of the soul are less conspicuous than those the ego because they have less of an emotional charge. Even though they are less conspicuous, they still play an important role in organizing our thoughts and behaviours. The emotions of the soul are usually brought on by actions or behaviours of the ego that either suppress opportunities for the soul to fulfil its desires—sadness, or enhance opportunities for the soul to fulfil its desires—joy.

Four of the emotions I have listed—happiness, anger, fear and sadness—are the basic emotions that Rachael Jack and her team identified recently in their study of facial expressions at the Institute of Neuroscience and Psychology in Glasgow.[5] The six emotions I am proposing are shown in Table 8.1.

Table 8.1: The six basic emotions.

	Ego emotion	Body emotion	Soul emotion
Needs/desires met	Happiness	(Alive)	Joy
Needs might not be met	Anxiety	Fear	N.A.
Needs/desires not met	Anger	(Distress)	Sadness

Happiness

Happiness, as an emotion, is not well understood. Happiness is the automatic energetic reaction that arises when we release the anxieties we have about not being able to meet one of our deficiency needs or when a potential threat to a need we have already satisfied is removed. Once the anxiety is released, happiness is felt but quickly dissipates. When we are able to master our deficiency needs, we experience the feeling of contentment. Happiness is linked to the following feelings: relief, pride, pleasure, satisfaction and cheerfulness.

Fear

Fear is the basic emotion shared by all living organisms. Fear is a present moment experience of the possibility of not getting your needs met. As soon as a threat disappears, the fear associated with the threat dissipates quickly.

Fear is linked to the following feelings: shame, guilt, worry, distress, horror, shock, terror and fright. Thus, we can state:

A threat to our needs → Fear

Anxiety

Whereas fear is a present moment experience of the possibility of not getting your needs met, anxiety is a present moment experience of the possibility of not getting your needs met in the future. Anxiety about being punishmed for something you did, for example, is an experience of the possibility of not getting your love and safety needs met in the future.

Anger

Primarily, we get angry when our ego needs are not met. Anger can also be triggered when we start to believe our needs may not be met. Anger is closely correlated with fear and anxiety.[6] I believe the first reaction we have when we understand that a need has not been met is fear about what will happen to us without that need being gratified. Fear is quickly followed by anger. In this sense, anger is the emotional upset associated with coming to terms with the implications arising from a need not being met. The more attached we were to satisfying a particular need, the angrier we become when that need is not met or when we believe it might not be met.

Unmet need → Anger

Most people only express anger when they feel it is safe to do so. We suppress our anger when we feel vulnerable: when we believe that expressing our anger could compromise our ability to get one of our other deficiency needs met. This is why children suppress their anger towards their parents. If they expressed their true feelings, they would risk compromising getting their needs met in the future.

Anger is linked to the following feelings: irritation, envy, jealousy, disgust, bitterness, hatred, rage, dislike, resentment, guilt, blame and shame. Among these, rage is the most intense and hatred is the longest lasting. For this reason, hatred is also the most physiologically damaging of all the feelings associated with anger, especially when your hate is turned inwards; when you believe you are the cause of the reason for not getting your needs met. Hatred of others creates external separation; hatred of self creates internal separation; the ego's separation from the soul. Separation has major repercussions on our psychological and physiological health.

Joy

Joy arises from the delight of the soul about getting its desires satisfied. Joy is the longest lasting positive emotion[7] because it is linked to a sense of fulfilment. Happiness quickly dissipates because it is linked to the release of fear. Joy is associated with the following feelings: optimism, enthusiasm, commitment, expression, creativity, connection, trust, and contribution.

Sadness

When the ego is unable to get its needs met, it experiences anger. When the soul is unable to get its desires met, it experiences sadness. When the sadness of the soul accumulates, we experience depression.

Whenever the ego is involved in a constant struggle to get its survival, safety or security needs met, the soul experiences the energy of sadness. What it feels sad about is the possibility of not getting its self-expression, connection and contribution desires met. The soul cannot meet its self-expression needs if the ego does not master its survival needs; it cannot meet its connection needs if the ego cannot meet it relationship needs, and it cannot meet its contribution needs if the ego cannot meet its self-esteem needs.

Thus, we can state:

Unmet ego needs → Unmet soul desires → Sadness → Depression

When the anger and the hatred the ego feels about not getting its needs met are suppressed—when it is turned inwards—the sadness of the soul intensifies and depression deepens.

This leads to the following statement:

Depression = Anger/Hatred turned inwards.

Sadness tends to last much longer than all the other emotions; up to 240 times longer than the duration of our shortest emotions.[8] Sadness is always associated with high levels of rumination and is linked to the following feelings: depression, despair, hopelessness, grief, sorrow, misery, loneliness and isolation.[9]

Depression

When the soul continuously experiences sadness—when the ego consistently fails to get its deficiency needs met—the soul's will to be present in 3-D awareness begins to wane. When the soul's will to be present wanes, the body's will to stay alive weakens and the ego's will to survive declines. When the body's will to stay alive weakens, the body's immune system becomes compromised. When the ego's will to survive declines, the ego begins to contemplate suicide.

Mastering your emotions

To lead a healthy and happy life we need to reduce the occurrence of negative emotions and increase the occurrence of positive emotions. We need to be able to master our deficiency needs and satisfy our soul's desires. When we are optimistic and focus on the positive, we accentuate the possibility of success (meeting our needs). When we are pessimistic and focus on the negative, we accentuate the possibility of failure (not meeting our needs).

Feelings/sensations

While I was developing my theory of emotions, I found myself asking the question: "If the number of emotions is so few, why do we experience a wide range of feelings?" On reflection, I realized it is because there are different dimensions to our feelings.

- Feelings/sensations can be positive or negative.
- Feelings/sensations can be felt in the body-mind, the ego-mind or the soul-mind.
- Feelings/sensations can be of different intensities.

Each of these dimensions is indicative of a particular quality of feeling, a particular source of feeling or a particular intensity of feeling. The way we can differentiate a strong positive body feeling such as exhilaration, from a weak negative ego feeling such as impatience, is through the frequency of vibration attached to the feeling/sensation.

Positive and negative

Positive feelings/sensations are an indication that your needs have been met. Negative feelings/sensations are an indication that your needs have not been met or might not be met. Positive feelings give you the energetic sensation of lightness: you feel aligned and content. Negative feelings give you the energetic sensation of heaviness: you feel misaligned and unhappy.

Body, ego and soul

Depending on the type of needs or desires that are met, not met or might not be met, you experience your feelings in the body-mind, ego-mind or soul-mind. Strictly speaking, the body-mind does not have feelings, it has sensations.

In Table 8.2 I have attributed feelings/sensations to the part of our energy field where you experience them: the body-mind, the ego-mind and the soul-mind. This table is further broken down into positive and negative feelings/sensations. Depending on your personal interpretation of these terms you may wish to allocate them differently.

Table 8.2: Feelings/sensations experienced by the body-mind, ego-mind and soul-mind.

	Body-mind sensations	Ego-mind feelings	Soul-mind feelings
Positive Feelings			
Lightness and alignment	Exhilarated Enlivened Rejuvenated Renewed Rested	Eager Happy Proud Satisfied Secure	Blissful Centered Compassionate Fulfilled Trusting
Negative Feelings			
Heaviness and misalignment	Exhausted Lethargic Listless Tired Weary	Afraid Anxious Annoyed Impatient Jealous	Bereaved Depressed Detached Dispirited Withdrawn

Intensity

Another important dimension to consider is the intensity of the feeling. Table 8.3 provides a schema of the intensity of feelings associated with the ego's and soul's emotions. Depending on your personal interpretation of these terms you may wish to allocate them slightly differently.

Table 8.3: Intensity of feelings.

Intensity	Ego emotions and feelings			Soul emotions and feelings	
	Happiness	Anxiety/fear	Anger	Joy	Sadness
High	Excited Thrilled Elated	Terrified Petrified Angry	Rage Hatred Exasperated	Ecstatic Euphoric Rapturous	Hopeless Despair Anguish
Medium	Delighted Gratified Cheerful	Insecure Apprehensive Uneasy	Upset Annoyed Irritated	Ebullient Exuberant Gleeful	Grief Diminished Discouraged
Low	Satisfied Fortunate Lucky	Worried Wary Nervous	Impatient Resentment Displeased	Blissful Radiant Blessed	Disappointed Dispirited Alone

The intensity of feeling associated with the emotion of happiness is related to the level of relief you experience when your need is satisfied. If the unmet need was important to you and the level of anxiety you had about not being able to meet the need was high, you would most likely feel very excited when the need is finally met.

The intensity of feeling associated with the emotion of anxiety/fear is related to the type of ego/body need that might not be met. If the need that is threatened is your ability to stay alive you will feel terrified: the highest intensity of anxiety/fear. If the need that is threatened is a lower order need, you will feel worried, wary or nervous.

The intensity of feeling associated with the emotion of anger is related to the extent to which you have suppressed your anger in the past and the type of need that has not been met. When anger is repeatedly suppressed over a long period, and you experience a life-threatening situation, your anger about that situation may come out as rage.

The intensity of feeling associated with the emotion of joy is related to the type of soul desire that has been met, and to a lesser extent, the level of expectation you had about meeting that desire. The highest levels of joy are experienced when you fulfil your soul's desire for self-expression. You feel ecstatic about your opportunity to express who you are.

The intensity of feeling associated with the emotion of sadness is related to the type of soul desire that has been undermined by the ego's failure to satisfy it deficiency needs. The highest intensity of sadness is experienced when the ego falls short of mastering its survival needs. This undermines the soul's ability to fulfil its desire for self-expression.

Frequency of vibration

In his book, *Power vs. Force*, Dr. David R. Hawkins classifies the principal human "emotions" according to their frequency of vibration.[10] His findings are reproduced in Table 8.4.[11] I have written "emotions" in inverted commas because I would classify most of the terms used in Hawkins' scale as feelings. The lower end of Hawkins' scale represents the presence of fear in our lives, and the upper end of his scale represents the presence of love.

Table 8.4: The relative levels of frequency of vibration of different "emotions."

Fear/Trust/Love	Emotion	Experience	Impact of Emotion
	Ineffable	Enlightenment	Pure
	Bliss	Peace	consciousness
	Serenity	Joy	Illumination
LOVE	Reverence	Love	Transfiguration
	Understanding	Reason	Revelation
	Forgiveness	Acceptance	Abstraction
	Optimism	Willingness	Transcendence Intention
TRUST	Trust	Neutrality	Release
	Affirmation	Courage	Empowerment
	Scorn	Pride	Inflation
	Hate	Anger	Aggression
	Craving	Desire	Enslavement
FEAR	Anxiety	Fear	Withdrawal
	Regret	Grief	Despondency
	Despair	Apathy	Abdication
	Blame	Guilt	Destruction
	Humiliation	Shame	Elimination

Prolonged periods of time spent at the lower end of the vibrational scale—below the level of trust—lead to sickness and disease in the body, and feelings of despair and hopelessness in the mind. Prolonged periods of time spent at the upper end of the vibrational scale—above the level of trust—lead to health in the body, and feelings of joy and well-being in the mind.

When our ego's motivations are in alignment with our soul's motivations, we experience high levels of energetic coherence and flow. Conversely, when our ego's motivations are out of alignment with our soul's motivations, we experience low levels of energetic coherence and flow.

There are two critical points[12] on Hawkins' vibrational scale that correspond to significant stages of psychological development.

- Self-empowerment: The willingness to stop blaming others and accept responsibility for our reality—when we stop being a victim.
- Non-judgmental forgiveness: Exercising understanding and unconditional kindness to all people without exception.

The first of these critical stages—self-empowerment—corresponds to the individuating stage of psychological development: the portal we pass through to access the energies of the soul. This is the stage where we develop the courage to face our fears and let go of negative parental programming and cultural conditioning that are keeping us focused on our deficiency needs.

The second of these critical stages—non-judgmental forgiveness—corresponds to the serving stage of psychological development. At the serving stage of development, we begin to recognize that everyone is simply a soul and an individuated aspect of the one-mind. Therefore, when I give to you, I give to myself. When I forgive you, I forgive myself.[13] At this stage of development, you no longer believe you have a soul; you know you are a soul, or to be more precise, you know your soul has you.

A summary of key points

Here are the main points of Chapter 8:

1. Over the past thirty years, it has become well accepted that our mental and physical health is linked to the way we manage our emotions.
2. Emotions and feelings are part of the same functional continuum. Emotions are visible, feelings are not. Your feelings are your conscious connection to the emotional shifts in your energy field.
3. Emotions do not arise from an actual change in circumstance; they arise from the meaning we give to a change in circumstance.
4. All emotions are a reflection of energy shifts: a sudden increase or decrease in the amplitude of vibration in our energy field caused by the body's or the ego's reaction to changes in their external environment that impact our needs.
5. The number of emotions we can experience is six. Meeting or not meeting the needs of the ego and the desires of the soul accounts for four emotions, and the ego believing it may not be able to get its needs met, and the body sensing it may not be able to get its needs met account for the other two.
6. Fear is a present moment experience of the possibility of not getting your needs met. As soon as a threat disappears, the fear associated with the threat dissipates quickly. Anxiety is a present

moment experience of the possibility of not getting your needs met in the future.
7. To lead a healthy and happy life, we need to reduce the occurrence of negative emotions and increase the occurrence of positive emotions. Positive feelings are an indication that your needs are met. Negative feelings are an indication that your needs have not been met or might not be met.
8. When our ego's motivations are in alignment with our soul's motivations, we experience high levels of energetic coherence and flow. Conversely, when our ego's motivations are out of alignment with our soul's motivations, we experience low levels of energetic coherence and flow.

References and notes

1. Robert Plutchik, *Emotions and Life: Perspectives from Psychology, Biology and Evolution* (Washington DC: American Psychological Association), 2002, p. 73.
2. Antonio Damasio, *The Feeling of What Happens: Body, Emotion and the Making of Consciousness* (London: Vintage Books), 2000.
3. Ibid., p. 42.
4. Ibid., p. 43.
5. Rachael Jack, Oliver Garrod and Philippe Schyns, *Dynamic Facial Expressions of Emotion Transmit an Evolving Hierarchy of Signals over Time*, Current Biology, 24 (2), p. 187–192, 20 January 2014.
6. Rick Naurert, Senior News Editor, *Link Between Anger and Anxiety?* Psych Central, December 5, 2012.
7. Philippe, Verduyn, Saskia, Lavrijsen, *Which Emotions Last Longest and Why: The role of event importance and rumination*, Journal of Motivation and Emotion, Volume 39 (1), February 1, 2015.
8. Ibid.
9. Ibid.
10. David R. Hawkins, Power vs. Force: *The Hidden Determinants of Human Behaviour* (Carlsbad: Hay House), 2002.
11. Ibid., pp. 68–69.
12. Ibid. p. 238
13. Forgiveness for believing you have the power to hurt me. In reality, I can only hurt myself by the thoughts that are attached to my belief in separation.

9

PROGRESSION THROUGH THE STAGES

> *Growth forward is made possible by the feeling of being safe, of operating out into the unknown from a safe home port, of daring because retreat is possible. If we never experienced a safe home port, then we will never venture out, and we will never grow.*

Having identified the needs and desires associated with the seven stages of psychological development and how they arise, let us now turn our attention to what motivates us to move forward on the journey of psychological development and what holds us back.

Before exploring this topic, I think it is important to remember that all psychological development involves emergent learning: constantly accumulating knowledge about how to meet your ego's needs and satisfy your soul's desires in the physical, social and cultural frameworks of your existence.[1] Even though we are all on the same journey of development, because we grow up in unique social, cultural and physical contexts, the routes we take—the ground we cover at each stage of our journey—is different.

Some people get bogged down in the early stages of their development: they may require coaching, counselling or therapeutic help to overcome obstacles. Some people find the journey so difficult and painful they decide to opt out by committing suicide. A small, but ever-increasing number of people, sail through the process, encountering only minor setbacks along the way.

Opportunities for emergent learning[2] occur every time we experience a change in our life conditions that either challenges our ability to maintain our internal stability or threatens our ability to maintain our external equilibrium. Whenever we encounter what we perceive as a threat or an opportunity for meeting our needs, there is a possibility for emergent learning.

As soon as we find a new way of interacting with our environment, which allows us to resolve a threat or take advantage of an opportunity, we commit the experience (the pattern of stimulus and response) to memory in the form of a belief or imprint. We can then use that belief or imprint to access the same response again if we are confronted with a similar situation in the future.

Rapid and normal emergent learning

There are two types of emergent learning: rapid emergent learning, which occurs during the period when the reptilian brain, the limbic brain and the neocortex brain are forming (0–24 years), and normal emergent learning (from 25 onwards).

During periods of rapid emergent learning, we lay down the foundations of our body's imprints and our ego's conscious and subconscious belief structures. During the period of normal emergent learning, we try to adapt or tweak our ego's belief structures to try to maximize our happiness and our potential for joy. Our focus during rapid emergent learning is on meeting our deficiency needs. Our focus during the normal emergent learning is on aligning our ego motivations with our soul motivations and activating our soul consciousness.

Everything we learn during the period of rapid emergent learning influences how we react or respond to changes in our life conditions later in life. If we learned, when we were young, that the world is a dangerous place and people are not to be trusted, then those beliefs will condition our reality and behaviours as adults. If we learned, when we were young, that the world is supportive of our needs and people can be trusted, then those beliefs will condition our reality and behaviours as adults. Fears prevent us from learning new ways of being; trust supports us in learning new ways of being.

Learning new ways of being is called adaptation. The most successful individuals are those who can adapt their belief structures to maximize their potential for contentment and joy. Adaptation is not only the key to successful psychological development; it is also the key to successful ageing.³

What is psychological growth?

The basic thesis of this book is that growth, in psychological terms, is a natural evolutionary process that begins as a biological imperative—the need to survive; then becomes a social imperative—the need for safety; then a cultural imperative—the need for security, and finally a spiritual imperative—the desire to understand and give meaning to our life's experiences.

Maslow explains this evolutionary process in the following way:

> The single holistic principle that binds together the multiplicity of human motives is the tendency for a new and higher order need to emerge as a lower order need fulfils itself by being sufficiently gratified.⁴

In other words, Maslow is postulating that there is a natural hierarchy of human motivations (needs). In answer to the question, "How does growth take place?" Maslow responds in the following way:

> ...growth takes place when the next step forward is subjectively more delightful, more joyous, more intrinsically satisfying than the previous gratification with which we have become familiar and even bored.⁵

During the early stages of our psychological development, we are not aware that we are on an evolutionary journey, and we are not aware that the journey is fundamentally psychological in nature. All we know is what is happening to us: what is changing inside (emotions) and what is changing outside (situations); what needs we have that are currently satisfied, and what needs we have that are not currently satisfied. We have no idea where our needs are coming from, we just feel them. We have no way of knowing that our needs are determined by the stage of psychological development we are at, and that at some point in the future, when those needs have been met, we will develop a new set of needs. We are operating blind because no one gave us an instruction manual when we were born. Maslow puts it this way:

> Growth is not in the pure case a goal out ahead, nor is self-actualization, nor is the discovery of Self. In the child, it is not specifically purposed; rather it just happens. [A child] doesn't so much search, as find.[6]

What prevents growth?

Having established that psychological growth is a natural process that simply happens to us during the first third of our lives, and something we choose during the second two-thirds of our lives, it is important to ask the question, "What prevents growth?"

Once more, I would like to draw on Maslow's wisdom:

> …growth forward is made possible by the feeling of being safe, of operating out into the unknown from a safe home port, of daring because retreat is possible. … Assured safety permits higher needs and impulses to emerge and to grow towards mastery.
> …in the choice between giving up safety or giving up growth, safety will ordinarily win out. Safety needs are pre-potent over growth needs; only a child that feels safe dares to grow forward healthily … The more safety needs are gratified, the less valence they have for the child.[7]

What Maslow is saying here is that we must have a firm psychological foundation—something that gives us stability—to grow. What constitutes a firm foundation? Maslow responds:

> Here we must become fully aware of the fixative and regressive power of ungratified deficiency-needs, of the attraction of safety and security, of the functions of defence and protection against pain, fear, loss and threat, of the need for courage to grow.[8]

Every human being has both sets of forces within him: the ego's need for survival, safety and security, and the soul's need for actualization.

> One set [of forces] clings to safety and defensiveness out of fear, tending to regress backward, hanging on to the past, afraid to grow ... afraid to take chances, afraid to jeopardize what he already has, afraid of independence, freedom, separateness.[9]
>
> The other set of forces impels him forward toward wholeness of Self and uniqueness of Self, toward full functioning of all his capacities, toward confidence in the face of the external world at the same time that he can accept his deepest, real, unconscious self.[10]
>
> This basic dilemma or conflict between the defensive forces and the growth trends I conceive to be existential, imbedded in the deepest nature of the human being.[11]

What Maslow is saying is that fear holds us back, and trust enables us to grow. Whenever we encounter a new situation—a set of circumstances we have never encountered before, we must decide if the situation presents a potential threat or a potential opportunity for meeting our needs. If we see the situation as a potential threat, we must decide whether to advance and overcome the threat, or whether to do nothing, retreat and run to safety.

We will only advance if we have built up confidence in our abilities to cope with the difficulties the situation may present and the courage to face the fears we are feeling; this advance constitutes growth. We retreat when the level of fear we feel is greater than our belief in our ability to cope with failure. Continuously choosing safety prevents us from growing.

If we see a situation as a potential opportunity for meeting our needs; we will only seek to take advantage of it if we believe we can be successful without expending too much energy. We hold back when we judge the amount of energy we would have to expend would be greater than the potential value we believe the opportunity presents. In other words, when our mind enhances the attractiveness and minimizes the dangers of a situation, we will move towards the opportunity. When our mind enhances the dangers and minimizes the attractiveness of a situation, we will retreat from it. Whichever of these alternatives we choose depends on our history. Maslow summarizes what healthy growth is in the following way:

> Therefore, we can consider the process of healthy growth to be a never ending series of free choice situations, confronting each individual at every point throughout his life, in which he

must choose safety or growth, dependence or independence, regression or progression, and immaturity or maturity.[12]

Facing our fears

What Maslow is saying is that we only grow when we are willing to embrace the changes that are happening around us, even if they bring up fear. We regress when we resist the changes that are happening around us and give in to our fear. The fear we are giving in to is the fear of not being able to cope if we fail; not believing we have the strength, skills or resources that we believe are necessary to achieve a successful outcome. Maslow states:

> ...if free choice is really free, and if the chooser is not too sick or frightened to choose, he [she] will choose wisely, in a healthy, growth direction, more often than not.[13]

A major determinant in our choice of safety over growth is the presence, and degree, of any early maladaptive schema (limiting beliefs), lodged in the subconscious mind. If we failed as a child to get one of our needs met or were told that we were wrong, not good enough, ugly or stupid, then we will be predisposed, as an adult, to choose safety. The beliefs we learned when we were young become self-fulfilling prophecies when we are older.

When we are young, and those who failed to support us in meeting our survival, safety or security needs are our parents, we get into a bind. We need to express our anger (internal instability) at not getting our needs met, but if we direct the anger towards our parents, we may compromise our ability to get our future survival, safety and security needs met. I believe this is part of what Maslow was referring to when he spoke of "neurotic compromises".

Once we have become adults, the nature of growth changes; if we are no longer pressured by our ego's need to survive, stay safe and feel secure, we can choose to experience the delights of self-expression, connection and contribution; to explore who we might become beyond our parental programming and cultural conditioning. We make this choice at the individuating stage of development.

We individuate when we feel confident enough to choose independence over dependence; when we are willing to risk separation from the safety and security of the social and cultural milieu in which we were raised, so we can experience the delight of our independence and find answers to the most basic of questions, "Who am I?" and "Why am I here?"

A summary of key points

Here are the main points of Chapter 9:

1. All psychological development involves learning, and all learning associated with psychological development is emergent.
2. There are two types of emergent learning: rapid emergent learning, which occurs during the period when the reptilian brain, the limbic brain and the neocortex brain are forming (0–24 years), and normal emergent learning (from 25 onwards).
3. Opportunities for emergent learning occur every time we experience a change in our life conditions that either challenges our ability to maintain our internal stability or external equilibrium or provides an opportunity to enhance our internal stability or external equilibrium.
4. The most successful individuals are those who can adapt their belief structures to maximize their potential for happiness and joy. Adaptation is not only the key to successful psychological development; it is also the key to successful ageing
5. The single holistic principle that binds together the multiplicity of human motives is the tendency for a new and higher order need to emerge as a lower order need fulfils itself by being sufficiently gratified.
6. Growth takes place when the next step forward is subjectively more delightful, more joyous, more intrinsically satisfying than the previous gratification with which we have become familiar and even bored.
7. Growth forward is made possible by the feeling of being safe, of operating out into the unknown from a safe home port, of daring because retreat is possible.
8. We only grow when we are willing to embrace the changes that are happening around us, even if they bring up fear.

9. We retreat when the level of fear we feel is greater than our belief in our ability to cope with failure.
10. A major determinant in our choice of safety over growth is the presence, and degree, of any early maladaptive schema (limiting beliefs) that are lodged in the sub-conscious mind.

References and notes

1. It also sometimes involves unlearning. We will discuss the topic of unlearning later.
2. Marilyn Taylor, *Emergent Learning for Wisdom* (New York: Palgrave MacMillan), 2011.
3. George E. Vaillant, *Adaptation to Life* (Boston: Harvard University Press), 1977.
4. Abraham Maslow, *Toward a Psychology of Being* (New York: Van Nostrand), 1968, p. 55.
5. Ibid., p. 45.
6. Ibid., p. 44.
7. Ibid., p. 48.
8. Ibid., p. 46.
9. Ibid.
10. Ibid.
11. Ibid.
12. Ibid., p. 48.
13. Ibid.

10

ENERGETIC INSTABILITY

Energetic instability and pain are synonymous, and all pain is positive. Pain tells us exactly what aspects of our mind or anatomy need energetic healing so we can stay in alignment with our soul.

Having explored the link between needs, desires, emotions and feelings, and how a failure to establish a safe base blocks the progress of our psychological development, I now want to explore how the negative emotions of fear, anxiety and anger impact our physiological and psychological functioning, in particular the manner in which the energetic instability caused by these emotions impairs the functioning of our minds. In the following chapter, I will explore how energetic instability impairs the functioning of our bodies.

There are two basic signs of energetic instability:

- Psychological pain: the struggle to maintain rational functioning when the ego's needs are not met.
- Physiological pain: the struggle to maintain homeostatic functioning when the body's needs are not met.

Additionally, when we let the mind dwell on the downside of our experience of physiological pain, we create the psychological pain known as suffering. Ruminating on our psychological pain also leads to suffering.

Every time the body-mind or ego-mind fails to get its needs met, or they believe they may not get their needs met, we experience energetic instability (anger and fear) that affects the functioning of our energy field. What our mind does with that energetic instability directly impacts our mental and physical health.

The human mind/brain

Most scientists have a tendency to think of our mind/brain as a single operating whole, but it is not. We have three brains and four minds that directly impact the decisions we make in our lives. The four minds and three brains are:

- The neocortex mind/brain: rational mind.
- The limbic mind/brain: emotional mind.
- The reptilian mind/brain: body-mind.
- The soul-mind.

In addition, the soul-mind is also part of the mind of humanity, which is part of the species-mind, which is a part of the one-mind, as described in Chapter 3. Whenever you grow and evolve in consciousness, the consciousness of the one-mind changes. When you consciously heal your separation from your soul, you impact the operation of the mind of humanity.

If you have difficulty grasping this idea, think of it like this. When you heal a diseased part of your body, your whole body feels the benefit. The reason your body feels the benefit is that the energy that consumed in struggling to maintain the homeostatic functioning of the diseased part of the body is now available for useful purposes that support the thriving of the body.

My company, the Barrett Values Centre,[1] has used this principle to heal and support the thriving of thousands of leaders and organizations all over the world. We call the energetic instability in the "diseased" part of an organization, cultural entropy. We call the energetic instability in the "diseased" part of the leader, personal entropy. Entropy is the degree of disorder and dysfunction caused by ego-driven, fear-based motivations. When the energetic instability in the leaders is healed, the energetic instability in organization reduces, and the organization begins to thrive.[2]

Dominant minds

Each part of the individual human mind has its own operating system, and each mind becomes dominant (the conscious interface with our external world) during different periods of our lives. When a new mind becomes dominant the mind that was previously dominant becomes the subconscious of the new dominant mind, and the mind that was the subconscious of the old dominant mind, now becomes the unconscious of the dominant mind, in alignment with the filtering process that I explained in Chapter 3.

I think it is also important at this point to be clear about what I mean by the term "dominant mind". I am using this term to refer to the mind that has primary executive control over our *conscious* awareness at a given moment in time. Table 10.1 shows the ages and stages of development when the different minds are dominant.

Table 10.1: Stages of development, levels of consciousness and dominant minds.

Approx. age range	Stage of development	Dominant mind	Ego/Soul development
60+	Serving	Soul	
50–59	Integrating	↑	Soul activation
40–49	Self-actualizing	Neocortex	
25–39	Individuating	Neocortex	Ego-soul alignment
8–24	Differentiating	Neocortex	
3–7	Conforming	Limbic	Ego development
0–2	Surviving	Reptilian	

Even though one mind is dominant, the next mind is conscious and growing: the reptilian mind/brain is dominant during the first two years of our lives and at the same time the limbic mind/brain (emotional mind) is growing and developing in the background. Similarly, when the limbic mind/brain becomes dominant, the neocortex mind/brain is growing and developing in the background. The needs of the dominant mind always dictate our primary needs, and the needs of the nascent mind will dictate our most important secondary needs.

The reptilian mind/brain

The first mind/brain to develop is the reptilian mind/brain (the body-mind). This mind/brain becomes dominant from about the end of the first trimester of gestation and remains dominant until we reach the age of about two. The purpose of this mind/brain is to keep the body alive. To do this, it relies on two forms of memory—species-wide memory (instincts) and personalized memory (imprints) that is built up through rapid emergent learning—learning that occurs while the mind/brain is growing and developing. Every living creature has a reptilian mind/brain that takes care of the biological functioning of its body. Later in life when we move beyond the age of puberty, this mind becomes actively engaged in assuring the continuation of the species.

If the reptilian mind/brain, for whatever reason has to struggle to keep the body alive or perceives a threat that could challenge its ability to keep the body alive, it experiences fear. Fear is the body's energetic reaction to the belief (instinctual response) that the needs associated with keeping the body alive may not be met.

The period of our evolutionary history that relates to the formation of the body-mind is the reptilian period. Typical behaviours associated with the reptilian mind include defence of territory, aggression, courtship, mating and procreation. The reptilian mind lives in present moment awareness and all the actions it initiates are designed to support the body in staying alive. The reptilian mind/brain houses the vital control centres that keep the heart beating the lungs breathing and the chemical composition of the blood in balance. When the reptilian mind/brain experiences fear, the operation of all these vital control centres is affected.

The fact that the reptilian mind/brain does not become operational until the end of the first trimester of gestation raises the question: "What mind is dominant before the formation of the reptilian mind/brain—from the moment of conception to the end of the first trimester of gestation?" I believe the answer to this question is the "soul-mind.

The soul-mind

The soul-mind provides the energetic template around which the physical body grows, and the character template around which the personality forms. The subconscious of the soul-mind—the species-mind—provides the evolutionary blueprint that guides the development of the embryo into a human foetus and from there on into a child, a pubescent teenager, and eventually into an adult human being. Three dimensional "material" scientists call this energetic blueprint, DNA.

The species blueprint influences our body immediately after conception. The soul's character blueprint influences our mind around the time the embryo becomes a foetus, approximately three months after conception. From that moment on, the personality begins to form around our character. The personality is formed through rapid emergent learning over the first 24 years of your life. If your ego personality swamps your soul character, you will have difficulty individuating. If your ego personality more or less aligns with your soul character, you will move more gracefully through the individuating stage of development.

Your adult personality is your autobiography of experiencing being in a human body in your current lifetime, and your character is your soul's autobiography of experiencing life in a human body over many lifetimes.

After the reptilian mind/brain (body-mind) has become dominant, the soul-mind goes on operating in the background as the subconscious of the body-mind and the species-mind becomes the unconscious of the body-mind.

The limbic mind/brain

The next mind/brain to develop is the limbic mind/brain (the emotional mind). The limbic mind/brain becomes dominant about 18–24 months after the baby is born, and remains dominant until we reach the age of about seven. The purpose of the limbic mind/brain is to keep the body physically and emotionally safe.

After the limbic mind/brain (emotional mind) has become dominant, the body-mind goes on operating in the background as the subconscious of the emotional mind, and the soul-mind becomes the unconscious of the emotional mind. As the limbic mind/brain grows and develops, the sensations of the body-mind and the feelings of the soul-mind gradually take on less importance because they are filtered out of our awareness.

The limbic mind/brain houses our nurturing instincts. The period of our evolutionary history that relates to the formation of the limbic mind/brain is the mammalian period. Mammals form close-knit social groups—families—in which members spend time caring for each other. Adult mammals care and protect each other from hostile external forces and keep their young safe. They also teach their young rules of behaviour that preserve the internal cohesion of the family group.

Most mammals can communicate with each other through the sounds they make with their vocal chords. They can play and have pleasurable experiences. Mammals live in present moment awareness; their actions are governed by their emotions, which are dictated by whether or not they get they can get their physical, and emotional needs met. Mammals are always seeking to maximize pleasure—to satisfy their needs, and minimize pain—avoid not getting their needs met. Getting their needs met creates happiness and contentment; not getting their needs met creates anger and sadness.

The neocortex mind/brain

The next mind/brain to develop is the neocortex mind/brain (rational mind). This mind/brain becomes dominant from the age of about eight until well into our adult years, when, if we are successful in mastering our psychological development, the soul-mind once again becomes dominant. Otherwise, the ego and the rational mind stay dominant for the rest of our lives.

The purpose of the neocortex mind/brain is to keep the body physically and emotionally secure while the limbic mind/brain keeps the body physically and emotionally safe, and the reptilian mind/brain keeps the body alive.

The neocortex mind/brain is the source of our imagination and our ability to mark the passage of time, think about the future, think about the past, and partake in abstract thought. The period of our evolutionary history that relates to the formation of the rational mind/brain is the hominoid period; primates that belong to the family of great apes (hominidae). Homo sapiens represent the pinnacle of evolution of the hominidae and the pinnacle of evolution of consciousness in three-dimensional physical awareness.

After the neocortex mind/brain (rational mind) has become dominant, the emotional mind goes on operating in the background as the subconscious of the rational mind. The body-mind becomes the unconscious of the rational mind, and the soul-mind becomes the super unconscious of the rational mind. The human personality is now fully formed, and the soul's character is hidden in the background behind the layers of the ego's personality waiting to re-emerge.

The override function

While each mind/brain has its software system designed to meet specific needs, evolution created an overall operating system linking the three mind/brains together. First it linked the reptilian mind/brain with the limbic mind/brain to create mammals, and then it linked these two brains to the neocortex mind/brain to create hominidae. One of the key features of the overall operating system of the human mind is the override function.

The override function allows a higher order mind to correct the decision-making (reactions) of a lower order mind when the decision of the lower order mind could prevent the higher order mind from getting its needs met.

For example, the override function might kick-in when the reptilian mind/brain makes a decision to react in a manner that would compromise the emotional mind from getting its safety needs met, and the rational mind might kick-in when the limbic mind/brain makes a decision to react in a manner that would compromise the rational mind from getting its security needs met.

If, while the limbic mind/brain mind and neocortex mind/brain are dominant, their operation becomes impaired by the emotions of fear, anger, hatred, jealously, etc., the override function will become compromised. During these times the override function is no longer available, and we may take unnecessary risks, commit crimes, and allow our fear, anger, hatred or jealousy to govern our decision-making. Only later, after the fear, anger, hatred or jealousy has dissipated, can we regain conscious control of our decision-making.

This leads me to the question: "What override function is available if the neocortex mind/brain gets overwhelmed and runs amok?" The answer to this question is the collective mind: the mind of the group or community that is affected by the behaviour of the irrational individual. Rules, regulations and laws which contain the threat of punishment are used to influence the decision-making of impaired ego-minds. Because the rules don't work so well, and the punishments may not deter anti-social behaviour, we have created police forces at the community level and armies at the national level. We also have prisons and mental institutions where we can lock these people away.

The ego-mind

The emotional mind and the rational mind together are often referred to as the ego-mind. Whereas the ego-mind is responsible for the survival, safety and security of the body in its physical, social and cultural framework of existence, the body-mind is responsible for the homeostatic functioning of the body—keeping the body alive. The ego begins to form soon after the limbic mind/brain becomes dominant around the age of two and continues developing until our early 20s. I will explain how and why the ego develops in a moment.

With this brief overview of how our four minds and three brains operate, we can now return our attention to understanding the two components of energetic instability: psychological and physiological pain.

Pain

In their book, *Pain: Psychological Perspectives*, Hadjistavropoulos and Craig say "pain is primarily a psychological experience"[3]. They make the case that pain is a product of the brain, because for them, like almost all medical and psychological scientists, both consciousness and mind are epiphenomena of the brain.

Since I fundamentally disagree with this materialistic world view, I would say that from the perspective of the 4-D awareness, *pain is an experience of energetic instability* and that energetic instability is either *a product of the impairment of the functioning of the body-mind, the ego-mind (the emotional or rational minds) or the soul-mind.* Whereas psychological pain refers to the pain of the ego-mind and the soul-mind, physiological pain refers to the pain of the body-mind.

Neuroscience indirectly supports the idea that that all pain is due to energetic instability because both physiological and psychological pain activate exactly the same region of the brain. One would expect physiological pain to show up in the region of the brain that is linked to the body-mind—the reptilian mind-brain, and physiological pain to show up in the region of the brain that is linked to the emotional mind—the limbic mind/brain, but this is not what happens. The same region of the brain is activated for both types of pain.

Psychological pain

Psychological pain (energetic instability) arises in the ego-mind from an overload of negative emotional experiences that cause an impairment of the rational mind; a negative overload that influences the decision-making of the rational mind. Negative emotional experiences include:

- The anger associated with the ego not getting its survival, safety or security needs met.
- The fear/anxiety/anger associated with the ego's belief that it may not get its survival, safety or security needs met.

Thus, we can state:

Energetic instability → Struggle to function → Psychological pain

Whenever we get angry or experience fear or anxiety, we are being reminded through a process called triggering, of our repressed memories of similar situations in the past where we failed to get our needs met and suppressed our anger, or where we believed we would not get our needs met and suppressed our fear.

If we had expressed these emotions in the past, when we experienced them they would not be present in our subconscious or unconscious mind. In other words, our present moment awareness would not be impaired, and we would be able to evaluate what is happening with an open mind. We would be able to look at our present moment experiences rationally, without judgement. We would be able to say: "Every event is neutral, what meaning do I want to give to this experience?" Because of our emergent learning, this is not possible. Our history has taught us what meaning to give to the situation. Whenever we get angry or experience fear, our history is speaking through us. We are being re-minded, of our past failures to get our needs met. The cause of energetic instability in the ego-mind is always repressed emotions. Consequently, we can re-write the causal statement in the following way:

Repressed emotions → Energetic instability → Struggle to function → Psychological pain

As long as the repressed emotions are held in the subconscious or unconscious of the dominant mind they do not compromise the operation of the dominant mind or inhibit the override function. They only affect the operation of the level of the mind in which they are located. A repressed emotion from the rational mind impairs the operation of the subconscious emotional mind, which in turn impairs the functioning of the body-mind. These impairments are the source of all our mental and physical disorders.

Only when a repressed emotion is triggered into the dominant mind does it impair our consciousness awareness.

Repression

There are two types of repressed psychological pain:

- The emotions and feelings associated with not getting our needs met that we are afraid to express.
- The emotions and feelings associated with not being able to make meaning of our negative experiences.

Many psychology textbooks refer to repression as a defence mechanism; I believe it is more of a "misguided" but a successful survival mechanism. Repression involves relegating the emotional turmoil (energetic instability) we have about not getting our needs met or the emotional turmoil (energetic instability) associated with not being able to make meaning of our negative experiences to the subconscious of the dominant mind.

When the dominant mind cannot ascribe meaning to a situation, when something occurs which the dominant mind has never experienced before, it brings up its greatest fear and it represses the energetic turmoil thus created to the subconscious of the dominant mind so it can go on functioning. The natural default mechanism when we cannot make meaning is to assume the worst, to interpret what happened in the most detrimental way. The most detrimental interpretation the subconscious mind can give to a situation is always its greatest fear. Thus, we can state:

Inability to make meaning → Energetic instability → Struggle to function → Psychological pain

When the body-mind fails to make meaning, it brings up the fear of death and represses this psychological pain to the soul-mind. This saddens and depresses the soul because it goes directly against its intention of being present in 3-D awareness.

When the emotional mind fails to make meaning, it defaults to the fear of physical or emotional harm and represses this fear to the body-mind thereby activating the sympathetic nervous system (fight, flight or freeze response).

When the rational mind fails to make meaning, it defaults to the fear of physical or emotional insecurity and represses this fear to the emotional mind thereby activating increased vigilance and caution in matters to do with relationships.

If the dominant mind fails to repress the fear it has given to the situation, the dominant mind will become overwhelmed with psychological pain and will be unable to function. If the dominant mind does repress the fear it is experiencing to its subconscious mind, then later, when the dominant mind has a similar experience, the repressed pain will be triggered into conscious awareness, and the functioning of the dominant mind will become impaired.

Whenever the rational mind becomes impaired with the psychological pain that has been triggered into conscious awareness, the override function is compromised, and we do stupid things, things we may later regret. During such moments, the feelings of anger or hatred stored in our emotional mind, body-mind or soul-mind takes over our rational mind and dominates our decision-making. We completely lose our ability for rational thought. That's when we abuse, maim, murder, rape, torment and persecute people.

Meaning making

Given the importance of meaning-making to decision-making, I think it is important to go deeper into this topic. Meaning-making is one of the primary functions of the human mind; perhaps *the* most important function. Without meaning-making evolution would never have happened.

Meaning-making occurs at every level of our being: in the soul-mind, body-mind, emotional mind, and the rational mind. The basis of all meaning-making is memories—species memories (instincts), soul memories (past lives), body memories (this life), emotional memories and rational memories.

The mind is synonymous with consciousness; consciousness is synonymous with meaning-making, and meaning-making is synonymous with memory-making. Without species memories, soul memories, body memories, emotional memories and the memories of the rational mind, we would not be able to make meaning, and we would not be able to survive.

Even at the most basic level of life, homeostasis—the ability to regulate the internal functioning of the body—could not happen without the body-mind being able to make meaning of what is happening in its external environment and regulate its internal functioning accordingly.

The way we create meaning is by making a connection between the information patterns developed by the conscious awareness of the dominant mind about a present moment experience, and the information patterns stored in the conscious or subconscious memory of the dominant mind that were formed during periods of rapid emergent learning or normal emergent learning.

In other words, meaning arises when your dominant mind can link a current experience with the memory of an experience in the past when you were either successful in getting your needs met (a positive experience) or struggled or failed to get your needs met (a negative experience). This is true at all levels of the mind: the soul-mind, the body-mind, the emotional mind and the rational mind. The body-mind can also rely on instincts—species memories—to make meaning.

When the dominant mind makes a match between what is happening and a past experience where it took action and was able to get its needs met, it believes it understands what is happening and can make a decision that will enable it to maintain its internal stability.

We can state that meaning-making leads to understanding, which leads to decision-making and decision-making, leads to action. If the meaning given to the situation is correct, then action taken will ensure internal stability is maintained.

Meaning-making → Understanding → Decision-making → Action → Energetic stability

If the dominant mind makes a match between what is happening and an experience in the past, where, even though it took action, it struggled or failed to get its needs met—when you experienced physiological or psychological pain—the emotion of anger is released. The anger leads to energetic instability in the dominant mind.

Thus, we can state:

Unmet needs → Anger → Energetic instability

I now want to get back to the question: "What happens if the dominant mind cannot find a match between its present moment experience and its storehouse of memories—if the dominant mind cannot make meaning?"

As indicated earlier, the answer is the dominant mind shifts into default mode. It ascribes its greatest fear to the situation. Consequently, when the body-mind struggles to make meaning it moves into a high state of alert and vigilance and triggers the fight, flight or freeze survival reaction. When the emotional mind struggles to make meaning, it shifts into a state of high alert and vigilance and triggers the defence or protection reaction. When the rational mind struggles to make meaning, it shifts into a state of high alert and vigilance and triggers the caution or carefulness response.

If you want to see an example of the effect of not being able to make meaning on the decision-making of a body-mind, I recommend you watch

Cats vs. Cucumbers on Youtube[4] For those who are unable to watch this video, let me explain what it is about.

The video shows the reactions of cats to a cucumber placed behind them while they are eating their food. The cats turn around when they are finished eating to walk away and notice the cucumber. They react by jumping into the air and fleeing as fast as they can: they react with fear. Since cats do not have a history of being attacked by cucumbers, this behaviour is not an instinctive reaction: it is a default body-mind reaction brought on by its inability to make meaning, a form of negative surprise. Surprise, positive and negative, is synonymous with the inability to make meaning. In other words, surprise is the outward expression of a failure to make meaning.

The emotional and rational minds behave in a similar manner to the body-mind; they abhor a vacuum in decision-making. Whenever they cannot make meaning, they impose a meaning which most closely aligns with their greatest fear: the fear that is most deeply imprinted in our minds. These are usually the imprints from the very earliest periods of our life; the period of rapid emergent learning. It takes a high degree of personal mastery to overcome this natural tendency. Optimists can do it; pessimists can't. The only reason optimists can do it is because the pain imprints are not significant.

People suffering from neurosis follow this meaning-making trajectory frequently. As soon as they are not sure what is happening, they assume the worst and start worrying. Instead of reflecting on the possible reasons why something is not happening, they become fearful and jump to the worst conclusion they can imagine thereby creating energetic instability.

People suffering from psychoses do the same, except the fears they have are so deep and intense, they become delusional. Their early experiences of fear were so traumatic, that fear-based memories are the only means they have of interpreting their reality.

Since the reptilian mind/brain is the least competent at meaning-making and the neocortex mind/brain is most competent, with the limbic mind/brain falling somewhere between, it follows that the pain of the struggle to make meaning experienced by babies and toddlers will be greater than the pain experienced by children, which in turn will be greater than the pain experienced by teenagers and adults.

This statement is borne out by research; the experience of acute pain decreases with the age of a child. In other words, the human pain threshold is lowest at birth.[5]

Extrapolate back a few months and one can imagine that pain experienced by a baby during the birth process and pain experienced by the foetus in the womb could be overwhelming for the reptilian mind/brain and the soul-mind. The memories of our earliest pain are the most deeply embedded in our psyche and the most potentially damaging to our physical and mental health.

The consequences of fear

Whenever we experience a situation where the instincts or imprints of the body-mind or the beliefs of the ego-mind suggest that our ability to stay alive or keep safe could be compromised, we experience the fear-based reaction of fight, flight or freeze. The dominant mind becomes hypervigilant, and the body-mind prepares itself for action: it pumps out chemicals to prepare the body for fight or flight and shuts down systems that require energy. These actions create instability in our energy field. As soon as the threat goes away, the body-mind quickly returns to normal functioning, and the instability in the energy field dissipates.

When a threat does not go away—when the emotional mind or rational mind experiences an ongoing situation that they believe could compromise their ability to meet their needs the body-mind remains in a state of heightened vigilance and energetic instability, pumping out chemicals and shutting down systems. This is called anxiety. Whenever we worry—when we let fear dominate our thinking—we experience anxiety. Because anxiety can stay with us for long periods of time, its impact on the homeostatic functioning of the body-mind is more significant than fear. The same thing happens when we repress our negative emotions and feelings. Fear, anxiety and repressed anger all compromise the working of the body-mind and impair the functioning of the dominant mind.

Healing of trauma

The only way to prevent impairment through the triggering of repressed emotions is to heal the negative imprints and beliefs. We do that by re-experiencing the sensations, emotions and feelings that have been repressed and bring them into the conscious awareness where they can be re-experienced, put into a historical context, and given meaning. When this is done, the impairment of consciousness is removed, and the psychological and physiological malfunctions associated with the energetic instability are healed. The following comments by Dr. Arthur Janov illustrate my point:

> Profound personality change is impossible on the level of words, or even on the level of emotions; there is no venting or "getting it out" such as crying and screaming, that will bring about any true or lasting change.[6]
>
> For true and lasting change to occur, deep levels of the brain must change physiologically ... no amount of talk-based therapy will ever bring about such a connection because there is little activation of the subcortical structures [and the levels of mind] that mediate the deeply imprinted memories.[7]
>
> Our job is to merge the unconscious with the conscious, to put us in touch with what our bodies are saying. For that, we need to learn the language of the deep brain [mind]... We cannot learn it through words, only through feelings. Relief comes when the [repressed] feeling is addressed and felt.[8]

Dr. Bessel van der Kolk says something very similar concerning trauma.

> We have begun to understand how overwhelming experiences affect our innermost sensations and our relationship to our physical reality—the core of who we are. We have learnt that trauma is not just an event that took place sometime in the past; it is also the imprint left by that experience on the mind, brain and body. This imprint has ongoing consequences for how the human organism manages to survive in the present.[9]
>
> Trauma results in a fundamental reorganization of the way mind and brain manage perceptions. It changes not only how we think and what we think about, but also our very capacity to think. We have discovered that helping victims of trauma find the words to describe what has happened to them is profoundly meaningful, but usually is not enough. The act of telling the story doesn't necessarily alter the automatic physical and hormonal responses of the bodies that remain hypervigilant, prepared to be assaulted or violated at any time. For real change

to take place, the body has to learn that the danger has passed and to live in the reality of the present.[10]

Only when we bring the deeply hidden feelings of our past, into the awareness of the rational mind, and give them a historical context, are we able to heal the energetic instability of the subconscious emotional mind and unconscious body-mind.

Like the soul-mind, the body-mind and the emotional mind exist in an everlasting moment of awareness. Therefore, all the memories of our repressed psychological pain accumulate in the same "space": the space of the everlasting moment. Only the neocortex with its understanding of the past, present and the future can unlock the door to this space and bring what was trapped in the past into the light of rational consciousness and the context of our personal history.

Physiological pain

Physiological pain arises from energetic instability in the body-mind. There are two sources of this energetic instability: the pain caused by the impairment of functioning when the body-mind is overloaded with homeostatic tasks (due to sickness, repairing damaged tissues or correcting malfunctions in the body) and the psychological pain associated with the anger and fear of the body-mind not getting its needs met.

Struggle to maintain homeostasis
Psychological pain of unmet needs $\rightarrow$ Energetic instability in the body-mind

The potential for energetic instability in the body-mind—the impairment of its functioning—is greatest when the reptilian mind/brain is dominant; when it is responsible for internal functioning (internal stability) and also the principal conscious interface with the outside world (external equilibrium): it feels physiological and psychological pain. Consequently, the potential for the onset of physiological disorders (energetic instability in the energy field of the body) is greatest during the survival stage of development (0–2 years old). These disorders may not show up until much later in life.

A summary of key points

Here are the main points of Chapter 10:

1. There are two basic signs of energetic instability: physiological pain and psychological pain.
2. Every time the body-mind or ego-mind fails to get its needs met, or believe they may not get their needs met, we experience energetic instability (anger and fear) that affects the functioning of our energy field. What our mind does with that energetic instability directly impacts our mental and physical health.
3. We have three brains and four minds: The first mind/brain to develop is the reptilian mind/brain (the body-mind). The second mind/brain to develop is the limbic mind/brain (the emotional mind). The third mind/brain to develop is the neocortex mind/brain (the rational mind). The soul-mind is present from the start of our life.
4. Each part of the individual human mind has its operating system, and each mind becomes dominant (the conscious interface with our external world) during different periods of our lives. When a new mind becomes dominant, the mind that was previously dominant becomes the subconscious, and the mind that was previously subconscious, becomes the unconscious of the dominant mind.
5. One of the key features of the overall operating system of the human mind is the override function. The override function allows a higher order mind to override or correct the decision-making (reactions) of a lower order mind.
6. When our dominant mind is energetically unstable, when it is overwhelmed with emotions of fear and anger, we take unnecessary risks, commit crimes, and allow our anger and hatred to govern our decision-making. During these times, the override function is no longer available to us. Only later, after the energetic instability has dissipated can we regain conscious control of our decision-making.
7. All psychological pain arises from energetic instability in the ego-mind: the impairment of the functioning of the ego-mind caused by an overload of experiences of not being able to get its needs met or an inability to make meaning of its negative experiences.
8. All physiological pain arises from energetic instability in the body-mind: the impairment of the functioning of the body-mind when

it struggles to function either from an overload of homeostatic tasks or a struggle to make meaning of the psychological pain it is experiencing from not getting its needs met.
9. When the body-mind fails to make meaning, it defaults to the fear of death and represses this energetic instability to the soul-mind. When the emotional mind fails to make meaning, it defaults to the fear of physical or emotional harm and represses this energetic instability to the body-mind. When the rational mind fails to make meaning, it defaults the fear of physical or emotional insecurity and represses this energetic instability to the emotional mind.
10. When we are young, and those who have failed to meet our survival, safety or security needs are our parents, we get into a bind. We need to express our anger (internal instability) at not getting our needs met, but if we direct the anger towards our parents, we may compromise our ability to get our future survival, safety and security needs met.

References and notes

1. www.valuescentre.com
2. Richard Barrett, *The Values-Driven Organization: Unleashing Human Potential for Performance and Profit* (Bath: Fulfilling Books), 2014.
3. T. Hadjistavropoulos and K. D. Craig, *Pain:Psychological Perspectives* (New York: Psychology Press), 2004, p. 1.
4. https://uk.search.yahoo.com/search?fr=mcafee&type=C114GB739D20151203&p=cats+vs+cucumbers
5. T. Hadjistavropoulos and K. D. Craig, *Pain: Psychological Perspectives* (New York: Psychology Press), 2004, p. 119.
6. Dr.Arthur Janov, *Primal Healing: Access the Incredible Power of Your Feelings to Improve Your Health* (Franklin Lakes: Career Press), 2007, p. 21.
7. Ibid.
8. Ibid., p. 24.
9. Dr. Bessel van der Kolk, *The Body Keeps the Score: Mind, Brain and Body in the Transformation of Trauma* (Penguin Books: New York), 2014, p. 21.
10. Ibid.

11

The impact of energetic instability

The source of our energetic instability is either the fear or anxiety we experience about the possibility of not getting our needs met or the anger and sadness we have when we don't get our needs met.

In order to fully understand how physiological and psychological pain affects our lives, we need to consider the impact that energetic instability has on the functioning of our four minds: the soul mind, the body-mind, the emotional mind and the rational mind.

I am going to explore this idea by splitting our lives into seven periods that relate to the times when the four minds are dominant and forming (during periods of rapid emergent learning) or simply dominant (during periods of normal emergent learning).

- Period 1: From the moment of conception to the end of the first trimester (the embryo period) when the soul-mind is dominant.
- Period 2(a): From the end of the first trimester to the moment of birth (the foetus period) when the body-mind is dominant and forming.
- Period 2(b): From birth to the age of two (the baby period) when the body-mind is still dominant and still forming. This represents the surviving stage of psychological development.
- Period 3: From the age of 2 to the age of 7 (the toddler and young child period) when the emotional mind is dominant and forming.

This represents the conforming stage of psychological development. The emotional mind starts forming earlier but is not dominant.
- Period 4: From the age of 7 to the early 20s (the child/teenager period) when the rational mind is dominant and forming. This represents the differentiating stage of psychological development. The rational mind starts forming earlier but is not dominant.
- Period 5: From the mid-20s to late-30s when the rational mind is fully dominant.
- Period 6: From the 40s to the late-50s when the rational mind becomes less dominant, and the soul-mind becomes more dominant.
- Period 7: From the early-60s onwards when the soul mind becomes dominant.

Whereas the first five periods are relatively constrained in their timing due to the species timetable for physical maturing, the last two periods are not as fixed; they may not occur at all. Many people have difficulties activating their soul-mind because they always allow their ego needs to take priority. Table 11.1 summarizes the impact of three types of energetic instability on the four minds during each period.

Table 11.1: Summary of potential sources of energetic instability.

Period	Energetic instability due to physiological pain	Energetic instability due to psychological pain
Period 1: Soul mind (from conception to end of the first trimester of gestation).	Energetic instability caused by ill-health, smoking, drug and alcohol abuse by the mother, as well as medical drugs used by mother and viruses contaminating the mother's blood.	Energetic instability caused by psychological pain (energetic instability) of mother transmitted to the energy field of the embryo.

Period 2(a): Body-mind (from second trimester of gestation to birth).	Energetic instability caused by the struggle to maintain homeostatic functioning due to energetic instability caused by ill-health, smoking, drug and alcohol abuse by the mother, as well as medical drugs used by mother and viruses contaminating the mother's blood.	Energetic instability caused by the experience of anger, fear and sadness associated with the body mind not getting its survival needs met.
Period 2(b): Body-mind (from birth to age of two). Surviving stage of development.	Energetic instability caused by the struggle to maintain homeostatic functioning caused by overload due to sickness, repair of damaged tissues or attempts to correct the internal malfunctions of the body.	Same as 2(a).
Period 3: Emotional mind (from age 2 to age 7). Conforming stage of development.	Same as 2(b).	Energetic instability caused by the experience of anger, fear and sadness associated with the emotional mind not getting its safety needs met.
Period 4: Rational mind (from age 7 to mid-20s) Differentiating stage of development.	Same as 2(b).	Energetic instability caused by the experience of anger, fear and sadness associated with the rational mind not getting its security needs met.
Period 5: Rational mind (from mid-20s to the late 30s). Individuating stage of development.	Same as 2 (b).	Same as Period 4. Work on releasing psychological pain sometimes begins in this period.
Period 6: Rational and soul mind (from the 40s to late-50s). Self-actualizing and integrating stage of development.	Same as 2(b).	Same as Period 5. Because of work done by releasing psychological pain, there is less frequent and less severe energetic instability.

Period 7: Soul-mind (from early-60s onwards). Serving stage of development.	Same as 2(b).	Rare occurrences of energetic instability.

Energetic instability in the soul-mind

The soul-mind is the most fragile of our minds because it's consciousness is easily impaired by 3-D material existence. It is not used to living in a material world and not used to the experience of energetic instability. It lives inside an energy field of love; any experiences the body has (physiological or psychological) of not getting its needs met are experienced by the soul as a lack of love.

Generally speaking, Period 1 is the honeymoon period of the soul in the body. The only energetic instability the soul can experience as an embryo is when the mother's energetic stability is compromised by ill-health, smoking, drug and alcohol abuse, the use of medical drugs or viruses affecting the mother's blood, such as the Zika virus. During this period the limbs, fingers and toes of the baby begin to appear, the lungs, ears, eyes, upper lip and nose start to form, and the reptilian mind/brain starts to develop. One example of the disastrous effect that "medicinal" drugs can have on the early development of the human embryo was the thalidomide debacle.

Thalidomide

In the late 1950's the drug thalidomide was marketed as a sedative to help people sleep. It was also discovered that the drug helped expectant mothers prevent morning sickness. In the early 1960s doctors began to associate thalidomide with severe birth defects: shortened or absent limbs. Very soon after that, the drug was taken off the market. In all, about 100,000 pregnant women took the drug. Most of them had lost their babies before they were born. Today about 6,000 "thalidomide children" are still alive in nearly 60 countries.

A lack of love

At the end of Period 1, the soul-mind hands over responsibility for staying present in a 3-D material awareness to the reptilian mind/brain. This is experienced by the body-mind as the will to stay alive. During Periods 2(a) and 2(b), after the reptilian mind/brain becomes functional and dominant, the main source of the energetic instability (pain) in the soul-mind is the repressed psychological pain (anger and fear) of the body-mind. This repressed pain is always associated with the fear of death, which for the soul means that its attempt to stay present in 3-D awareness could come to an end. This causes the soul-mind to feel sadness.

The energetic instability (pain) of the soul-mind is held in the layer of the energy field that contains the heart. This layer of the energy field is associated with the individuating stage of psychological development and is known as the upper etheric field (I will explain what this terminology means in the following chapter). Therefore, any energetic instability (pain) in the soul-mind will have a significant impact on our cardiac health.

Energetic instability in the body-mind

The functioning of the body-mind is most easily impaired during Periods 2(a) and 2(b) when the reptilian mind/brain's neurological functions are developing. Consequently, energetic instability during this period can impair the functioning of the body-mind for the rest of our lives.

The pre-natal period

The most likely cause of energetic instability before birth (Period 2(a)) is the homeostatic imbalance caused by the mother worrying and being anxious, and by the mother being sick or ingesting alcohol, drugs or smoke, or having viruses in her blood. Other causes of energetic instability in the body-mind occur when the mother fails to eat nutritional food or suffers from a chronic disease.

The birth process

The birth process is potentially the most dangerous and stressful period of our lives. So many things can go wrong during the birth process causing the body-mind to experience energetic instability—homeostatic overload (physiological pain) and psychological overload due to the difficulty in making meaning of the physiological pain—the fear of death. The emotions associated with this pain are repressed to the soul-mind where they are stored in the soul's memory. This pain can be triggered in later in life when conditions similar to those that caused the pain are encountered.

The normal birth process is naturally painful for the mother and the baby. The mother struggles with the pain of giving birth, and the baby struggles through the pain of travelling through the constriction of the uterus and birth canal. The pain of the mother is assuaged by her joy at the new arrival. The pain of the baby is not assuaged unless it is immediately comforted and held by the mother. If the baby is born prematurely and needs intensive care, separation is unavoidable. It would be highly beneficial if some way could be found for the mother to comfort the baby even in such situations.

If the birth process goes well, the baby learns (through emergent learning) that it can successfully struggle through difficulties and pain.

Dr. Arthur Janov considers the birth process to be so important to our adult health that he devotes a whole chapter to this brief period of our lives in his book *The Biology of Love*.[1] He particularly draws attention to the problem of anoxia—an absence of oxygen in the lungs, and hypoxia, deficiency of oxygen reaching the body's tissues.

> Oxygen deficit at birth forces the foetus to produce high levels of stress hormones these hormones prepare the system for flight or fight from danger; in this case the danger of death through anoxia.[2]

Dr. Janov suggests that sustained oxygen deprivation can also occur in the womb if the mother smokes. He states:

> Anoxia hinders cortical development, which can result in poor controlled impulses and lifelong tension and anxiety.[3]

The sympathetic branch (the fight reaction) of the autonomic nervous system helps the baby to get through the pain of being born. Once the baby is born, it wants to be held by its mother to soothe away the pain of the trauma of the birth experience. The baby is frightened by the painful sensations involved in the birth process. These painful sensations are experienced by the soul as a lack of love. The soul needs to be comforted so it can be reassured. If the baby is not immediately soothed, the trauma of the birth process is magnified in the soul-mind. Not only does the pain of the birth process cause the soul to experience a lack of love, once the struggle to stay alive is over, its immediate separation from the energy field of the mother is perceived as abandonment and is also felt in the soul-mind as a lack of love.

Our bodies have several requirements for staying alive (maintaining their internal stability through homeostatic functioning): they need oxygen, water, food, sleep, and warmth. Our soul has only one requirement: LOVE.

When the mother (and foetus) experiences a prolonged painful period of labour, one of the choices the mother can make is to have an epidural to deaden the pain. If she makes this choice, not only does she deaden her pain, she deadens the pain of the unborn baby, and the autonomic nervous system of the baby shuts down. Dr Janov explains:

> A mother heavily tranquilized or anesthetized leaves the baby "feeling" overwhelmed, literally unable to struggle to save its life, so that later it is finally articulated as, "What's the use [of struggling]?"[4]

A neurological link is made in the baby's developing reptilian mind/brain that struggles to survive do not require the services of the sympathetic nervous system. The baby learns to give in and not fight when faced with fear-inducing situations. The learned imprint, "What's the use of struggling?" can have serious consequences later in life. A study by L. P. Lipsitt of the Child Study Centre at Brown University shows a dramatic relationship between the suicidal tendencies (What is the use of struggling) of adults and problem births.

> The key meaning of the Lipsitt study is that trauma, once imprinted, follows us throughout life and can affect us enough to deny our lives.[5]

The work of Lee Salk at Cornell University Medical School and researchers at the Karolinska Medical Centre in Stockholm verify the effects of birth trauma on suicide. In particular, Salk's studies show that 60 percent of the people with suicidal tendencies experienced either a lack of prenatal care for the first twenty weeks of pregnancy, respiratory distress at birth, or chronic disease in the mother.[6]

It is not just the risk of suicide that increases with early trauma; a host of other physiological malfunctions are also associated with distress experienced during Period 2.

> ...womb-life profoundly affects later adult life and in a host of ways. Deformation of cells leading to cancer, later on, may well take place in the womb and not become evident until age fifty.[7]
>
> Heart disease in later life can be related to birth trauma and life in the womb [and] strokes at fifty can be the logical denouement of events at six months of gestation.[8]

As we shall see later, the suppression of the immune system and elevated blood pressure due to heightened stress lie at the root of the early onset most diseases and disorders in the body.

The post-natal period

When the baby is born, the greatest risk of energetic instability is the lack of attention the mother (or caregiver) pays to the baby's needs: the need for touching, feeding and cleaning is paramount for the healthy (psychological) development of the baby. Babies who are neglected suffer significantly as children and later as adults. Research shows that if a child has been neglected or inadequately cared for before the age of six, their chances of having overall poor physical health increases two-fold.[9]

When the will of the soul to be present in 3-D awareness is not strong and the pain (lack of love) experienced by the soul in the womb or during the birth process is significant, the soul can become so overwhelmed by the energetic instability it is experiencing that it chooses to withdraw from the baby's body. Usually, this happens during the first few months of life. This is known as Sudden Infant Death Syndrome or SIDS for short.

Let me reassure you, no matter how caring and vigilant you are as a parent, simply being in a physical body will affect the energetic stability of the soul and impair the functioning of its consciousness. When the pain of this impairment becomes too great for the soul to bear, particularly a "young" or less resilient soul, it will withdraw from the body.

If the soul is able to bear the pain (energetic instability) and stay present in the body, sometime beyond the age of 2, after the limbic mind/brain has become dominant, the soul creates a psychic entity we call the ego. The ego acts as a buffer, preventing the soul from experiencing any further energetic instability. I will explain how the soul creates the ego shortly.

We know we have energetic instability stored in our body-mind if we experience outbursts of physiological pain that cannot be diagnosed. This pain is due to the triggering of the memory of a trauma lodged in our body-mind.

Energetic instability in the body-mind in later in life

The most frequent experience of energetic instability in the body-mind is known as a "psychosomatic disorder". A psychosomatic disorder is one in which physical symptoms of disorder originate from mental or emotional causes; when the impairment of mind function causes impairment of body function.

I prefer to think of the "psycho" component of "psychosomatic" as energetic instability in the energy field of the body caused by anger, fear or anxiety, and the "somatic" component, as energetic instability in the energy field of the body caused by the body's struggles to maintain homeostatic functioning caused by the stress of anger, fears and anxiety. In other words, psychosomatic symptoms emerge as a physiological concomitant of psychological dysfunctions involving fear, anxiety or anger.

> In a state of rage, for example, the angry person's blood pressure is likely to be elevated and his pulse and respiratory rate to be increased. When the anger passes, the heightened physiologic processes usually subside. If the person has a persistent inhibited aggression (chronic rage), however, which he is unable to express overtly, the emotional state remains unchanged, though unexpressed in the overt behaviour, and the physiological symptoms associated with the angry state persist. With time, such a person becomes aware of the physiological dysfunction. Very often he develops concern over the resulting

physical signs and symptoms, but he denies or is unaware of the emotions that have evoked the symptoms.[10]

Whenever we experience fear and anger or any feeling that is a derivative of fear and anger, such as irritation, impatience, anxiety or rage, the energy field of the body-mind immediately becomes energetically unstable and starts to create stress hormones, preparing the body for fight or flight. The sympathetic branch of the autonomic nervous system stays in this mode of operation until the perceived threat dissipates.

If the sympathetic nervous system becomes permanently activated due to traumatic imprinting or severe early maladaptive schema, the body will experience an ongoing chemical imbalance and suppression of the immune system, thereby increasing the chance of disease and sickness.

One of the chemicals produced by the adrenal gland, which suppresses the immune system when the sympathetic nervous system is aroused, is cortisol. In addition to suppressing the immune system, cortisol increases blood sugar, aids the metabolism of fat, protein and carbohydrate as well as decreasing bone formation. All these actions have a negative impact on the long-term functioning of the body.

Psychosomatic disorders occur as a result of inappropriate activation of the autonomic nervous system by stress arising from the ego's unresolved fears. In other words, the pain and stress we keep locked up in our bodies about our inability to get our needs met is the cause of psychosomatic disorders.

Psychosomatic disorders include, but are not limited to, hypertension, respiratory ailments, gastrointestinal disturbances, migraine and tension headaches, pelvic pain, impotence, frigidity, dermatitis and ulcers. I will show in the following chapters that the precise nature and location of psychosomatic disorders is directly related to deficiency needs that you have not been able to meet, which in turn is related to the time in your life when those deficiency needs were most important to your psychological development.

The hypothesis I am putting forward in this book is that *all* physiological disorders are, at their core, psychosomatic in nature. They begin in the mind and manifest in the body. Every illness, sickness and physical dysfunction has its roots in either the energetic impairment of or overload of the body-mind's ability to function due to homeostatic or psychological causes, physical accidents or inappropriate nutrition.

The body-mind is particularly sensitive to experiences that involve a struggle to stay alive: if we fail we will die, and the soul's intention of experiencing 3-D awareness will be thwarted. It follows therefore that the highest levels of fear we experience are associated with meeting the needs of the body-mind.

Energetic instability in the emotional mind

The functioning of the emotional mind is most easily and frequently impaired during Period 3 when the limbic mind/brain's neurological functions and personal belief systems about how to interpret its experiences are developing. Consequently, energetic instability during this period can impair the functioning of the emotional mind for the rest of our lives.

The emotional mind is sensitive to experiences that involve struggles to keep safe: if we fail in these struggles—if we are physically or emotionally abused during Period 3—our consciousness can be permanently impaired. Such impairment lies at the root of almost all long-term psychological dysfunctions (mental disorders) including psychoses and neuroses.

The sources of energetic instability in the emotional mind are two-fold: the instability engendered by the anger, fear and anxiety about not getting our safety needs met and the instability engendered by rational mind's repressed psychological pain about not getting its security needs met.

The energetic instability associated with anger, fear and anxiety is experienced by the reptilian mind as *sensations*, by the limbic mind as *emotions*, and by the neocortex as *feelings*.

The creation of the ego

The creation of the ego-mind occurs early in Period 3 after the limbic mind/brain starts to become dominant. The reason the soul creates the ego-mind is to reduce the level of energetic instability—the pain of the lack of love it is feeling—by building a psychic layer of protection that we call the ego-mind. Over the next few years, the soul gradually hands over control of its survival in 3-D awareness to the ego-mind. It has already handed over control for staying alive to the body-mind.

The soul, as an individuated aspect of the universal energy field, lives in a state of oneness and abundance—a timeless world of connection—where its needs are instantly gratified through its thoughts. Therefore, the soul has no needs and experiences no separation. For the soul, any lack of gratification of the body's needs or feelings of separation the ego experiences are indicative of a lack of love. In attempting to explore the 3-D physical reality, the soul is moving from a world of "connection" and "abundance" to a world of "separation" and "limitation."

It follows that when the body's physiological needs and ego's psychological needs are not met—when the body-mind and emotional mind experience anger and fear the soul feels an acute sense of pain (energetic instability). Experiences of the foetus or baby that cause the body-mind to struggle to maintain homeostasis, or experiences that cause the infant to experience separation, result in energetic discomfort in the soul-mind. If these needs are not gratified, the discomfort in the body-mind turns into sadness, depression and despair in the soul-mind. From the soul's perspective, we can express the relationship between the body's unmet needs and love in the following way:

Unmet body and emotional needs → Lack of love

Therefore, when the survival and safety needs of the foetus or young infant are not attended to or are ignored—when the foetus or young infant's need for love is left ungratified or its biological needs are compromised, for example, by the mother smoking, drinking alcohol or taking drugs—the body-mind finds it difficult to maintain biological homeostasis and the emotional mind finds it difficult to maintain energetic stability. In other words, when the body-mind experiences physical discomfort or the emotional mind experiences separation, the soul feels a lack of love.

Dr. Arthur Janov puts it this way:

> Love ... means taking care of oneself during pregnancy, when the neurons in the foetus's brain are developing at an incredibly rapid rate. The mother must not do things that threaten the baby's development, such as taking alcohol and tranquilizers that will find their way into the baby's system. Love means wanting the baby, because mothers who do not want their child find that their children have more health problems,

> both physical and psychological. Above all, there should be no smoking while pregnant. The foetus feels it and can choke and gasp in the womb.[11]

Love also means taking good care of the baby when it is born. Without the love of a mother (or mother surrogate) the future health of the body is compromised. A recent research study carried out by the New York University Langone Medical Center supports this statement.[12]

This study found that when rat pups experienced pain, hundreds of genes in the rat pups brains were modified by the mother's presence. This is the first time that scientists have shown how an infant's brain reacts to the presence or absence of its mother when it in distress. Professor Regina Sullivan, who led the study, explains:

> Our study shows that a mother comforting her infant in pain does not just elicit a behavioural response, but also the comforting itself modifies critical neural circuitry during early brain development.[13]

So how does the soul deal with the traumas (physical and emotional demonstrations of a lack of love) it experiences during its time in the womb, the birth process, and the first two-to-three years of life? It absorbs the hurt and pain into its energy field causing malfunctions in the circuitry of the developing reptilian mind-brain, and later on, in the circuitry of the developing limbic mind/brain.

When the soul starts to become overwhelmed by the pain of separation, it dissociates from 3-D awareness by creating an energetic buffer that we call the ego. Once the ego is created, it protects the soul by absorbing the psychological pain associated with the child's development: first, the pain of anger, fear and loneliness associated with not getting our safety needs met during the conforming stage of development, then the pain of anger, fear and isolation associated with not getting our security needs met during the differentiating stage of development.

To keep functioning, the ego represses the pain of separation (loneliness and isolation) from its conscious mind to its subconscious mind. When the emotional mind is dominant, the pain (energetic instability) is repressed to the body-mind, and while the rational mind is dominant, the pain (energetic instability) is repressed to the emotional mind.

Dissociative Identity Disorder (DID)

When young children experience repeated physical or sexual abuse or are ignored by their parents, the dominant emotional mind first represses the pain it is experiencing to the body-mind, and if the experiences continue, it dissociates itself from the pain by creating an alter ego. By making the alter ego the repository of the pain, the ego-mind (the emotional mind and later the rational mind) can go on functioning in a normal manner. Children who experience different forms of repeated traumatic experience may have several alter egos.

According to the American Psychiatric Association (APA), the essential features of dissociative disorders are "a disruption in the usually integrated functions of consciousness, memory, identity and perception".

The APA goes on to say:

> Dissociate Identity Disorder (or Multiple Personality Disorder) is characterized by the presence of two or more distinct identities or personality states that recurrently take control of the individual's behaviour, accompanied by an inability to recall important personal information that is too extensive to be explained by ordinary forgetfulness. It is a disorder characterized by identity fragmentation, rather than proliferation of separate personalities.[14]

What is striking about alter egos is that they display different physical symptoms to the host personality, the ego personality that protected itself by forming the alter egos.

> The alter carries all the time-encapsulated memories including body memories [energy field memories] and with an intensity that has never been diluted because it has never been shared. The host has avoided trauma incidents and has left the alter ego to deal with them.[15]

Alter-egos absorb the repressed emotions and feelings of the host ego and accommodate them in their energy fields. When an alter ego shows up, the physical symptoms of the illness and diseases caused by the energetic instability associated with the repressed painful experiences are now found in the body-mind of the alter ego.

When an alter ego shows up as the dominant personality, the body experiences the physical symptoms associated with energetic instabilities of the alter ego. When the alter ego is not present, the body experiences the physical symptoms associated with the energetic instabilities of the host ego. One personality can be blind whereas the host personality can have perfect vision.

In my mind, the fact that alter egos can experience different symptoms in the same physical body proves without a doubt that the operation of the energy field of the body is dependent on, and contained within, the energy field of the ego. When an alter ego assumes conscious awareness (become dominant), it appears with its own body template of dysfunctions and symptoms.

The implications of this are enormous: it means that the so-called "physical" body is a complete reflection of the personal history of the energy field of the ego-mind. Change your personality and you change your physical symptoms.

Psychosis

Another significant form of conscious impairment that has its origins in Period 3 is psychosis. Psychosis is a mental state that impairs thought, perception and judgement. A person experiencing a psychosis loses a solid connection to reality; he or she becomes delusional. A person experiencing psychosis may hallucinate, become paranoid or experience a change of personality. Psychoses—such as schizophrenia, delusional disorder or bipolar disorder—can significantly interfere with our daily functions.

> For whatever reason (and the events can be legion) the sufferer from psychosis has mis-learned the nature of human beings. Instead of learning that human beings are born lovable, sociable and non-violent—the sufferer has picked up the message that reality is dangerous; that powerful human beings, including everyone else, are consistently malign. Such others may appear benign; they may say they are friendly—but the basic trust has been broken, and they are not to be believed.[16]

There are some similarities *and* some differences between psychosis and dissociative identity disorder. The main similarity is that they are both caused by early trauma—experiences of the pain of being of not getting our safety needs met or the experience of separation caused by the feeling of being unloved. The main difference is people experiencing DID split their minds into parts so the host ego can go on functioning in a normal manner, whereas people with psychosis do not split their minds into parts; they attempt to go functioning despite the fact that their meaning-making has been severely impaired.

Neurosis

A less serious form of impairment that usually has its origins during Period 3 and the early stages of Period 4 is something we all suffer from to some degree, we call it neurosis.

Whereas a psychosis significantly disrupts our daily functioning, a neurosis does not. A neurosis may impair our daily functioning but does not disrupt it. We can go on operating, but because of the neurosis the decisions we make can inhibit our ability to find happiness in our lives. Neuroses arise from our early childhood experiences of struggling and failing to get our safety and security needs met. These struggles condition our emotional and rational minds into specific modes of thinking based on our past experiences. The Encyclopedia Britannica defines neuroses in the following way:

> Neuroses are characterized by anxiety, depression, or other feelings of unhappiness or distress that are out of proportion to the circumstances of a person's life. They may impair a person's functioning in virtually any area of his life, relationships, or external affairs, but they are not severe enough to incapacitate the person. Patients with neuroses do not suffer from the loss of the sense of reality seen in persons with psychoses.[17]

Maslow speaks of neuroses as I do, as a failure of personal growth:

> It is a falling short of what one could have been, and even, one could say, of what one should have been, biologically speaking, that is if one had grown and developed in an unimpeded way. Human and personal possibilities have been lost. The world has been narrowed, and so has consciousness. Capacities have

been inhibited. The cognitive losses, the lost pleasures, joys, and ecstasies, the loss of competence, the inability to relax, the weakening of will, the fear of responsibility—all these are diminutions of humanness.[18]

Maslow also states that the fear of one's own greatness or the evasion or the limits we place on our possible destiny are also a sign of psychological impairment:

> If you deliberately plan to be less than you are capable of being, then I warn you that you'll be deeply unhappy for the rest of your life. You will be evading your own capacities, your own possibilities.[19]

Early Maladaptive Schema

Another term that is sometimes used to describe the impairment of functioning of consciousness is Early Maladaptive Schema (EMS). EMS places emphasis on exploring the childhood and adolescent origins of psychological problems and maladaptive coping styles.[20]

Early Maladaptive Schemas are fear-based thought patterns usually formed during Periods 3 and 4. EMS is called *Early* because it originates when we are young. It is called *maladaptive* because it arises from an impairment in the functioning (meaning-making) of the dominant mind, and it is called a *schema* because it relates to a way of being that we always deploy when we are confronted by a particular set of circumstances that remind us of situations in our childhood when we experienced emotional hurt or pain in attempting to get our safety or security needs met.

Jeffrey Young, Founder and Director of the Cognitive Therapy Centres of New York and Fairfield County (Connecticut), describes EMS in the following way:

> Early Maladaptive Schemas [a theme not just a belief] seem to be the result of dysfunctional experiences with parents, siblings, and peers during the first few years of an individual's life. Most schemas are caused by ongoing everyday noxious experiences with family members and peers who cumulatively strengthen the schema. For example, a child who is constantly criticized

when performance does not meet parental standards is prone to develop the incompetence/failure schema.[21]

If you developed an Early Maladaptive Schema during your formative years, your mind wils constantly be on the lookout for incoming information patterns that correspond to these schema.

Abraham Maslow describes how our failure to get our needs met in our childhood years contributes to our neuroses later in life:

> The child who is fortunate enough to grow normally and well get satiated and bored with the delights he has savoured sufficiently, and eagerly goes on to higher more complex, delights as they become available to him without danger or threat. He wants to go on, to move, to grow.[22]
>
> Only if frustration, failure, disapproval, ridicule come at the next step does he [she] fixate or regress, and we are then faced with the intricacies of pathological dynamics of neurotic compromises in which the impulses remain alive but unfulfilled, or even of loss of impulse and capacity.[23]

These early negative experiences may never occur again but their effects remain; they become hard-wired into your brain as neural pathways. The memories of these experiences and the associated emotions become embedded stimuli that shape or distort your present reality in line with the past. This means that you will be predisposed, even as an adult, to believe that you will still be inadequate to the task of meeting these needs.

Based on this, we can see that the common thread linking psychosis, neurosis and EMS is an impairment of meaning-making related to experiences when we did not get our needs met during periods of rapid emergent learning. These experiences condition the way in which our minds create reality through the formation of fear-based beliefs. When we have such beliefs, subconscious or conscious, they affect us in two ways. We are constantly vigilant—always on the lookout for opportunities to satisfy our unmet needs—and the memories of the hurt and pain we originally experienced and repressed are frequently triggered, impairing our ability to make decisions.

Energetic instability in the rational mind

The functioning of the rational mind is normally impaired later in Period 3 and during Period 4 when the neocortex mind/brain's neurological functions and personal belief systems about how to interpret its experiences are developing. Consequently, energetic instability experienced during these periods can impair the functioning of the rational mind for the rest of our lives.

The rational mind is sensitive to experiences that involve a struggle to maintain security. If we fail in this struggle—if we are not respected, acknowledged or recognized—our consciousness becomes impaired. Such impairment lies at the root of almost all long-term mental neuroses concerned with self-worth.

The sources of energetic instability (pain) in the rational mind are twofold: the instability engendered by the fear and anxiety we have about not getting our survival, safety and security needs met in the present moment, and the instability engendered when the psychological pain of the rational mind that has been repressed to the emotional mind is triggered into the conscious awareness of the rational mind.

Post-traumatic stress disorder (PTSD)

A more serious impairment of the rational mind than neurosis is a condition called Post-Traumatic Stress Disorder (PTSD). PTSD is described officially in the following way:

> PTSD is a psychiatric disorder that can occur following the experience or witnessing of life-threatening events such as military combat, natural disasters, terrorist incidents, serious accidents, or physical or sexual assault in adult or childhood. People who suffer from PTSD often relive the experience through nightmares and flashbacks, have difficulty sleeping, and feel detached or estranged, and these symptoms can be severe enough and last long enough to significantly impair the person's daily life.[24]

PTSD symptoms arise when the pain of the fear associated with the struggle to make meaning of a traumatic experience (often involving death) that is repressed from the rational or emotional mind is triggered into present moment awareness by a sound, sight, or situation that acts as a reminder of the traumatic experience. The symptoms of PTSD usually begin to appear a few months after the traumatic experience and can continue for many years.

As soon as the memory of the traumatic experience is triggered our whole being, including our dominant conscious mind, becomes overwhelmed by the emotions of guilt, shame, fear, anger and rage. During such times, we lose our ability to think clearly, and our override function closes down.

People usually develop post-traumatic stress disorder (PTSD) when they have been the victim of, or witness to, a traumatic event or a series of traumatic events. A traumatic event could be a serious accident, a natural disaster, a rape or other violent crime, military combat, torture, a terrorist attack, physical or sexual abuse in childhood, domestic violence, etc. Some people, for example, refugees and asylum seekers, may have experienced several traumatic events in their lives.

One of the main symptoms of PTSD is re-experiencing the trauma. People have vivid "flashbacks" that can include seeing, smelling, hearing and feeling things that were part of the original trauma. These intrusive memories feel real as if they are happening in the present moment. If someone felt they were going to die at the time, they feel as if they are going to die every time they have a flashback. People can also experience vivid and terrifying nightmares in which they re-experience the trauma. They often thrash around in their sleep or cry out, and wake up feeling disorientated.

People who have PTSD may feel constantly threatened; they feel that their lives are damaged. They may blame themselves for what happened, think they didn't do the right thing at the right time, they may feel shame because they didn't resist an attack on their person, or guilt because they didn't stop what happened. They may find it hard to sustain relationships and tend to withdraw from encountering other people. Consequently, PTSD can have a devastating effect on relationships.

Researchers have shown that experiencing traumatic events in childhood increases the risk of developing the symptoms of psychosis later in life.[25]

The history of our understanding of PTSD is intimately linked to traumatic experiences of war veterans. The first time this condition was noticed was in survivors of World War I. In those days PTSD was called "shell shock". Attempts at that time by researchers to understand this condition were mostly ignored by the military establishment. The first big push to understand PTSD came after the Vietnam War when many returning veterans started taking their lives. More recently, in 2012, the number of US soldiers committing suicide was more than the number killed in active combat.

For William Nash, a retired Navy psychiatrist who directed the US Marine combat stress control programme, expressions of torment due to PTSD were very familiar. He worked with hundreds of service members who grappled with suicidal thoughts, particularly when he was posted to Fallujah in Iraq during the height of the fighting in 2004.

Nash concluded that contrary to widely held assumptions, it is not the fear and the terror that service members endure in the battlefield that inflicts the most psychological damage, but the feelings of shame and guilt related to the moral injuries they suffer. Top of the list of such injuries, by a long shot, is when one of their own people is killed.

> I have heard it over and over again from Marines—the most common source of anguish for them was failing to protect their "brothers". The significance of that is unfathomable; it's comparable to the feelings I've heard from parents who have lost a child.[26]

In the *Body Keeps The Score*, Bessel Van Der Kolk, states that:

> Trauma results in a fundamental reorganization of the way mind and brain manage perceptions. It changes not only how we think and what we think about, but also our very capacity to think. We have discovered that helping victims of trauma find the words to describe what has happened to them is profoundly meaningful, but usually is not enough.
>
> The act of telling the story doesn't necessarily alter the automatic physical and hormonal responses of bodies that remain hypervigilant, prepared to be assaulted or violated at any time. For real change to take place, the body needs to learn that the danger has passed and to live in the reality of the present.[27]
>
> Gradually, the psychological profession has begun to understand that the symptoms associated with trauma have

their origins in the entire body's response to the original trauma.[28]

You don't have to be a war veteran or an abused child to experience PTSD. Any experience of significant trauma can impair your daily functioning.

What I believe is happening in the minds of those who experience PTSD is a struggle to make meaning of their experiences. When we cannot make meaning of someone's death or our own brush with death, we jump into default mode and fill the void of not being able to make meaning by assuming the worst fears we have: the fear of death, and the fear that there is no meaning to life. This throws our mind into extreme turmoil and chaos because it contradicts the soul's impulse of being present in 3-D awareness and the body's will to stay alive. Therefore, with PTSD, it is not enough to put words to the thoughts and feelings of the traumatic experience, you have to release viscerally the fear of extinction from the energy field of the body by re-experiencing the trauma and consciously giving the experience a new meaning.

Fear as the cause of energetic instability

Throughout this chapter, I have mainly focused on how the early experiences of the body-mind, the emotional mind and the rational mind are impaired by the imprints of traumas and the beliefs developed when we have had repeated experiences of not getting our needs met.

The reason early traumas and experiences of not getting our needs met have such a significant impact on our later physiological and psychological functioning is that they occur when the reptilian mind/brain, limbic mind/brain and neocortex mind/brain are growing and developing. In other words, while memories and neural pathways are forming that condition our meaning-making for the rest of our lives. Early experiences of trauma and unmet needs have a significant impact on the calibration of the meaning-making and decision-making that governs our physiological (body-mind) and psychological (ego-mind) reactions to situations. The cause of these impairments is the impact of the emotion of fear, anger and sadness on our developing mind/brains. We can summarise these impacts in the following way:

Struggle to make meaning → Worst fears → Energetic instability

Needs might not be met → Fear/anxiety → Energetic instability

Needs not met → Fear/Anger → Energetic instability

When we struggle to make meaning, our mind always defaults to our greatest fears. When our needs might not be met, we experience fear about our ability to satisfy our survival, safety or security needs. When our needs are not met, we are fearful of the consequences and get angry.

Fear, anxiety and anger, no matter where or how they arise, induce the fight (aggression), flight or freeze reaction in the body-mind, the protection and defence reaction of the emotional mind, and the caution and carefulness response in the rational mind. All of these reactions and responses cause the body-mind and the ego-mind to experience energetic instability that impairs the homeostatic functioning of the body and the mental functioning of the emotional and rational minds. This energetic instability is experienced by the soul as a lack of love.

Normally, fear is a life-saver. It tells us to pay attention to what is happening because our survival, safety or security may be under threat. When the threat goes away, the fear dissipates. But when the threat is repressed, the fear and associated anger do not go away. They continuously impair the homeostatic functioning of our body-mind, thereby affecting our physical health. When the memories of the repressed fear and anger are triggered, they impair the decision-making of the dominant mind.

The impact of fear on the early stages of psychological development

From a developmental perspective, the impact of fear is most significant during the first two years of our lives (the surviving stage of development) when the reptilian mind/brain (body-mind) is dominant.

Body-mind

The reptilian mind/brain is designed for one main purpose: to keep the body alive in its physical environment. It reacts to getting its needs met or not getting its needs met through sensations: energetic feelings in the body. The reptilian mind/brain is also designed for procreation.

Experiences that engender life-enhancing sensations, such as care for our nourishment and physical comfort, keep the reptilian mind/brain in a state of energetic stability. At the subconscious level of the body-mind—the soul-mind—life-enhancing sensations are interpreted as love, releasing the emotion of joy, which engenders the bodily sensation of vitality.

A lack of care for our nourishment or physical comfort is experienced by the body-mind as life-suppressing sensations. To maintain normal functioning, the memories of these life-suppressing sensations are repressed to the subconscious of the body-mind—the soul mind—where they are interpreted as a lack of love, releasing the emotion of sadness, which engenders the bodily sensation of tiredness.

Emotional mind

Meaning-making from 2 to 7 (the conforming stage of psychological development), when the limbic mind/brain is dominant, is more sophisticated than the meaning-making of the body-mind because our needs at this stage of development are more complex. A more complex environment requires a more complex mind to maintain energetic stability. The limbic mind/brain is primarily designed to keep the body safe in its social (family) environment.

Experiences that engender pleasurable feelings, such as safety and acceptance, keep the limbic mind/brain in a state of energetic stability. At the subconscious level of the emotional mind—the body-mind—pleasurable feelings are interpreted as life-supporting sensations. At the unconscious level of the emotional mind—the soul-mind—life-supporting sensations are interpreted as love, releasing the emotion of joy, which engenders the feeling of belonging in the emotional mind.

A lack of care for our safety and acceptance needs is experienced by the emotional mind as unpleasant feelings. To maintain normal functioning, unpleasant feelings are repressed to the subconscious of the emotional mind—the body-mind—where they are experienced as life-suppressing sensations. At the unconscious level of the emotional mind—the soul-mind—life suppressing sensations are interpreted as a lack of love, releasing the emotion of sadness, which engenders the feelings of loneliness in the emotional mind.

Rational mind

Meaning-making from the age of 8 onwards, when the neocortex mind/brain is dominant, has to be more sophisticated than the limbic mind/brain because our ego's needs at this stage of development are more complex. A more complex environment requires a more complex mind to maintain energetic stability. The neocortex mind/brain is primarily designed to keep the body secure in its cultural environment.

Experiences that engender happy thoughts, such as security, respect and recognition, keep the neocortex mind/brain in a state of energetic stability. At the subconscious level of the rational mind—the emotional mind—happy thoughts are interpreted as pleasurable feelings, and at the unconscious level of the rational mind—the body-mind—pleasurable feelings are interpreted as life-enhancing sensations. At the super unconscious level of the rational mind—the soul mind—life-enhancing sensations are interpreted as love, releasing the emotion of joy, which engenders thoughts of contentment.

A lack of care for our security, respect and recognition needs is experienced by the rational mind as unhappy thoughts. To maintain normal functioning unhappy thoughts are repressed to the subconscious of the rational mind—the emotional mind—where they are interpreted as unpleasant feelings. At the unconscious level of the rational mind—the body-mind—unpleasant feelings are experienced as life suppressing sensations, and at the super unconscious level of the rational mind—the soul-mind—life suppressing sensations are interpreted as a lack of love releasing the emotion of sadness, which engenders thoughts of despair.

Table 11.2 shows the impact on our body-mind, emotional mind, rational mind and soul-mind of our needs being met, not being met and potentially not being met.

Table 11.2: The impact of the satisfaction of needs on our four minds.

Mind/Brain	Needs met	Needs not met or might not be met
Neocortex (rational mind)	Happy thoughts and contentment	Unhappy thoughts and despair
Limbic (emotional mind)	Pleasurable feelings and belonging	Unpleasant feelings and loneliness
Reptilian (body-mind)	Life-enhancing sensations and vitality	Life-suppressing sensations and tiredness
Soul-mind	Energy of love	Energy of fear

Table 11.2 shows how our needs being met promote the life-enhancing energy of love and our needs not being met promote the life-suppressing energy of fear. Fear leads to tiredness, loneliness and despair, and love leads to vitality, belonging, and contentment.

Since love is the life source of the soul and since the body is the physical manifestation of the soul's energy field, then it follows that love is also the life source of the body. It also follows that fear-induced, life-suppressing sensations block the flow of love energy, and love-induced, life-enhancing sensations open up the flow of energy.

Let us, at this point, recall the words of Dr. Barbara L. Fredrickson, cited in the foreword. She calls love the "supreme emotion"[29]. She states:

> ...[love] is perhaps the most essential emotional experience for thriving and health. Your body was designed to harness this power—to live off it. ... love is far more ubiquitous than you ever thought possible for the simple fact that love is connection.[30]

Dr. Arthur Janov agrees with Fredrickson but goes further. He states:

> Love in the early stages of life literally shapes the brain and affects us for a lifetime.[31] It determines how long we live and what illnesses we will fall prey to later in life. It is no exaggeration to say that very early lack of love already sets the limits on how long we will live and how happy our lives will be.[32]

The findings of the Harvard Grant Study reach a similar conclusion:

> The seventy-five years and twenty million dollars expended on the Grant Study points, at least to me, to a straightforward conclusion: "Happiness is love. Full stop." ... Love conquers all.[33]

A summary of key points

Here are the main points of Chapter 11:

1. The soul-mind is the most fragile of our minds because its consciousness is easily impaired. It is not used to living in a material world and not used to any form of energetic instability. Any experiences of the body not getting its needs met are experienced by the soul as a lack of love.
2. The functioning of the body-mind is most easily impaired when the reptilian mind/brain's neurological functions are developing. Consequently, energetic instability during this period can impair the functioning of the body-mind for the rest of our lives.
3. The functioning of the emotional mind is most easily impaired when the limbic mind/brain's neurological functions and personal belief systems about how to interpret its experiences are developing. Consequently, energetic instability during this period can impair the functioning of the emotional mind for the rest of our lives.
4. The functioning of the rational mind is most easily impaired when the neocortex mind/brain's neurological functions and personal belief systems about how to interpret its experiences are developing. Consequently, energetic instability during this period can impair the functioning of the rational mind for the rest of our lives.
5. The creation of the ego-mind occurs after the limbic mind/brain starts to become dominant. The reason the soul creates the ego-mind is to reduce the level of energetic instability—the pain of the lack of love it is feeling—by building a psychic layer of protection that we call the ego-mind.
6. When young children experience repeated physical or sexual abuse or are ignored by their parents, the dominant emotional mind represses the pain it is experiencing to the body-mind, and if the

experiences continue, it dissociates itself from the pain by creating an alter ego.
7. A lack of care for our nourishment or physical comfort is experienced by the body-mind as life-suppressing sensations.
8. A lack of care for our safety and acceptance needs is experienced by the emotional mind as unpleasant feelings.
9. A lack of care for our security, respect and recognition needs is experienced by the rational mind as unhappy thoughts.
10. Since love is the life source of the soul and since the body is the physical manifestation of the soul's energy field, then it follows that love is also the life source of the body.

References and notes

1. Dr. Arthur Janov, *The Biology of Love* (New York: Prometheus Books), 2000.
2. Ibid., pp. 219–227.
3. Ibid., p. 192.
4. Ibid., p. 193.
5. Ibid., p. 207.
6. Ibid., p. 207.
7. Ibid., p. 206.
8. Ibid., p. 203.
9. Flaherty, Thompson, Litrownik, English, Black et al., *Effect of Early Childhood Adversity on Child Health*, Archives of Pediatrics and Adolescent Medicine, 160, 1232–1238.
10. International Encyclopaedia of Rehabilitation.
11. Dr. Arthur Janov, *The Biology of Love* (Amerhurst: Prometheus Books), 2000, pp. 264–265.
12. Ibid.
13. *The Amazing Effect of Mother's Mere Presence on Infant Pain and Brain Development*, Psyblog, published: 9 December 2014.
14. American Psychiatric Association
15. Jo L. Ringrose, *Understanding and Treating Dissociative Identity Disorder* (London: Karnac), 2012, p 3.
16. www.truthtrustconsent.com/public_html/psychiatry/the-cause-and-cure-of-psychosis

17. Encyclopaedia Britannica.
18. Abraham Maslow, *The Farther Reaches of Human Nature* (New York: Penguin Books), 1977 edition, pp. 32–33.
19. Ibid., p. 35.
20. Jeffrey E. Young, Janet S. Kolsko and Marjorie E. Weishaar, *Schema Therapy: A Practitioner's Guide* (New York: The Guilford Press), 2003, p. 5.
21. Jeffrey E. Young, *Cognitive Therapy for Personality Disorders: A schema-focused approach* (revised edition) (Sarasota: Professional Resource Press), 1994, p. 11.
22. Abraham Maslow, *Toward a Psychology of Being* (New York: Van Nostrand), 1968, p. 56–57.
23. Ibid.
24. http://www.ptsd.ne.gov/what-is-ptsd.html
25. http://www.mentalhealthcare.org.uk/post_traumatic_stress_disorder_and_psychosis
26. http://www.theguardian.com/world/2013/feb/01/us-military-suicide-epidemic-veteran
27. Dr. Bessel van der Kolk, *The Body Keeps the Score: Mind, Brain and Body in the Transformation of Trauma* (Penguin Books: New York), 2014, p. 21.
28. Ibid., p.11.
29. Dr. Barbara Fredrikson, *Love 2.0* (New York: Hudson Street Press), 2013, p. 10.
30. Ibid., p. 18.
31. Dr. Arthur Janov, *The Biology of Love* (New York: Prometheus Books), 2000, p. 15.
32. Ibid., p. 39.
33. George E. Vaillant, *Adaptation to Life* (Boston: Harvard University Press), 1977, Preface to the 1995 Edition, p. 52.

12

THE HUMAN ENERGY FIELD

Every part of our anatomy is linked to a stage of psychological development. When you fail to master a stage of development, the chakras in that part of the anatomy become overactive or underactive providing too much or too little life-enhancing energy to those parts of your anatomy. This energy imbalance is the source of all our physiological disorders.

We now reach, what for me, is perhaps the most exciting part of the book: the linking of the Seven Stages of Psychological Development to the human energy field. This is something I have been thinking about and studying for almost 15 years. To make this link we must first understand how the human energy field is structured and then how it operates.

The model of the human energy field I am proposing is the classical Eastern model. It comprises seven layers. The four upper layers correspond to our soul's "spiritual" body and the three lower layers correspond to our ego's "earthly" body. When we die, the soul lets go of the three lower layers of the energy field and continues to function from the four upper layers of the energy field. We don't lose consciousness when we die; we just lose our 3-D awareness and our attachment to materiality.

Each layer of the energy field operates at a different frequency of vibration that is in harmony with the other layers. The outer layers of the energy field, furthest away from the body, operate at the highest frequencies of vibration and the inner layers closest to the body operate at the lowest frequencies of vibration. Each chakra is represented by a different colour, and each colour has its own wavelength and frequency, with violet at the upper end of the spectrum and red at the lower end.

Each layer of the energy field corresponds to a specific level of consciousness that is linked to every other layer through an energy vortex known as a chakra. The term "chakra" is a Sanskrit word meaning wheel. Chakras are channels/gates through which the life force (prana/love energy) from the universal energy field passes to activate our spiritual and earthly bodies.

The five middle layers of the energy field have two chakras; one at the front and one at the back of the body. The upper and lower layers of the energy field each has one chakra; the upper chakra pointing towards the heavens, and the lower chakra pointing towards Earth. Each chakra is connected to one of the major glands associated with the endocrine system. Endocrine glands secrete hormones directly into the blood to regulate and support our physiology and behaviour.

To stay healthy our chakras need to be balanced and open, so they can receive energy from the universal energy field. If they are not balanced—if they are overactive or underactive—then our health is affected. When they are overactive they draw in too much energy; when they are underactive, they draw in too little energy.

One of the ways of balancing the chakras is through is through acupuncture; another way is through colour therapy. The lower chakras are represented by red, orange and yellow, and the upper chakras by blue, indigo and violet. The middle (heart) chakra is represented by green.[1]

The source of the chakras' energetic instability is our reaction to fear. If we fight and struggle to overcome our fears, our chakras become overactive: they draw in too much life-giving energy to the parts of the body associated with the chakra. If we freeze and give into our fears, our chakras become underactive—they fail to draw in enough life-giving energy to the parts of the body associated with the chakra. If we release the energy associated with our fears, our chakras can go on functioning normally. If we identify with the soul and learn to trust our soul, we will not experience fear.

The autonomic nervous system

To understand the impact that overactive or underactive chakras have on our physical body, we need to become familiar with the body's autonomic nervous system (ANS). The ANS is responsible for regulating the body's reactions to external changes in our environment. There are two branches of the autonomic nervous system; one is controlled by the meaning-making and decision-making of the reptilian mind/brain, and the other is controlled by meaning-making and decision-making of the limbic mind/brain.

The part that is controlled by the reptilian mind/brain is known as the sympathetic nervous system. This is the part that makes our chakras become overactive and is linked to hyperactivity. The part that is controlled by the limbic mind/brain is known as the parasympathetic nervous system. This is the part of the ANS that modulates the energy flow to our chakras so we can rest, stay calm and meditate.

The sympathetic nervous system is responsible for dealing with danger and emergencies: it stimulates the body's glands to release hormones that increase the heart rate, cause us to bring more oxygen into our lungs and makes us more vigilant whenever the body-mind experiences fear; whenever we perceive some form of threat to meeting our needs.

The parasympathetic system is the system responsible for the healing and recovery of the body from physical trauma: it stimulates the body's glands to release hormones that reduce the heart rate, relax our breathing, and facilitate digestion. In a normal day, both systems will be activated as we deal with the stresses of work and appreciate the pleasures of relaxation when we get home.

When we learn during periods of rapid emergent learning that struggling or fighting is useless, or trying to get our needs met is hopeless or a waste of effort, the imprints and beliefs that are formed cause our sympathetic nervous system to switch off leaving the parasympathetic system dominant and causing our chakras to become underactive. In such circumstances, our chakras will no longer draw in enough energy to vitalize the parts of the body associated with those chakras. We may also shift into an altered state where we detach from current experiences that remind us of these struggles.

If we learn through our experiences that we live in a hostile world where people cannot be trusted, the sympathetic nervous system permanently switches on, constantly overriding the parasympathetic system's relaxation response. This causes our chakras to become overactive. They draw in too much energy, constantly stimulating the parts of the body associated with the overactive chakra.

If we learn during periods of rapid emergent learning that fighting is not useless, and we can get our needs met even if we have to struggle, then the imprints and beliefs we learn will cause our chakras to act normally.

To have a healthy body we need to keep our chakras balanced. We do this by learning how to master our fears and embracing the energy of love in everything we do. The activation of the parasympathetic nervous system through mindfulness and meditation are extremely useful in this regard. They allow us to calm our fears and access the energy of love.

A summary of the behavioural characteristics associated with an overactive and underactive chakra for each stage of psychological development/level of consciousness is shown in Table 12.1.

Table 12.1: Characteristics of over active and under active chakras.

Stages/levels	Overactive chakra (Too much life-force)	Underactive chakra (Too little life-force)
Serving/service	Over intellectualize, frustrated by unrealized potential, addicted to spirituality, ignore the needs of the body. Overly righteous.	Difficult to make decisions, lack a sense of fulfilment, feel exhausted or overwhelmed and become rigid in the way of thinking.
Integrating/ making a difference	Live in a world of fantasy, dreams and illusions. Lack clarity. Gullible. Much too open to the influence of gurus or authority figures.	Not good at thinking for yourself, and tend to defer to authority. Rigid in thinking. Easily get confused. Find it difficult to integrate.
Self-actualizing/ internal cohesion	Talkative, dominate conversations, a poor listener. You may also be dogmatic and not very adaptable. Seek success through achievement.	Do not voice opinions or ideas, introverted, reticent and shy. Reluctant to ask for support and nourishment. Low on creativity.
Individuating/ transformation	Easily upset and angry. Getting needs met is primary, compared to others getting their needs met. Impatient, aggressive and hostile.	Cold, keep to yourself, do not allow people to get too close to you. Avoid closeness and sharing. Fear rejection and feel unworthy to receive love.
Differentiating/ self-esteem	Arrogant, domineering, and judgemental of others. Consider yourself superior. Demands attention. The sense of entitlement and narcissistic.	Negative self-image. Passive, compliant, lack of confidence and indecisive. Sensitive to criticism. Need reassurance. Fear of rejection and being alone.

Conforming/ relationship	Jealous or possessive, with a tendency to be unbalanced emotionally. Manipulate others to get your love and sexual needs met. Engage in unhealthy relationships.	A life devoid of intimacy; hard on yourself, avoid conflict, rigid and stiff and hide your emotions. Not very open and come across as frigid or impotent.
Surviving/survival	Materialistic, bullying and greedy. Take foolhardy risks, want to control things, and may be obsessed with accumulating wealth. Micromanage situations. Not trusting.	Easily feel unwelcome. Anticipate the worst. Avoid physical activity and find yourself low on energy. You are passive and not persevering. You give in too easily.

With this understanding of the workings of the sympathetic and parasympathetic nervous systems and their relationship to the operation of the chakras, we are now in a position to explore the link between the Seven Levels of Consciousness, the Seven Stages of Psychological Development and the human energy field.

A New Psychology of Human Well-Being

The layers of the energy field

The relationship between the seven levels of consciousness, the layers of the energy field and the chakras, are shown in Figure 12.1 and Table 12.2.

Figure 12.1: The human energy field, the chakras and levels of consciousness.

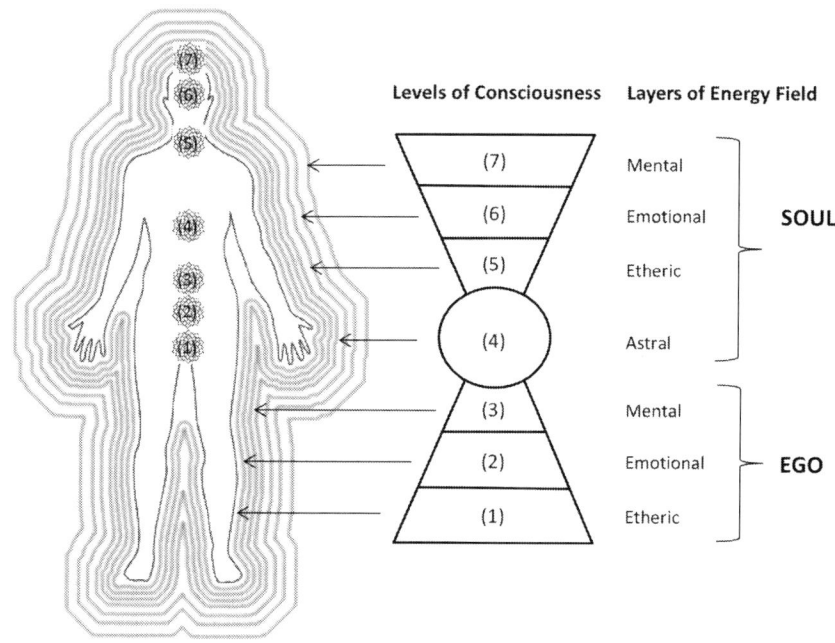

Table 12.2: The human energy field, the chakras, stages of psychological development and levels of consciousness.

Layer of energy field	Chakra	Stage of psychological development	Operating level of consciousness
Mental (higher)	Crown (7)	Serving	Service
Emotional (higher)	Brow (6)	Integrating	Making a difference
Etheric (higher)	Throat (5)	Self-actualizing	Internal cohesion
Astral	Heart (4)	Individuating	Transformation
Mental (lower)	Solar Plexus (3)	Differentiating	Self-esteem
Emotional (lower)	Sacral (2)	Conforming	Relationships
Etheric (lower)	Root (1)	Surviving	Survival

The ego layers

Layer 1: The lower etheric field

The lower etheric field, which is energized by the flow of energy through the root chakra, represents the surviving stage of psychological development and the survival level of consciousness. We are successful at mastering this stage of development when we feel in control of our lives and can meet our survival needs.

In her book, *Hands of Light: A Guide to Healing Through the Human Energy Field*, Dr. Barbara Brennan provides the following description of the lower etheric field:

> [The lower etheric field] consists of a definite structure of lines of force, or energy matrix, upon which the physical matter of the body tissues is shaped and anchored. The physical tissues exist only because of the vital field behind them; that is the field prior to, not a result of, the physical body.[2]

Brennan's description of the lower etheric field closely correlates with the latest thinking emanating from the study of pain. This new thinking came about by the challenge that the concept of the phantom limb posed to what was known as the "gate control theory". Although this theory has been in vogue for several decades, it could not adequately account for the pain experienced in the phantom body of those who had their limbs removed or the nerve connection to their lower limbs severed. To overcome this difficulty, researchers suggested that the brain contains a template of the body called a neuro-matrix and that pain in a phantom limb arises from the template in the brain.[3]

This is exactly what I am proposing here except the matrix is not contained in the brain; it is the energy field of the body.

The root chakra becomes overactive when you try to compensate for the difficulties you had in getting your needs met during the survival stage of development, when you overcompensate for the lack of control you felt you had in your early life. These difficulties may cause you to become materialistic, bullying and greedy, take foolhardy risks, want to control things, and you may become obsessed with accumulating wealth. You will want to micro-manage your life. You will not trust others. You will be demanding and extremely persistent.

The root chakra becomes underactive when you become resigned to the difficulties you had in getting your needs met during the survival stage of development; when you accepted the lack of control you felt you had in your life. These difficulties may cause you to become passive, low on energy, avoid activity, lacking in imagination and afraid to explore your creativity. You do not make a strong impression on others, and their lack of interest in you may make you feel unwelcome. You will anticipate the worst and give in too easily when faced with opposition.

Layer 2: The lower emotional field

The lower emotional field, which is energized by the sacral chakra, represents the conforming stage of psychological development and the relationship level of consciousness. The emotions we store in the lower emotional field affect the flow of energy into the lower etheric field. We are successful at mastering this stage of development when we love ourselves, express our emotions and feelings, and create emotional boundaries that enable us to fulfil our safety needs.

The sacral chakra becomes overactive when you try to overcompensate for the difficulties you had in getting your safety needs met during the conforming stage of development, when you overcompensate for the lack of love and connection in your life. These difficulties may cause you to become jealous or possessive and needy for love. You will have a tendency to manipulate others to get your sexual needs met, and engage in potentially unhealthy emotional relationships.

The sacral chakra becomes underactive when you become resigned to the difficulties you had in getting your needs met during the conforming stage of development, when you accept the lack of love and connections in your life and believe you are unlovable. These difficulties may cause you to feel your life is devoid of intimacy. You avoid conflicts and may come across as unemotional, rigid, stiff, frigid or impotent. You hide your emotions and feelings. You are hard on yourself and you may feel guilty for no apparent reason.

Layer 3: The lower mental field

The lower mental field, which is energized by the solar plexus chakra, represents the differentiating stage of development and the self-esteem level of consciousness. The thought forms we hold in the lower mental field influence the feelings we store in the lower emotional field, which in turn affect the energy flows in the lower etheric field. We are successful at mastering this stage of development when we can think clearly, hold heathy positive thoughts, and establish ourselves as a respected member of a community.

The solar plexus chakra becomes overactive when you try to overcompensate for the difficulties you had in getting your security needs met during the differentiating stage of development; when you overcompensate for the lack of self-esteem you feel in your life. These difficulties may cause you to become arrogant, domineering and judgemental of others, consider yourself superior, demand attention, and feel a sense of entitlement. You may become a workaholic, seeking power and intimidating people. You may become aggressive when you cannot get your needs met. You may also come across as narcissistic.

The solar plexus chakra becomes underactive or closed when you become resigned to the difficulties you had in getting your security needs during the differentiating stage of development—when you accept your feelings of low self-esteem. These difficulties may cause you to have a negative self-image, to be passive and compliant, docile and timid, lacking in confidence and having difficulties in being decisive. You will be sensitive to criticism about your performance or physical or mental attributes; you may constantly need reassurance, fear rejection and being alone.

The soul layers

Layer 4: Astral field

The astral field, which is energized by the heart chakra, represents the individuating stage of psychological development and the transformation level of consciousness. This layer of the energy field and the higher layers belong to the soul. We are successful at mastering this stage of development when we can operate with integrity and be truthful and honest with ourselves; when we achieve a high level of coherence between who we are as an ego and who we are as a soul. In other words, when the personality of the ego aligns with the character of the soul.

The astral field is where we hold the memories of our past experiences and previous lives. This is also the layer of the energy field where we store the memories from the first two years of our experience of being in a human body when the soul-mind was dominant or acted as the subconscious of the body-mind.

The astral field is the portal between the material world of the ego and the energetic world of the soul. This is where we transmute the energy of fear into the energy of love, where we begin to let go of our ego's fear-based motivations so we can align with the soul's love-based motivations.

The only way we can pass through this portal is by leading a life of energetic coherence, where we can maintain a high level of integrity with our true character in everything we do. To achieve this objective, the ego must first reunite with its alter ego(s) and then bond with the soul. Coherence is the energetic underpinning of health.

The heart chakra becomes overactive when you try to over compensate for the difficulties you have in letting go of your negative parental programming and cultural conditioning, when you over compensate for the lack of integrity in your life and unconsciously or unashamedly cover up your dishonesty and deceitfulness. These difficulties may also cause you to become angry and hateful, overly sensitive and easily upset, impatient, aggressive and hostile. Getting *your* needs met is primary, compared with others getting their needs met.

The heart chakra becomes underactive or closed when you become resigned to the difficulties you have in letting go of your negative parental programming and cultural conditioning, when you accept the lack of integrity in your life. These difficulties may cause you to keep to yourself and avoid closeness. You may come across as emotionless or cold. You fear rejection and feel unworthy to receive love.

Alice Miller is adamant that incoherence, which she defines as "the conflict between what we feel and what we think we ought to feel so as to comply with the moral norms and standards we learned in early childhood"—for example, the fourth commandment, honour your father and mother—is at the root of the majority of physical illness.

When your fundamental needs as a child—to be nourished, loved and respected—are disregarded by your parents and siblings, when you are not nurtured, not loved and not respected, the fourth commandment that thou should honour thy father and mother does not allow you to blame them, it only allows you to blame yourself.

To get around this problem, we unconsciously concoct a lie. We suppress our anger towards them and turn it inwards towards ourselves, by telling ourselves a story about how we were not dutiful enough, deserving enough or good enough to earn the love we so desperately needed. Not telling the true story about what we felt, closes down the heart chakra and makes us vulnerable to a heart attack.

To fully activate the astral layer of our energy field and master the individuating stage of development, we have to face the truth. This requires tremendous courage, especially when the repressed memories of not getting our needs met are so painful that we are afraid to bring them into our conscious awareness. It is extremely difficult to come to terms with the idea that we were not adequately loved by our parents, but so liberating when you are prepared to own this truth. Whenever we allow our fears to control what we say, when we commit lies of omission and commission, we disturb the energetic balance in this layer of our energy field.

Layer 5: The upper etheric field

The upper etheric field, which is energized by the throat chakra, represents the self-actualizing stage of psychological development and the internal cohesion level of consciousness.

Barbara Brennan describes the upper etheric field in the following way:

> It is the template of the physical body. It is the blueprint or the perfect form for the lower etheric layer to take.[4]

The throat chakra represents the soul's will to express itself in our 3-D material world. As Brennan indicates, this layer of the energy field is linked to the lower etheric field. If you are unable to master the survival stage of development, you will be unable to manifest your soul's desire for self-expression. If you have any unresolved issues from the surviving stage of development, they will show up when you reach the self-actualizing stage.

We are successful at mastering this stage of development, when we can express who we truly are: broadcast our thoughts, ideas and opinions to the world, share our feelings without fear and be open about our identity.

Whenever your actions and behaviours compromise the soul's ability for self-expression, you disturb the energetic balance in this layer of our energy field causing the throat chakra to become overactive or underactive.

The throat chakra becomes overactive when you try to compensate for the difficulties you have expressing your true nature during the self-actualizing stage of development, when you overcompensate for the lack of self-expression. These difficulties may cause you to become overly talkative and dominate conversations. You will be a poor listener. You may become dogmatic or righteous, not very adaptable and constantly seeking success through your achievements.

The throat chakra becomes underactive when you become resigned to the difficulties you have in expressing your true nature during the self-actualizing stage of development. These difficulties may cause you to hold back expressing your opinions or ideas. You may become introverted, reticent or shy and do not ask for support or nourishment when you need it. You will display low levels of creativity.

Layer 6: The upper emotional field or celestial body

The upper emotional field, which is energized by the brow chakra, represents the integrating stage of psychological development and the making a difference level of consciousness.

The brow chakra represents the soul's will to express unconditional love by connecting with others. This layer of the energy field is connected to the lower emotional field. If you are unable to master the conforming stage of development, you will be unable to manifest your soul's desire for connection. If you have any unresolved issues from the conforming stage of development, they will show up when you reach the integrating stage of development.

We are successful at mastering this stage of development when we can create empathic connections with other people, feel joyful without cause, and experience the inspiration of the soul.

Whenever your actions or behaviours compromise your soul's desire for connection and unconditional love towards others, you disturb the energetic balance in this layer of your energy field causing the brow chakra to become overactive or underactive.

The brow chakra becomes overactive when you try to compensate for the difficulties you have in establishing unconditional loving connections during the integrating stage of development, when you overcompensate for your feelings of separation and lack of connectedness. These difficulties may cause you to live in a world of fantasy and illusions. You may lack clarity and may seek to follow those who you consider an authority figure or a guru. You may be overly gullible.

The brow chakra becomes underactive when you become resigned to the difficulties you have in establishing unconditional loving relationships during the integrating stage of development. These difficulties may make it hard for you to integrate with others. You may defer to authority and easily get confused. You become rigid in your thought patterns and not willing to change your beliefs.

Layer 7: The upper mental field or causal body

The upper mental field, which is served by the crown chakra, represents the serving stage of psychological development and the service level of consciousness.

The crown chakra represents the soul's will to contribute to the well-being of the people of the community you belong to. This layer of the energy field is linked to the lower mental field. If you are unable to master the differentiating stage of development, you will be unable to manifest your soul's desire for contribution. If you have any unresolved issues from the differentiating stage of development, they will show up when you reach the serving stage of development.

We are successful at mastering this stage of development when we can feel a compassionate connection to those who are suffering, feel a deep sense of well-being, and experience moments bliss. To fully inhabit this layer of your energy field you need to surrender to the desires of your soul.

Whenever your actions or behaviours compromise your soul's desire for contribution, you disturb the energetic balance in this layer of your energy field causing the crown chakra to become overactive or underactive.

The crown chakra becomes overactive when you try to compensate for the difficulties you have contributing to the good of your community during the serving stage of development, when you overcompensate for your lack of confidence in being able to make a contribution. These difficulties may cause you to over-intellectualize. You may get frustrated by your sense of unrealized potential, or you may become addicted to a spiritual path, ignore your bodily needs and become overly righteous.

The crown chakra becomes underactive when you become resigned to the difficulties you have contributing to the good of your community during the serving stage of development. These difficulties may make it hard for you to make decisions; they may cause you to experience a lack of fulfilment in your life and feel exhausted or overwhelmed. You may become rigid in your way of thinking.

The organization of the human energy field

You will have noted by now that both the ego and the soul have etheric, emotional and mental fields and that difficulties in mastering the survival needs of the ego at the lower etheric level impairs your ability to satisfy the desires of your soul for self-expression at the upper etheric level. Similarly, difficulties in mastering the safety and security needs of the ego at the lower emotional and mental levels impair your ability to satisfy the desires of your soul for connection and contribution at the upper emotional and mental levels. These linkages are shown in Figure 12.2 and Table 12.3.

Figure 12.2: Linkages between the ego and soul layers of the energy field.

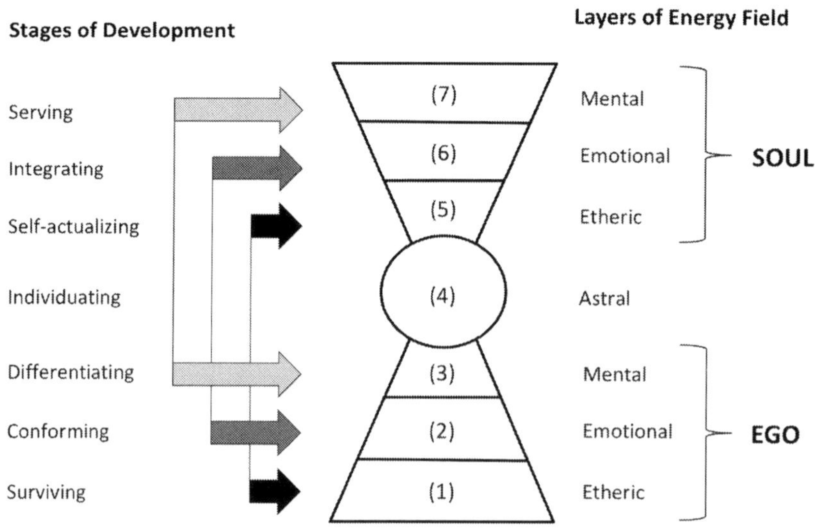

Stages of Development		Layers of Energy Field	
Serving		(7) Mental	
Integrating		(6) Emotional	SOUL
Self-actualizing		(5) Etheric	
Individuating		(4) Astral	
Differentiating		(3) Mental	
Conforming		(2) Emotional	EGO
Surviving		(1) Etheric	

Table 12.3: Linkages between the lower and upper chakras and parts of the body.

Paired layers of energy field	Soul and ego motivations.	Ego/soul chakras and endocrine glands.	Ego/soul related parts of the body and functions.
Upper mental layer	Soul's desire for contribution.	Crown chakra and pineal gland (governing body rhythms).	Neocortex (rational) brain and central nervous system.
Lower mental layer	Ego's ability to establish itself in a community.	Solar plexus chakra and pancreas gland (governing metabolism).	Digestion, oesophagus, stomach, small intestine, duodenum and gall bladder. Liver and pancreas.
Upper emotional layer	Soul's desire for connection.	Brow chakra and thyroid (governing metabolism and growth).	Limbic (emotional) brain, para sympathetic system. Eyes, face, lymphatic and endocrine system.
Lower emotional layer	Ego's ability to form loving relationships.	Sacral chakra and gonads—ovaries and testes (governing growth and sexuality).	Large intestine. Organs of reproduction. Kidneys and bladder.
Upper etheric layer	Soul's desire for self-expression.	Throat chakra and thyroid gland (governing metabolism, heart and digestive functions).	Reptilian (body-mind) brain, sympathetic system-fight or flight. Upper chest, lungs, breasts, bronchial and vocal apparatus, teeth and ears.
Lower etheric layer	Ego's ability to survive.	Root chakra and adrenal glands (governing metabolism and actions).	Rectum and anus. Parts of organs of reproduction, lower spinal column, bones, hips, legs, feet.

The structure and organization of the human energy field lead us to some interesting insights into how the human body works.

The brain in the gut

Although it is relatively logical that the lower and upper etheric fields are connected—the energetic template of the physical body and the energetic template of the soul body—and the lower emotional and upper emotional fields are connected—the emotions of the ego and the emotions of the soul—at first glance it seems somewhat less logical that the lower mental and upper mental fields should be connected. This is because our 3-D material awareness leads us to believe that the brain thinks and stomach digests. From the perspective of 4-D energetic awareness, every part of the body is an aspect of mind, and the mind in the head is linked to the mind in the gut. Recent research supports this idea.

Jay Pasricha, M.D. Director of the John Hopkins Centre for Neurogastroenterology, refers to the "brain in the gut" as the enteric nervous system. She says:

> The enteric nervous system doesn't seem capable of thought as we know it, but it communicates back and forth with the brain.[5]

An article by Justin and Erica Sonneburg in Scientific American suggests that:

> Our brain and gut are connected by an extensive network of neurons and a highway of chemicals and hormones that constantly provide feedback about how hungry we are, whether or not we're experiencing stress, or if we've ingested a disease-causing microbe. This information superhighway is called the brain-gut axis, and it provides constant updates on the state of affairs at [the two ends of the highway] … [When you are] stressed your gut knows it—immediately.[6]

The heart chakra

You may have noticed in Table 12.3 that one layer of the energy field is missing: the astral field. This layer of the energy field is not paired with any other layer. The astral field, which links to the heart chakra, corresponds to the individuating stage of development and the transformation level of consciousness.

As already stated, this stage of development and layer of consciousness plays a very special role in the operation of the human energy field. It is the portal your ego must pass through to activate the soul layers of your energy field. The only way you can pass through this portal is by leading a life of energetic coherence, where you are honest with yourself and with others, and where you can maintain a high level of integrity in everything you do.

This is also the layer of the energy field where you store your anger and hatred at not getting your needs met during your time in the womb and during the first two years of your life, when the soul was the dominant or subconscious mind. If you have any stored up anger and hatred in this layer of your of your energy field, it is likely to increase your risk of an early heart attack.

Patterns of dysfunction

When we fail to master any of the ego stages of psychological development during the early years of our lives, the unresolved issues associated with our unmet needs are likely to show up as psychological and physiological dysfunctions later on in our lives. They are like ticking time bombs waiting to explode.

This is why Dr Janov states:

> It is no exaggeration to say that very early lack of love already sets the limits on how long we will live and how happy we will be.[7]

A research team in San Diego came up with a similar conclusion. When they asked 17,000 people with an average age of 57, what their childhood was like, they found the incidence of severe illnesses was many times higher in people who had been abused in their childhood than in people who had grown up free of such abuse.[8]

Because of the paired linkages between the upper and lower layers of the energy field, the structure of the human energy field gives us significant clues as to when the ticking time bombs of our failures to master the ego stages of development will go off.

Energetic weakness in the lower etheric field (the survival level of consciousness) will tend to show up as psychological or physiological dysfunctions during, or a few years after, the end of the surviving stage of development or after we reach the self-actualizing stage of development. Similarly, weakness in the lower emotional field (the relationship level of consciousness) will tend to show up as psychological or physiological dysfunctions during the conforming stage of development, or a few years after, or after we reach the integrating stage of development. Weakness in the lower mental field (the self-esteem level of consciousness) will tend to show up as psychological or physiological dysfunctions during the differentiating stage of development, or a few years after, or after we reach the serving stage of development. I will be testing this hypothesis on real data in the following chapter.

Gender differences

Generally speaking, women have greater difficulty mastering the tasks involved with the surviving level of consciousness than men, and men have greater difficulty mastering the tasks involved with the relationship level of consciousness than women. As a consequence, later in life women find the self-actualization stage of development more difficult to master than men, and men find the integrating stage of development more difficult to master than women.

Because of parental programming and cultural pressures, it is more difficult for girls to express who they are and establish control of their lives than boys, and it is more difficult for boys to express how they relate to others and display their emotions than girls. Boys are expected to be tough and strong; girls are expected to be pliable and servient. Emotional outbursts involving tears are tolerated in girls but not so in boys.

A summary of key points

Here are the main points of Chapter 12.

1. The model of the human energy field I am proposing is the classical Eastern model. It is comprised of seven layers. The four upper layers correspond to the soul's "spiritual" body and the three lower layers correspond to the ego's "earthly" body.

2. Each layer of the energy field corresponds to a specific level of consciousness and is linked to every other layer through an energy vortex known as a chakra.
3. To stay healthy our chakras need to be balanced and open to receive energy from the universal energy field. If they are not balanced—if they are overactive or underactive—then our health is affected.
4. The autonomic nervous system (ANS) has two branches; one is controlled by the reptilian mind/brain, and the other is controlled by the limbic mind/brain. The part that is controlled by the reptilian mind/brain is known as the sympathetic nervous system. The part that is controlled by the limbic mind/brain is known as the parasympathetic nervous system.
5. The sympathetic nervous system is responsible for dealing with danger and emergencies: it stimulates the body's glands to release hormones that increase the heart rate, cause us to bring more oxygen into our lungs and makes us more vigilant whenever the body-mind experiences fear; whenever we perceive some form of threat to meeting our needs.
6. The parasympathetic system is the system responsible for the healing and recovery of the body from physical trauma: it stimulates the body's glands to release hormones that reduce the heart rate, relax our breathing, and facilitate digestion.
7. In a normal day, both systems will be activated as we deal with the stresses of work and appreciate the pleasures of relaxation when we get home.
8. When we learn during periods of rapid emergent learning that struggling or fighting is useless or trying to get our needs met is hopeless or a waste of effort, the imprints and beliefs we learn will cause our sympathetic nervous system to switch off leaving the parasympathetic system dominant and causing our chakras to become underactive.
9. If we learn through our experiences that we live in a hostile world where people cannot be trusted, the sympathetic nervous system permanently switches on, constantly overriding the parasympathetic system's relaxation response. This causes our chakras to become overactive. They draw in too much energy, over stimulating the parts of the body associated with the overactive chakra.

10. If we learn during periods of rapid emergent learning that fighting is not useless, and we can get our needs met even if we have to struggle a bit, then the imprints and beliefs we learn will cause our chakras to act normally.
11. To have a healthy body, we need to keep our chakras balanced. We do this by learning how to master our fears and embracing the energy of love in everything we do. Mindfulness and meditation are extremely useful in this regard. They allow us calm our fears and access the energy of love.
12. Because of parental programming and cultural pressures, it is more difficult for girls to express who they are and establish control of their lives than boys, and it is more difficult for boys to express how they relate to others and display their emotions than girls. Boys are expected to be tough and strong; girls are expected to be pliable and servient. Emotional outbursts involving tears are tolerated in girls but not so in boys.

References and notes

1. Kath Roberts & Kate Griffiths, *Colourful Boardrooms: Transforming leaders from the inside out* (Waye Forward Publishing: Cardiff), 2016
2. Barbara Brennan, *Hands of Light: A Guide to Healing Though the Human Energy Field* (Bantam: New York), 1988, p. 49.
3. T. Hadjistavropoulos and K. D. Craig, *Pain: Psychological Perspectives* (New York: Psychology Press), 2004, p. 22–23.
4. Barbara Brennan, *Hands of Light: A Guide to Healing Though the Human Energy Field* (Bantam: New York), 1988, p. 52.
5. http://www.hopkinsmedicine.org/health/healthy_aging/healthy_body/the-brain-gut-connection
6. http://www.scientificamerican.com/article/gut-feelings-the-second-brain-in-our-gastrointestinal-systems-excerpt
7. Dr. Arthur Janov, *The Biology of Love* (New York: Prometheus Books), 2000, p. 19.
8. Alice Miller, *The Body Never Lies: The Lingering Effects of Hurtful Parenting* (New York: W. W. Norton), 2006, p. 29.

13

THE IMPACT OF PSYCHOLOGY ON PHYSIOLOGY

To achieve optimum physical health, we must learn to master each stage of psychological development. We must learn to let go of the ego's fears about meeting our survival, safety and security needs and fully embrace the soul's desires for self-expression, connection and contribution.

In the last chapter, I explored the links that exist between the layers of the human energy field, the chakras, and the Seven Levels of Consciousness. In this chapter I want to go one stage further: I want to relate the difficulties we have in mastering each of the Seven Stages of Psychological Development to the onset of specific diseases in the body. My basic hypothesis is:

> Physiological dysfunctions associated with difficulties in mastering a particular stage of psychological development start to become significant 5 to 10 years after the start of that stage of development and peak 10 to 15 years later.

To test my hypothesis, I first identified the leading causes of death in Western society and then identified the ages when the symptoms of these diseases became prevalent. I then linked the ages associated with the onset of the symptoms of specific diseases to the layers of the energy field and chakras associated with the stages of development. This allowed me to show how the difficulties we have in mastering specific stages of psychological development result in specific physiological dysfunctions in specific parts of the human body.

I was aware before I began my investigation that there were multiple factors that could make it difficult to find the correlations I was looking for; primary among them being the impact that addictions to alcohol, recreational drugs, and tobacco have on the early onset of specific physiological disorders. Nevertheless, despite these difficulties, I decided to go ahead with my investigation.

One of the factors that encouraged me to move forward was a large amount of evidence that the science of psychoneuroimmunology (PNI) has discovered that suggests that the mind and the body can be regarded as an irreducible whole. Michael Lerner addresses this topic in *Choices of Healing*. In speaking of PNI, he states:

> It is now beginning to appear that mind-body interactions are so ubiquitous that it may no longer be possible to refer to the body and mind as separate entities but only as body-mind. For psychology, this means emotional states of mind and behavioural patterns may profoundly affect not only symptoms [of disease] but the progress of disease itself.[1]

This connection between psychology and diseases is what I am proposing to explore in this chapter.

Leading causes of death

According to the United Nations, the top three leading causes of death in the world are heart disease (7.4 million per year), stroke (6.7 million per year) and lung disease (3.1 million per year).[2] You will see, by referring to Table 13.1, that these diseases are also the leading causes of death in five industrialized nations: US, UK, Canada, Australia and Sweden. Other leading causes of death in these nations are Alzheimer's disease, dementia, pneumonia and lung cancer, stomach and colon cancer, diabetes, prostate cancer and breast cancer, and kidney and liver disease.

Table 13.1: The leading causes of death in five industrialized nations.

Importance	USA	UK	CANADA	AUSTRALIA	SWEDEN
1	Heart disease	Heart disease	Heart disease	Heart disease	Heart disease
2	Alzheimer's	Stroke	Lung cancer	Stroke	Stroke
3	Lung cancer	Pneumonia	Stroke	Lung cancer	Alzheimer's
4	Stroke	Lung cancer	Alzheimer's	Alzheimer's	Lung cancer
5	Lung disease	Alzheimer's	Lung disease	Lung disease	Colon cancer
6	Colon cancer	Lung disease	Colon cancer	Colon cancer	Prostate cancer
7	Hypertension	Colon cancer	Diabetes	Diabetes	Lung disease
8	Pneumonia	Breast cancer	Pneumonia	Prostate cancer	Pneumonia
9	Kidney disease	Prostate cancer	Breast cancer	Breast cancer	Diabetes

Source: United Nations, World Health Organization.

I have categorized the leading causes of death in Table 13.1 into four groupings using various shadings, from dark to light:

- Dysfunctions that affect the mind/brain: stroke, dementia, Alzheimer's disease.
- Dysfunctions that affect the organs located in the chest: coronary heart disease, lung disease (pneumonia, asthma, etc.), lung cancer and breast cancer.
- Dysfunctions that affect the organs located in the abdomen: diabetes, stomach cancer, colon cancer, liver cancer, kidney disease and prostate cancer.
- Other issues: hypertension, associated with the heart and high blood pressure, and diabetes, associated with difficulties in producing insulin in the pancreas or the cells of the body not responding properly to the insulin that is produced.

Apart from heart disease, the other leading causes of death follow a pattern. The highest risk of death is from diseases of the organs associated with the head. The second highest risk of death is from diseases of the organs associated with the chest (except the heart), and the third highest risk of death is from diseases associated with the abdomen. I believe this progression of increased risk of death from disorders in the lower abdomen to disorders of the mind/brain reflects the increasing difficulties attached to mastering the higher stages of psychological development.

The majority of the physiological dysfunctions associated with the leading causes of death occur during the self-actualizing, integrating and serving stages of psychological development, in the latter part of our lives. Therefore, to make my investigation more complete, I have also included some of the leading causes of death and physiological dysfunctions experienced during the surviving, conforming, differentiating and individuating stages of psychological development, in the earlier part of our lives.

Because of the high incidence of suicide in all parts of the world, especially among young people, I have devoted Chapter 14 to a discussion on the linkages between psychological development and the risk of taking of one's life.

Also, since cancer affects many parts of the body, and different age groups, I have devoted a separate section at the end of this chapter to the link between cancer and psychological dysfunction.

Leading causes of death in the US (2013) and UK (2014)

To correlate *specific* physiological dysfunctions with difficulties in mastering *specific* stages of psychological development, I have used data about the leading causes of death by age from the US and the UK. The top five leading causes of death in the US and the UK by age group and stage of psychological development are shown in Table 13.2a and 13.2.b respectively.

Since data in the US was not specifically available for the 0–2 years group—the surviving stage of development—nor for the 3–7 years group—the conforming stage of development, but was available for the first year of life, the 1–4 age range and 5–9 age range, I decided to use data from the first year of life to represent the surviving stage of development, and data from the 1–4 and 5–9 age ranges to represent the conforming stage of development.

The data for the UK is presented slightly differently; I have grouped all age ranges into the stages of psychological development and separated males from females. I had similar difficulties in the UK to the US in relating the early age group data to the stages of psychological development. So I have included all data from the 1–4 and 5–9 age ranges in the conforming stage of psychological development and have ignored the surviving stage of development. It was also difficult to relate the differentiating stage of development to the data, so I shortened the differentiating stage and lengthened the individuating stage so it would fit with the age ranges of the data sources.

In both tables, I have highlighted cancer, heart disease and suicide, by using different shades of grey. I have highlighted cancer because it tends to be ubiquitous across all age ranges, I have highlighted heart disease because it is the leading cause of death in the world, and I have highlighted suicide because it is not a physiological issue, but a psychological issue.

Causes of death not directly related to physiological or psychological factors such as accidents and homicides have been indicated in a grey lettering and are ignored in the remainder of the analysis.

Table 13.2a: Causes of death by stage of psychological development in the US in 2013.

	Primary	Secondary	Tertiary	Quaternary	Quinary
	SURVIVING STAGE OF DEVELOPMENT				
Less than 1	Congenital	Low weight	SIDS	Complications	Accidents
	CONFORMING STAGE OF DEVELOPMENT				
1–4	Accidents	Congenital	Homicide	Cancer	Heart disease
5–9	Accidents	Cancer	Congenital	Homicide	Lungs
	DIFFERENTIATING STAGE OF DEVELOPMENT				
10–14	Accidents	Cancer	Suicide	Congenital	Homicide
15–19	Accidents	Suicide	Homicide	Cancer	Heart disease
20–24	Accidents	Suicide	Homicide	Cancer	Heart disease
	INDIVIDUATING STAGE OF DEVELOPMENT				
25–29	Accidents	Suicide	Homicide	Cancer	Heart
30–34	Accidents	Suicide	Cancer	Heart disease	Homicide
35–39	Accidents	Cancer	Heart disease	Suicide	Homicide

	SELF-ACTUALIZING STAGE OF DEVELOPMENT				
40–44	Accidents	Cancer	Heart disease	Suicide	Liver
45–49	Cancer	Heart disease	Accidents	Suicide	Liver
	INTEGRATING STAGE OF DEVELOPMENT				
50–54	Cancer	Heart disease	Accidents	Liver	Suicide
55–59	Cancer	Heart disease	Accidents	Liver	Lungs
	SERVING STAGE OF DEVELOPMENT				
60–64	Cancer	Heart disease	Lungs	Diabetes	Accidents
65–69	Cancer	Heart disease	Lungs	Diabetes	Stroke
70–74	Cancer	Heart disease	Lungs	Stroke	Diabetes
75–79	Cancer	Heart disease	Lungs	Stroke	Diabetes
80–84	Heart disease	Cancer	Lungs	Stroke	Alzheimer's
85–89	Heart disease	Cancer	Stroke	Lungs	Alzheimer's
90–94	Heart disease	Cancer	Alzheimer's	Stroke	Lungs
95–99	Heart disease	Alzheimer's	Cancer	Stroke	Lungs
100+	Heart disease	Alzheimer's	Stoke	Influenza	Cancer

Source: CDC/NCHS, National Vital Statistics System, Mortality 2013 (US).

Table 13.2b: Causes of death by stage of psychological development in the UK in 2014.

	Primary	Secondary	Tertiary	Quaternary	Quinary
	CONFORMING STAGE OF DEVELOPMENT (1–4)				
MALE	Congenital	Lungs	Accidents	Cancer	Cancer
FEMALE	Congenital	Lungs	Homicide	Accidents	Cancer
	DIFFERENTIATING STAGE OF DEVELOPMENT (5–19)				
MALE	Suicide	Transport (2)	Cancer	Congenital	Cancer
FEMALE	Transport (2)	Suicide	Cancer	Congenital	Cerebral Palsy

INDIVIDUATING STAGE OF DEVELOPMENT (20–34)					
MALE	Suicide	Poisoning (1)	Transport (2)	Homicide	Liver
FEMALE	Suicide	Poisoning (1)	Liver	Transport (2)	Breast cancer
SELF-ACTUALIZING STAGE OF DEVELOPMENT (35–49)					
MALE	Suicide	Heart disease	Liver	Poisoning (1)	Stroke
FEMALE	Breast cancer	Liver	Suicide	Poisoning (1)	Heart disease
INTEGRATING STAGE OF DEVELOPMENT (50–64)					
MALE	Heart disease	Prostate cancer	Liver	Colon	Lung
FEMALE	Breast cancer	Cancer	Heart disease	Lung	Liver
SERVING STAGE OF DEVELOPMENT (65–79)					
MALE	Heart disease	Prostate cancer	Lung	Stroke	Prostate cancer
FEMALE	Breast cancer	Heart disease	Lung	Stroke	Alzheimer's

Source: Office for National Statistics, UK.
Notes: (1) Poisoning refers to accidental poisoning; (2) Transport refers to transport accidents.

Leading causes of death by stages of psychological development in the US and the UK

Surviving and conforming stages of development

The leading causes of death during the surviving (US) and conforming stages (US and UK) are congenital disorders and cancer. This is true for males and females. SIDS is the third highest cause of death for infants in the first year of their lives in the US and is also significant in the UK.

Differentiating stage of development

The leading cause of death during the differentiating stage of development in the US and the UK is suicide. The second leading cause of death is cancer. Diabetes is also a significant cause of death during this stage of psychological development in the US. Other dysfunctions during this stage of development are obesity, anorexia nervosa and bulimia nervosa.

Individuating stage of development

The leading cause of death during the individuating stage of development in the US and the UK is suicide. The second leading cause of death in the US is cancer. The second leading cause of death in the UK is liver disease. Diabetes and liver disease are also significant causes of death in the US at this stage of development.

Self-actualizing stage of development

The leading causes of death for males in the US during this stage of psychological development are heart disease followed by cancer. The leading cause of death for females is cancer followed by heart disease. The form of cancer that most affects females at this stage of development is breast cancer. Other leading causes of death for males and females in the US are liver disease, diabetes and suicide. In the UK, suicide and heart disease are the leading causes of death for males. For females the leading cause of death is cancer.

Integrating stage of development

The leading causes of death in the UK and US for males and females during this stage of psychological development are heart disease and cancer. Liver disease is also prominent in males and females. The form of cancer that most affects males at this stage of development is prostate cancer. Diabetes and liver disease are also leading causes of death in the US.

Serving stage of development

The leading causes of death in the UK and US for males and females during this stage of psychological development are heart disease and cancer. Other leading causes of death for both males and females are lung disease, strokes and different forms of dementia. Diabetes, liver and kidney disease are also leading causes of death in the US.

My hypothesis

The details of the hypothesis I am attempting to test—the age at which physiological dysfunctions associated with each stage of development begin to appear and the age beyond which they peak—are shown in Table 13.3.

Table 13.3: Stages of psychological development, ages at which physiological dysfunctions begin to appear and the age beyond which they peak.

Stage of Development	Age range of stage of development	Age at which disease begins to appear	Age beyond which disease peaks
Serving	60+	65	75
Integrating	50–59 years	55	65
Self-actualizing	40–49 years	45	55
Individuating	25–39 years	35	45
Differentiating	8–24 years	18	28 and/or 60s
Conforming	3–7 years	13	23 and/or 50s
Surviving	0–2 years	5	15 and/or 40s

Because of the linkages between the lower (ego) and upper (soul) etheric, emotional and mental fields (shown in Figure 12.2), I am suggesting that when you reach the upper (soul) stages of development any weakness or impairment in your ability to meet the needs of the corresponding lower (ego) stage of development can put additional pressure (instability) on the lower etheric, emotional or mental layers of the energy field causing physiological dysfunctions in the body asscociated with those levels.

Difficulties in mastering the self-actualizing stage of development could show up as physiological issues in the parts of the body connected to the throat chakra or the root chakra. Similarly, difficulties in mastering the integrating stage of development could show up as physiological issues in the parts of the body connected to the brow chakra or the sacral chakra; difficulties in mastering the serving stage of development could show up as physiological issues in the parts of the body connected to the crown chakra or the solar plexus chakra.

This also means that physiological issues associated with surviving (root chakra) could reach their peak either during the surviving stage or the self-actualizing stage of development; physiological issues associated with relationships and the conforming stage of development (sacral chakra) could reach their peak either during the conforming or the integrating stage of development; and physiological issues associated with the self-esteem and differentiating stage of development (solar plexus chakra) could reach their peak either during the differentiating or serving stage of development.

Body organs and endocrine functions served by each chakra

The link between the stages of psychological development, the chakras and body organs/endocrine functions associated with each layer of the human energy field are shown in Table 13.4. The endocrine glands are important because they regulate the homeostatic functioning of the body.

Table 13.4: Physiological issues associated with each stage of psychological development.

Stage of development/ Energy layer	Chakra	Endocrine glands	Body organs/ parts of anatomy	Physiological issues
Serving/ Higher mental	Crown (7)	Pineal:[3] biological cycles and sleep (Melatonin)	Neocortex	Alzheimer's disease, dementia, Parkinson's disease, migraines.
Integrating/ Higher emotional	Brow (6)	Pituitary: regulation of physical growth	Limbic brain, eyes, ears, nose.	Infections and problems with sight and hearing.

Self-actualizing/ Higher Etheric	Throat (5)	Thyroid: regulation of body temperature and metabolism	Reptilian mind/brain, neck, mouth, vocal chords, lungs, breasts, oesophagus.	Breast cancer, asthma, lung, neck and thyroid problems Infections of mouth and throat.
Individuating/ Astral field	Heart (4)	Thymus: immune system	Heart, circulation system, arms and hands.	Heart disease, blood pressure.
Differentiating/ Lower mental	Solar Plexus (3)	Pancreas: metabolism (Insulin)	Stomach, duodenum, pancreas, liver, gall bladder, upper spine.	Stomach ulcers, colon cancer, irritable bowel, diabetes, hypoglycaemia and liver disease.
Conforming/ Lower emotional	Sacral (2)	Gonads: reproductive system	Prostate, ovaries, bladder, colon, lower intestine, spleen, pelvic region.	Prostate cancer, ovarian cancer, urinary problems, pelvic pain, anorexia, bulimia and obesity.
Surviving/ Lower Etheric	Root (1)	Adrenals: stress response	Rectum, anus, lower spine, legs, feet.	Osteoarthritis, varicose veins, rectal tumours, lower back pain.

The following sections of this chapter link specific physiological disorders and diseases to the stages of psychological development.

Physical disorders associated with the serving stage of development

The serving stage of psychological development, which begins in the 60s, relates to the upper mental field and the crown chakra. This stage of development is about using your thoughts and intentions to contribute to the greater good of your community, society, humanity or the planet. The area of the body and the homeostatic functions associated with the crown chakra are shown in Table 13.5.

Table 13.5: Characteristics of the serving stage of psychological development.

Stage of Development	Serving
Energetic impulses	Thoughts and intentions
Energy field	Higher mental
Developmental task	Contribution: using your skills and talents to alleviate suffering and improve the well-being of others. Intentions and thoughts directed towards serving your community, society, humanity, future generations or the planet.
Chakra	Crown
Endocrine system	Pineal gland
Endocrine function (homeostatic functioning)	Biological cycles, sleep
Body parts	Neocortex
Body functions	Central nervous system
Physical/psychological issues	Alzheimer's disease, Parkinson's disease, migraines
Psychological issues	Dementia
Negative feelings	Sadness and depression
Positive feelings	Joy and compassion
Characteristics associated with balanced chakras	When the crown chakra is functioning normally, you can make a contribution to the well-being of your community. You have access to universal wisdom. You are at peace with yourself. You are compassionate, unprejudiced and non-judgmental, aware of the world around you and know yourself.

The crown chakra controls the flow of energy to the layer of the energy field that represents the serving stage of psychological development and the service level of consciousness. The parts of the anatomy energized by the crown chakra are the neocortex mind/brain and the pineal gland.

Progress at the serving stage of development (the upper mental field) is dependent on our ability to master the differentiating stage of development (the lower mental field). If we fail to develop our self-esteem (confidence through respect and recognition) at the differentiating stage, we will be ill-equipped and ineffective in making a contribution to our community at the serving stage.

If you want to avoid brain dysfunction in your older years, you should establish a healthy sense of self-esteem when you are young, and later, when you reach your 60s, devote your energies to supporting friends and members of the social, religious or spiritual communities to which you belong. The worst thing you can do when you reach retirement age is to reduce your sphere of influence or social radius. You must be able to connect with others so you can use your gifts and talents to make a positive contribution to your community.

Making a contribution to others brings meaning and purpose to your life, stabilizes the inflow of energy to your crown chakra and augments your will to live. When you fail to do this, the life-supporting energy of the universal energy field flowing through the crown chakra is reduced, and the brain shrinks. As the brain shrinks, various forms of dementia[4] and strokes begin.

In his book, *Anatomy of an Illness*, Norman Cousins speaks of the chemistry of the "will to live". He cites the work of Ana Aslan (1897–1988), who was one of Romania's leading endocrinologists. In reporting on a conversation he had with her, he states:

> She spoke of her belief that there is a direct connection between a robust will to live and the chemical balances in the brain. She is convinced that creativity—one aspect of the will to live—produced the vital brain impulses that stimulate the pituitary gland, triggering effects on the pineal gland and the whole of the endocrine system.[5]

Cousins also speaks of his meetings with Pablo Casals (1876–1973), a world renowned cellist and conductor, and Albert Schweitzer (1875–1965), best known for his work as a medical missionary in Africa. He met both of these highly creative men when they were octogenarians.

> What I learned from these two men is that a highly developed purpose and the will to live are among the prime raw materials of human existence. I became convinced that these materials may well represent the most potent force within human reach.[6]

These statements concur with the findings of the Terman Study and Grant Study mentioned in the Foreword. George Vaillant makes the following statement about these studies:

> Like creativity in the Terman women, creativity in the College men [Grant Study] was associated with successful aging.[7] To summarize creativity was positively correlated with generativity, sublimation, and altruism.[8]

Having discussed what happens when we struggle to master the serving stage of psychological development and the types of dysfunction that occur, let us take a look at the incidence of Alzheimer's disease, strokes and Parkinson's disease: all diseases that impair the functioning of the mind and damage the operation of the brain.

Alzheimer's disease

Alzheimer's disease is a progressive brain disorder that damages and eventually destroys brain cells, leading to memory loss and impaired thinking. Alzheimer's usually develops slowly and gradually gets worse as brain cells wither and die. Ultimately, Alzheimer's is fatal, and currently, there is no cure. Alzheimer's disease is the most common type of dementia, accounting for 50–80 percent of all deaths due to dementia in the US. One in three seniors in the US dies of Alzheimer's disease or another form of dementia. Two-thirds of those with Alzheimer's disease are women.

Figure 13.1 shows the prevalence of people in different age groups suffering from Alzheimer's disease in the US in 2015.[9] The risk of developing Alzheimer's disease increases significantly over the age of seventy. According to the World Health Organization, the incidence of dementia in Europe is similar to the US.[10]

Figure 13.1: Proportion of people with Alzheimer's disease in the US, 2015.

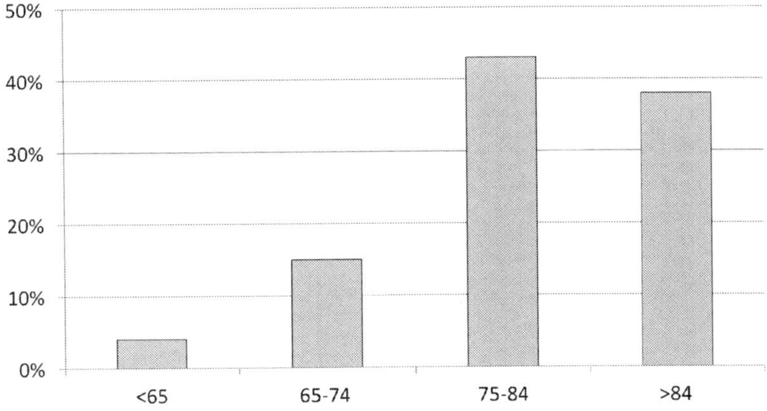

Source: American Alzheimer's Association.

Strokes

Strokes occur when the flow of the blood to the brain is cut off. Without blood, your brain cells cannot function. Figure 13.2 shows the prevalence of strokes in Australia in 2009. The age range for strokes peaks between the years 75–84.

Figure 13.2: Prevalence of strokes in Australia, 2009.

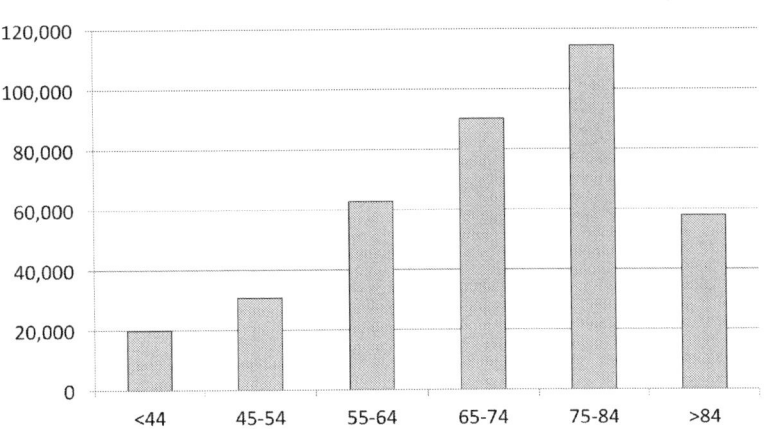

Source: Australia Institute of Health and Welfare.

Parkinson's disease

Parkinson's disease is a progressive neurological condition caused by the death of dopamine-producing nerve cells. Figure 13.3 shows the number of people suffering from Parkinson's disease in the UK in 2009. The number of people with Parkinson's disease increases gradually after the age of 60 and peaks between the years 75–79.

Figure 13.3: Number of people suffering from Parkinson's disease in the UK in 2009.

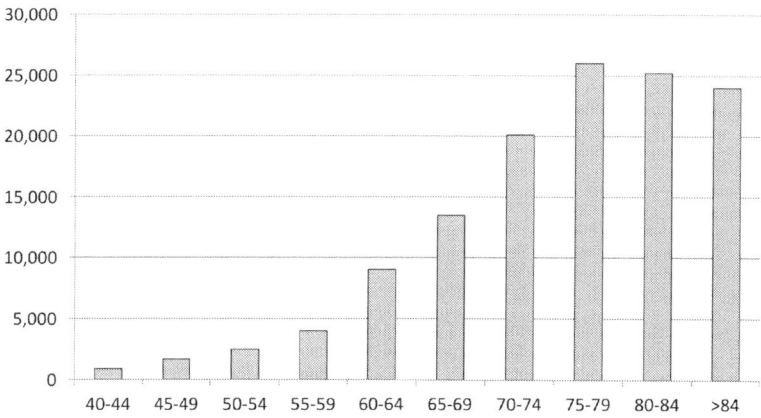

Source: UK National Health Statistics.

Conclusion

The leading causes of death linked to the serving stage of development—Alzheimer's disease, strokes and Parkinson's disease—show a significant increase in prevalence in the 60s, peaking between 75 and 84 in line with my hypothesis (see Table 13.3).

The conclusion I draw from this data is that a failure to master the serving stage of development frequently leads to diseases of the brain.

Physical disorders associated with the integrating stage of development

The integrating stage of psychological development, which begins in the 50s, relates to the upper emotional field and the brow chakra. This stage of development is about connecting with others and forming unconditional loving relationships. The area of the body and the homeostatic functions associated with the brow chakra are shown in Table 13.6.

Because our ability to master the integrating stage of development (the higher emotional field) is highly dependent on our ability to master the conforming stage of development (the lower emotional field), I have also included information about the areas of the body and homeostatic functions associated with both of these stages of development in Table 13.6.

The conforming stage of psychological development, which begins around age 2, relates to the lower emotional field and the sacral chakra. This stage of development is about learning how to manage your relationships so you feel accepted and safe.

The integrating and conforming stages of psychological development are linked because they both relate to the quality of our connections: the extent to which we can love ourselves (the conforming stage) and the extent to which we can love others (the integrating stage).

Table 13.6: Characteristics of the integrating and conforming stages of psychological development.

Stage of Development	Integrating	Conforming
Energetic impulses	Emotions and feelings towards others	Emotions and feelings towards self
Energy field	Higher emotional	Lower emotional
Developmental task	Connecting: building connections and empathising with others in unconditional loving relationships so you can make a difference in their lives.	Safety: feeling safe and protected by staying close to your kin and community and satisfying your need for loving relationships.
Chakra	Brow	Sacral
Endocrine system	Pituitary	Gonads
Endocrine function (homeostatic functioning)	Regulation of physical growth	Reproductive system

Body parts	Limbic brain, eyes, ears, nose	Female sexual organs, bladder, colon, bowel, bladder, prostate, kidneys and spleen
Body functions	Perception	Autonomic nervous system, parasympathetic system
Physical issues	Infections and problems with sight and hearing	Prostate cancer, ovarian cancer, urinary problems, pelvic pain, anorexia nervosa, bulimia nervosa and obesity
Psychological issues	I cannot connect with others	I am not loved enough
Negative feelings	Sadness and depression	Guilt and blame
Positive feelings	Empathy and connection	Safety and protection
Characteristics associated with balanced chakras	When the brow chakra is functioning normally, you can form unconditional loving relationships for the purpose of making a difference in people's lives. You easily make empathic connections and may be seen as charismatic. You have access to your intuition. You are clear about your purpose. You are not attached to the material world.	When the sacral chakra is functioning normally, you can form intimate, loving relationships. Your feelings flow freely and are expressed without being overly emotional. You are not afraid of conflict, and you can be passionate and lively. You have no problems dealing with your sexuality and feel comfortable in your body.

The brow chakra controls the flow of energy to the layer of the energy field that represents the integrating stage of psychological development and the making a difference level of consciousness. The parts of the anatomy energized by the brow chakra are the limbic mind/brain, the pituitary gland and the eyes, ears and nose.

The sacral chakra controls the flow of energy to the layer of the energy field that represents the conforming stage of psychological development. The parts of the anatomy energized by the sacral chakra are the female sexual organs, bladder, colon, bowel, kidneys, spleen and the prostate which helps to regulate the male sexual function.

Because these two layers of the energy field and their chakras are linked, issues at the integrating stage of psychological development can show up either as physiological dysfunctions in the area of the body linked to the brow chakra or the area of the body linked to the sacral chakra.

If we have struggled in our early life to build relationships that keep us safe, then the sacral chakra will be energetically unstable, and this instability will compromise our ability to make connections when we reach the integrating stage of development. The pressure to make connections at the integrating stage of development can further aggravate the instability of the lower emotional field resulting in disorders or disease in the parts of the body served by the sacral chakra. This is particularly true for men who are not encouraged to develop the emotional side of their character during the conforming stage of development.

Among the leading causes of death are two dysfunctions that relate to the operation of the sacral chakra: prostate cancer and ovarian cancer. There are no leading causes of death that relate to the operation of the brow chakra. Our ability to build relationships is linked to the development of the limbic mind/brain that is located in the part of the body energized by the brow chakra.

As you might expect, when you compare the incidence of prostate and ovarian cancer in Sweden (See Figure 13.4), an underactive sacral chakra is significantly more prevalent in males than females. In other words, the incidence of prostate cancer is significantly greater than the incidence of ovarian cancer.

Figure13.4: New cases of ovarian and prostate cancer in Sweden in 2012.

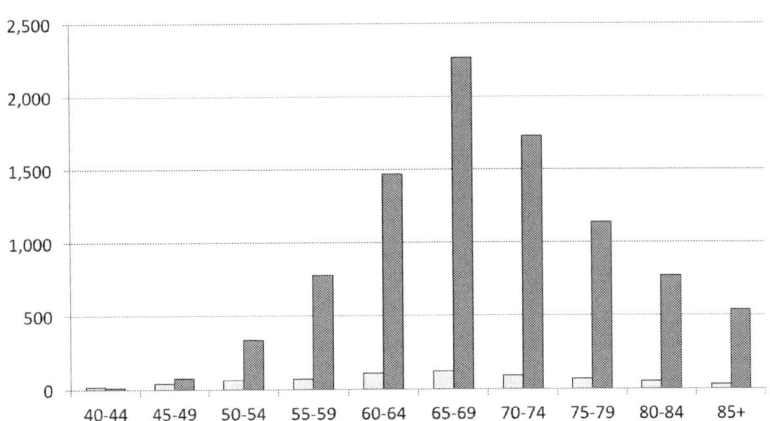

Source: National Board of Health and Welfare, Sweden.

I believe the reasons for these differences are twofold. First, females are more inclined to create loving connections because of the biological imperative of motherhood. Men, in general, do not experience this deep sense of connection. Second, women are treated differently from men. There is more pressure on women to conform—fit in with others, and more pressure on men to differentiate—stand out from others. Therefore, women tend to exercise their emotional connecting "muscles" earlier and more frequently than men.

The pressures on men to differentiate mean they must be seen to be strong: they cannot be seen to be weak if they are going to be respected in their communities, and they cannot show their emotions. They are pressured to suppress their feelings and be separate. In separating from their feelings, they get separated from their souls.

If you want to avoid dysfunctions related to your sacral chakra later in life, you should learn how to establish healthy loving relationships when you are young. This, unfortunately, is not something we have much control over. Only when you become an adult and find it difficult to build a committed relationship, do you become cognizant of your unmet (emotional) safety needs. If you do suffer in this way, it is important to seek professional help to release your fear-based relationship beliefs. Releasing the accumulated negative energies associated with the beliefs you have about not being lovable (an inability to meet your safety needs) will help you avoid physical disorders later in life.

Prostate cancer

The prostate is an exocrine gland[11] of the male reproductive system, which is found directly under the bladder in the front of the rectum. The prostate gland is about the size of a walnut. The urethra—a tube that goes from the bladder to the end of the penis and carries urine and semen out of the body—goes through the prostate. There are thousands of tiny glands in the prostate, that produce a fluid that forms part of the semen. This fluid protects and nourishes the sperm.

Prostate cancer arises from an abnormal and uncontrolled growth of cells. The growing cancer cells squeeze the urethra and disrupt the normal functioning of the prostate.

The impact of psychology on physiology

Figure 13.5 and 13.6 show the number of new cases of prostate cancer among the UK and Swedish males, respectively. The incidence of prostate cancer begins to become significant in the mid-50s and peaks in the late 60s and early 70s.

Figure 13.5: New cases of prostate cancer by age in the UK, 2009–2011.

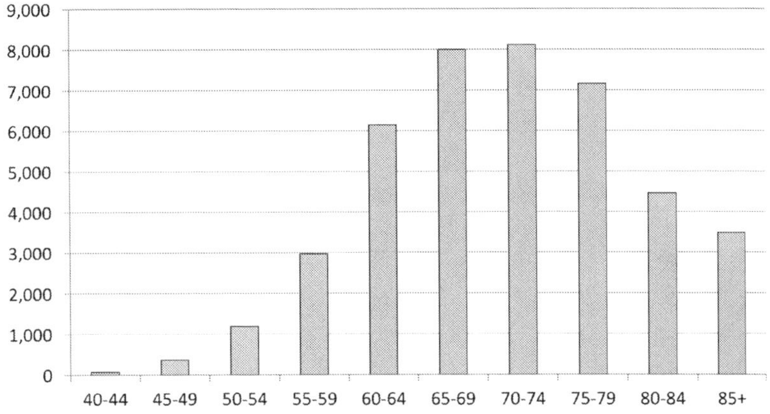

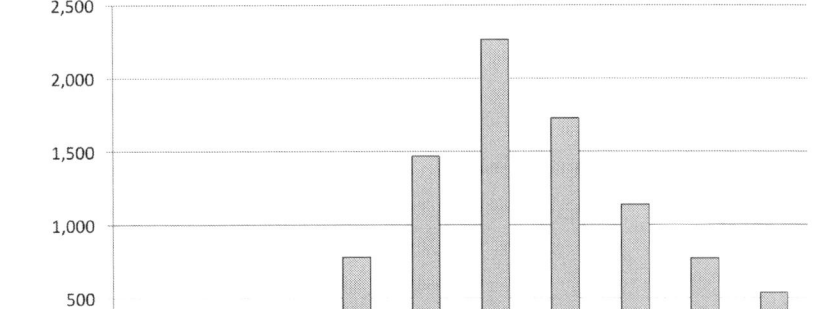

Source: Cancer Research UK.

Figure 13.6: New cases of prostate cancer by age in Sweden in 2012.

Source: National Board of Health and Welfare, Sweden.

Ovarian cancer

The distribution of the incidence of ovarian cancer in females by age is shown in Figure 13.7. This is almost the same as the distribution of prostate cancer in males. The data in 13.7 is the same data I presented in Figure 13.4, with an enlarged vertical axis. What this indicates, I believe, is that women who have difficulty mastering the conforming stage of development and inhibit the functioning of their sacral chakra, experience similar physiological dysfunctions as men when they reach the integrating stage of development.

Figure 13.7: New cases of ovarian cancer in Sweden in 2012.

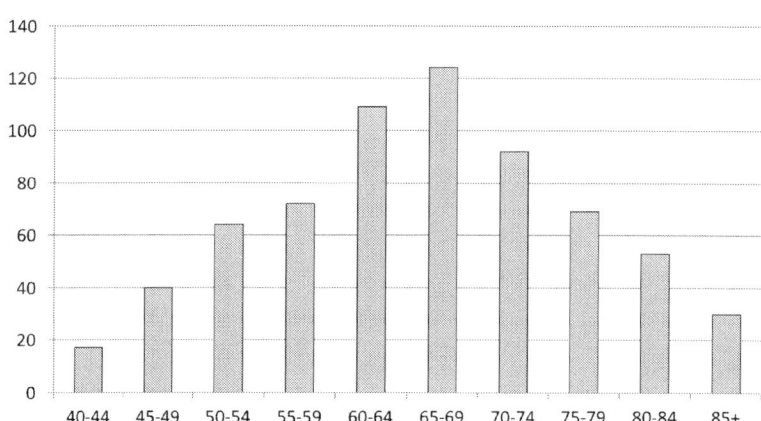

Source: National Board of Health and Welfare, Sweden.

Conclusion

The two leading causes of death linked to the individuating stage of development—prostate cancer and ovarian cancer—show a significant increase in prevalence in the 50s, peaking between 65 and 70 in line with my hypothesis (see Table 13.3).

In these two cases, the impact of not being able to master the higher emotional level shows up in the parts of the body associated with the lower emotional level, suggesting that psychological roots of prostate cancer and ovarian cancer began to form in our early life at the conforming stage of development.

The conclusion I draw from this data is that a failure to master the integrating stage of development is primarily linked to a failure to master the conforming stage of development and leads to diseases associated with the sexual organs.

Physical disorders associated with the self-actualizing stage of development

The self-actualizing stage of psychological development, which begins in the 40s, relates to the higher etheric field and the throat chakra. This stage of development is about expressing your soul's purpose so you can find meaning in your life. The area of the body and the homeostatic functions associated with the throat chakra are shown in Table 13.7. Progress at the self-actualizing stage of development (the higher etheric field) is dependent on our ability to master the surviving stage of development (the lower etheric field).

Table 13.7: Characteristics of the self-actualizing stage of psychological development.

Stage of development	Self-actualizing
Energetic impulse	Expression
Energy field	Higher etheric
Developmental task	Self-expression: express soul-self and stay present in physical/material reality. Actions to develop self. Expressing meaning and purpose.
Chakra	Throat
Endocrine system	Thyroid gland
Endocrine function (homeostatic functioning)	Body temperature and metabolism
Body parts	Reptilian mind/brain, neck, mouth, vocal chords, lungs, oesophagus and breasts
Body functions	Respiration, lactation
Physical issues	Breast cancer, asthma, lung, neck and thyroid problems. Infections of mouth and throat.

Psychological issues	I have no purpose
Negative feelings	Sadness and depression.
Positive feelings	Trust and enthusiasm
Characteristics associated with balanced chakras	When the throat chakra is functioning normally, you have no problems expressing yourself and vocalising your truth. You will often feel inspired and creative. You feel your life has purpose and meaning.

The throat chakra controls the flow of energy to the layer of the energy field that represents the self-actualizing stage of psychological development and the internal cohesion level of consciousness. The parts of the anatomy energized by the throat chakra are the reptilian mind/brain, lungs, vocal chords, oesophagus, breasts and the thyroid.

Success in mastering the self-actualizing stage of psychological development depends on success in mastering the surviving stage of psychological development. The self-actualizing stage of psychological development represents the soul's will for self-expression, the principal reason for the soul's incarnation. The surviving stage of development represents the ego's will to survive and establish control over its life; the soul's will to be present in 3-D awareness. If you cannot establish control over your life, then the soul cannot fulfil its desire for self-expression.

Compared to boys and men, who are normally given freedom to express themselves from an early age, girls and young women living in patriarchal societies—most of the Western world—tend to have their self-expression suppressed from an early age. This has major implications for the incidence of physiological dysfunctions in the chest area such as breast cancer.

Breast cancer

Breast cancer arises from an abnormal and uncontrolled growth of breast cells that form malignant tumours. Figure 13.8 shows the incidence of new cases of breast cancer among UK females during the period 2009–2011. Figure 13.9 shows the incidence of new cases of breast cancer among Swedish females during 2012.

Figure 13.8: New cases of breast cancer in the UK, 2009–2011.

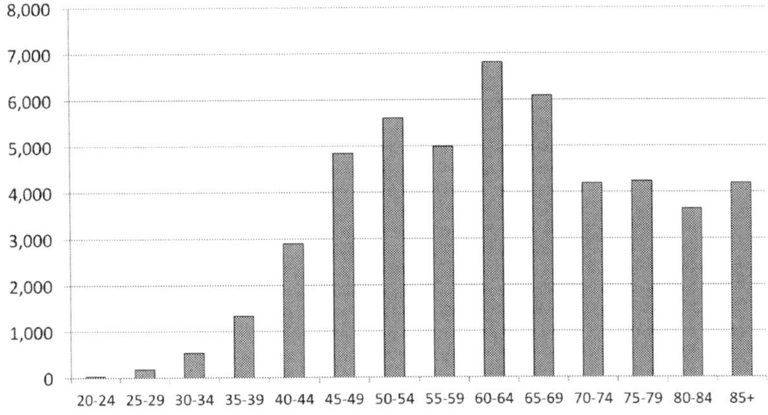

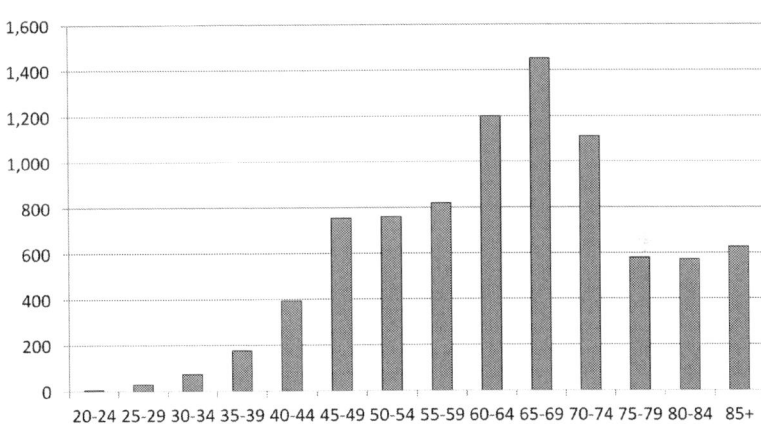

Source: Cancer Research UK.

Figure 13.9: New cases of breast cancer in Sweden in 2012.

Source: National Board of Health and Welfare, Sweden.

The distribution of new cases of breast cancer by age is very similar in the UK and Sweden. There are two periods when the increase in the number of women diagnosed with breast cancer is significant: during the self-actualizing stage of psychological development (40–49 years) and the serving stage of psychological development (60–69 years). The number of new cases flattens out during the integrating stage of psychological development (50–59 years) and drops to a much lower level during the 70s and 80s.

This suggests that women not only experience difficulties mastering the self-actualizing stage of development—finding meaning and purpose in their lives—but also experience difficulties mastering the serving stage of development—finding meaning and purpose after they have reached retirement age or after their children have left home.

Women encounter far fewer difficulties during the integrating stage of development because women are predisposed to be good at connecting with others. This is why, later in life, the number of women who have difficulties with mastering the integrating stage of psychological development is far fewer than those who have difficulties mastering the self-actualizing stage of development. Consequently, the proportion of women who suffer from breast cancer compared to ovarian cancer is much larger. This comparison is shown in Figure 13.10 using data from Sweden. In 2011, there were 6.44 times more women who developed breast cancer than developed ovarian cancer (8,382 compared to 1,301).

Figure 13.10: New cases of breast and ovarian cancer in Sweden in 2012.

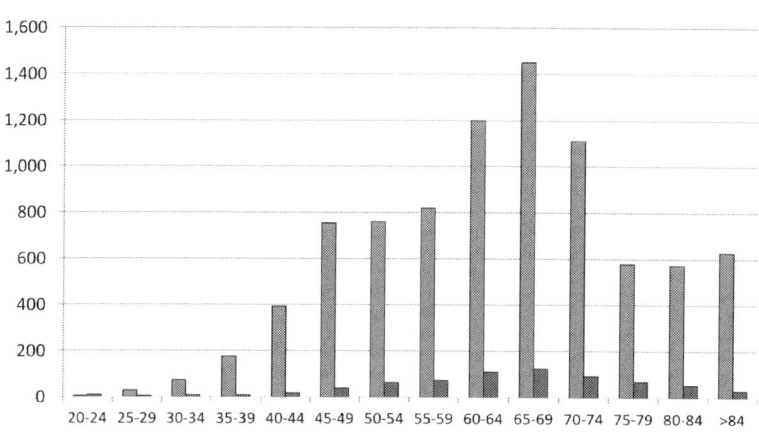

Source: National Board of Health and Welfare, Sweden.

Respiratory problems

All creatures need to breathe to stay alive. Without well-functioning lungs and an ample supply of oxygen, we cannot breathe, and if we cannot breathe, we die within a matter of minutes. There are several diseases that affect the lungs: lung cancer, asthma, influenza, pneumonia, cystic fibrosis and emphysema. Figure 13.11 shows the number of deaths from respiratory problems in Sweden in 2012. The incidence of deaths begins to become significant in the 40s and peaks in early 70s.

Figure 13.11: Number of deaths from respiratory problems Sweden in 2012.

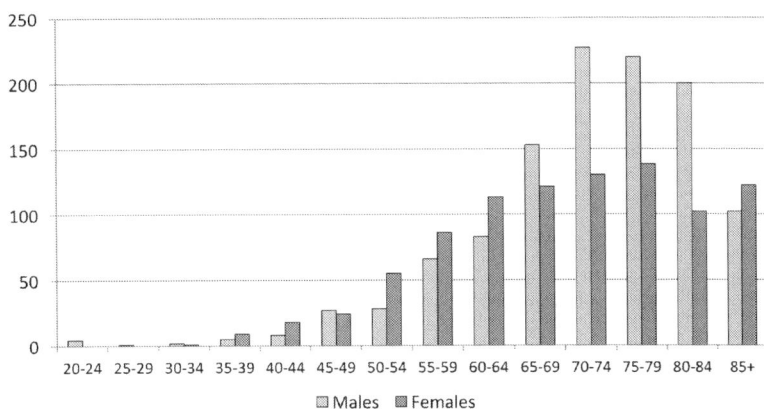

Source: National Board of Health and Welfare, Sweden.

Suicide

Although suicide is one of the leading causes of death at the self-actualizing stage of psychological development, it is a psychological issue rather than a physiological issue. For this reason, I discuss the relationship between suicide and the stages of psychological development in the following chapter.

Conclusion

The two leading causes of death linked to the self-actualizing stage of development—breast cancer and lung disease—begin to show a significant increase in prevalence in the 40s and early 50s, particularly respiratory problems for females, in line with my hypothesis (see Table 13.3).

Breast cancer appears to occur in peaks. One peak occurs in the late 40s exactly in line with my hypothesis, and the other peak occurs in the late 60s about ten years later. I believe this is because females not only experience difficulties mastering the self-actualizing stage of development; they also have difficulties mastering the serving stage of development. This would be in line with my hypothesis.

The conclusion I draw from this data is that a failure to master the self-actualizing stage of development frequently leads to breast cancer in females and respiratory problems in males and females.

Physical disorders associated with the individuating stage of development

The individuating stage of psychological development, which begins in the mid-20s, relates to the heart chakra. This stage of development is about learning how to live in a state of coherence. Coherence is the degree to which you can live your life as a unified whole. In other words, the degree to which you can heal the separation of your ego from your soul and align your ego's motivations with your soul's motivations.

The primary causes of separation are the fears you developed during the first three stages of development about being able to meet your deficiency needs. The individuating stage of development is where you begin to release these fears. This is a necessary prerequisite for accessing the higher stages of psychological development.

The area of the body and the homeostatic functions associated with the heart chakra are shown in Table 13.8.

Table 13.8: Characteristics of the individuating stage of psychological development.

Stage of development	Individuating
Energetic Impulse	Love
Energy field	Astral
Developmental task	Freedom: mastering the fears you learned in your childhood and teenage years about being able to satisfy your deficiency needs.
Chakra	Heart
Endocrine system	Thymus
Endocrine function (homeostatic functioning)	Immune system

Body parts	Heart, circulation system, arms and hands
Body functions	Blood circulation
Physical and mental issues	Heart disease and blood pressure
Psychological issues	Identity: I do not know who I am
Negative feelings	Anger and hatred
Positive feelings	Love and courage
Characteristics associated with balanced chakras	When the heart chakra is functioning normally you are honest with yourself and with others. Maintain a high degree of integrity in everything you do. You are willing to look at your shadow, and identify, face and overcome your fears.

The heart chakra controls the flow of energy to the layer of the energy field that represents the individuating stage of psychological development and the transformation level of consciousness. The parts of the anatomy energized by the heart chakra are the heart and the thymus gland. This is the first layer of the energy field that "belongs" to the soul. The lower layers of the energy field "belong" to the ego.

When you die the first three ego layers of the energy field are released, and your soul "life" continues to operate from the soul layers: the astral field and the higher etheric, emotional and mental fields.

The astral layer of the energy field is where the imprints of previous lives are held and where the imprints of your current life, that your soul will carry forward to your next life, are located. These imprints condition our "starting" physiological and psychological orientations in our life by being incorporated into the first three layers of our energy field. Therefore, who you are in your current life is not just based on your personal history in this life, but also on the psychological imprints from the personal histories of your previous lives. This means if we can heal negative imprints from previous lives in this life, and we can be free of them in future lives. It also means that "inherited" negative imprints from past lives can affect our physiological health in the early years of our current lives. This I believe has a lot to do with childhood deaths, such as cancer, which are not related to birth trauma.

The layer of our energy field associated with the heart chakra is where we store our anger and hatred at not getting our needs met during our time in the womb and during the first two years of our life, when the soul was the dominant or acting as the subconscious to the reptilian mind/brain. If you have stored up anger and hatred in this layer of your energy field, it is likely to increase your risk of an early heart attack. All forms of physiological or psychological pain are interpreted by the soul as a lack of love.

A study of childhood abuse and neglect carried by the University of Toronto showed that:

> Individuals who reported they had been physically abused as children had 45 percent higher odds of heart disease than their peers who had not been abused.[12]

A further study by the University of Toronto links male childhood sexual abuse to heart attacks.[13] According to this study, men who experienced sexual abuse in childhood were three times more likely to have a heart attack than men who were not sexually abused.

Another study carried out in the US reaches a similar conclusion:

> Adverse childhood experiences may cause psychological and physiological changes that eventually lead to heart disease.[14]

This study found that those who suffered emotional or physical abuse or grew up in a dysfunctional household were 30–70 percent more likely to have a heart attack or other cardiac problem. The study also found that children who are abused or neglected are three times more likely to struggle with drug addiction as adults and twice as likely to become alcoholics. They are also twice as likely to smoke or to be severely obese.

We can conclude that living in coherence with your soul-self means letting go of the fear, pain and anger stored in the energy field of your soul at the astral level. When you do not let go of this fear and anger; when you let this pain accumulate, and you live in a state of incoherence, the risk of a heart attack increases.

Researchers at the Harvard School of Public Health have found that in the two hours immediately following an angry outburst, the risk of a heart attack increases nearly five-fold and the risk of stroke increases more than three-fold. They say it is unclear why anger is dangerous. I believe it is unclear to them because they fail to appreciate the energetic dimensions of

The impact of psychology on physiology

our existence. Like most medical scientists, they look at the world around them through the lens of 3-D material reality.

Heart disease

Cardiovascular disease (CVD), also known as heart disease, is a class of diseases that affects the heart and blood circulation. CVD includes angina and myocardial infarction (heart attack). Other CVDs include stroke, hypertension and cardiomyopathy. Heart disease is the leading cause of death in the world. Figure 13.12 shows the number of US adults per 1000, by gender and age, diagnosed as having experienced a heart attack in 2015.

Figure 13.12: Number of US adults per 100,000 diagnosed with a heart attack by age and gender in 2014.

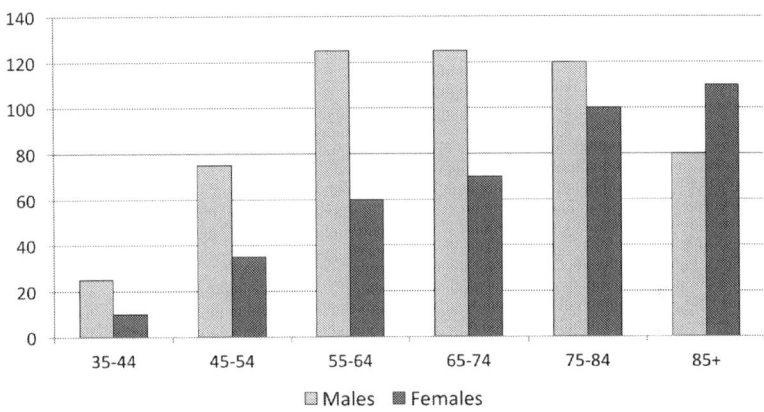

Source: American Heart Association.

Figure 13.13 shows the number of deaths, by gender and age, in the US due to heart disease in 2012, and Figure 13.14 shows the number of deaths, by gender, in the UK due to heart disease in 2014. It is important to remember that the incidence of deaths from a disease occurs much later than the prevalence of a disease; the disease has to be present and develop before it causes death.

Figure 13.13: Number of deaths by gender from heart related diseases in the US in 2012.

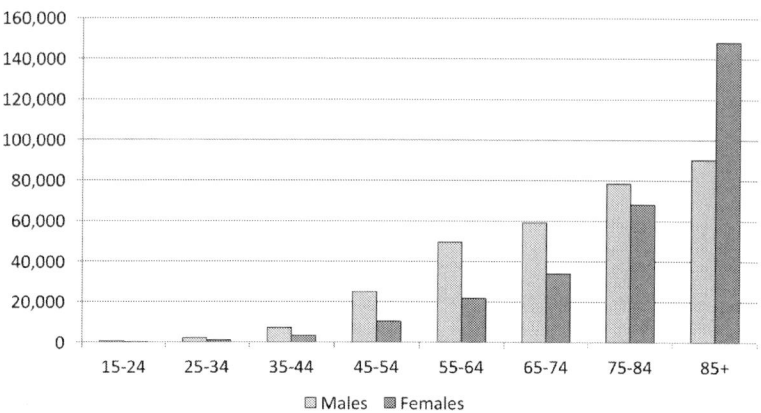

Source: National Vital Statistics, Vol. 64, No. 10, August 31, 2015.

Figure 13.14: Number of deaths by gender from heart-related diseases in the UK in 2014.

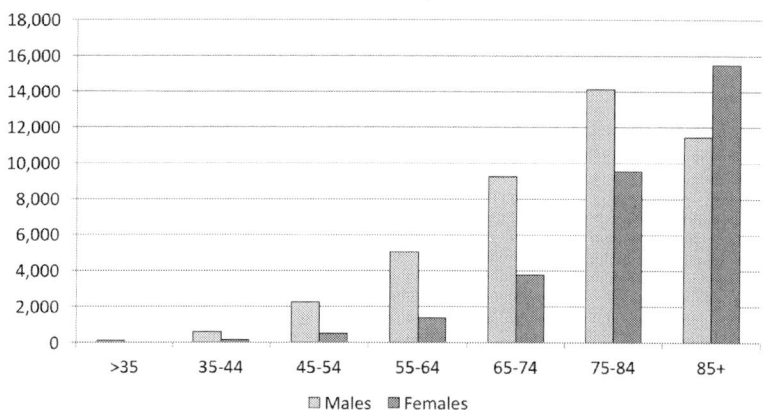

Source: British Heart Foundation, Cardiovascular Disease Statistics, 2014.

It is noticeable that the prevalence and incidence of heart attacks are significantly lower for females than males in all age ranges except the 85+ range when females are more inclined to suffer and die from heart disease than males.

Suicide

Although suicide is one of the leading causes of death at the individuating stage of psychological development, it is a psychological issue rather than a physiological issue. For this reason, I discuss the relationship between suicide and the stages of psychological development in the following chapter.

Conclusion

The leading cause of death related to the individuating stage of development is heart disease. Issues related to the heart—heart attacks and blood pressure—begin to show a significant increase in prevalence in the 30s (men and women) and tend to peak (in men) during the mid-50s and early 60s (Figure 13.12) in line with my hypothesis (see Table 13.3). Heart disease in women peaks twenty to thirty years later.

The conclusion I draw from this data is that a failure to master the individuating stage of development frequently leads to heart problems.

Physical disorders associated with the differentiating stage of development

The differentiating stage of psychological development, which begins in the mid-20s, relates to the lower mental field and the solar plexus chakra. This stage of development is about establishing a sense of identity and physical and emotional security in the cultural framework of your existence. Success at this stage of development requires confidence and self-esteem. The area of the body and the homeostatic functions associated with the solar plexus chakra are shown in Table 13.9.

Table 13.9: Characteristics of the differentiating stage of psychological development.

Stage of development	Differentiating
Energetic impulses	Thoughts and beliefs
Energy field	Lower mental

Developmental task	Security: developing your confidence in a community where you can display your skills and talents and feel respected and recognized. Intentions and thoughts directed towards feeling secure and serving yourself.
Chakra	Solar plexus
Endocrine system	Pancreas
Endocrine function (homeostatic functioning)	Metabolism
Body parts	Stomach, duodenum, pancreas, liver, gall bladder, and spine. Link to neocortex mind/brain (rational mind).
Body functions	Digestion
Physical issues	Stomach ulcers, colon cancer, irritable bowel, diabetes, hypoglycaemia and liver disease
Psychological issues	I am not good enough
Negative feelings	Shame and envy
Positive feelings	Power and confidence
Characteristics associated with balanced chakras	When the solar plexus chakra is functioning normally, you can establish yourself in a community where you gain respect and recognition. You can express your personal power. You feel in control, have confidence and hold yourself in positive regard. You are spontaneous and uninhibited.

The solar plexus chakra controls the flow of energy to the layer of the energy field that represents the differentiating stage of psychological development and the self-esteem level of consciousness. The parts of the anatomy energized by the solar plexus chakra are the "brain in the gut", the stomach, the upper intestine, liver, gall bladder and the pancreas, which regulates the digestive system and controls the blood sugar levels in the body.

The leading cause of death associated with the differentiating stage of psychological development and the self-esteem level of consciousness is suicide. Since this is a psychological issue rather than a physiological issue, as previously mentioned, I propose to deal with this topic in the following chapter, which is exclusively devoted to the link between suicide and the stages of psychological development.

Another psychological issue that shows up at the differentiating stage of development and the self-esteem level of consciousness is eating disorders (bulimia nervosa, anorexia nervosa and obesity): controlling or not controlling the amount of food that is taken into the stomach. Although the symptoms of bulimia nervosa, anorexia nervosa and obesity are all different, they all have a connection to self-esteem, discipline and control.

After suicide, the leading causes of death and physiological disorders associated with the differentiating stage of development are liver disease and diabetes.

Liver disease

The liver plays an important role in many body functions from protein production and blood clotting to cholesterol, glucose and iron metabolism. The operation of the liver is affected by certain drugs, alcohol abuse, hepatitis, etc. The incidence of death from liver disease in Sweden during 2012 is shown in Figure 13.15.

Deaths from liver disease start early in the 20s and 30s and continue increasing through the 40s and 50s reaching a peak during the 60s.

Figure 13.15: Number of deaths from liver disease in Sweden in 2012.

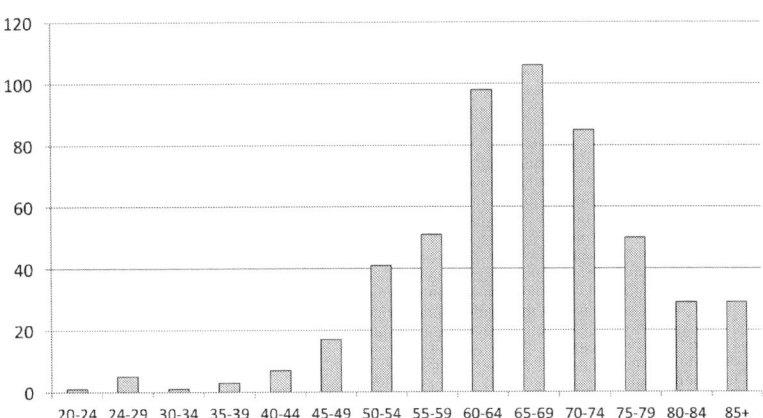

Source: National Board of Health and Welfare, Sweden.

Diabetes

Diabetes is a general term for a variety of different metabolic disorders that affect the ability of the body to digest and process sugar properly. Left untreated, diabetes can lead to serious long-term complications. Figure 13.16 shows the incidence of death from diabetes in the US in 2012. Deaths from diabetes start in the 20s and 30s and continue growing through the 40s and 50s, reaching a peak during the late 70s.

Figure 13:16: Number of deaths from diabetes in the US in 2012.

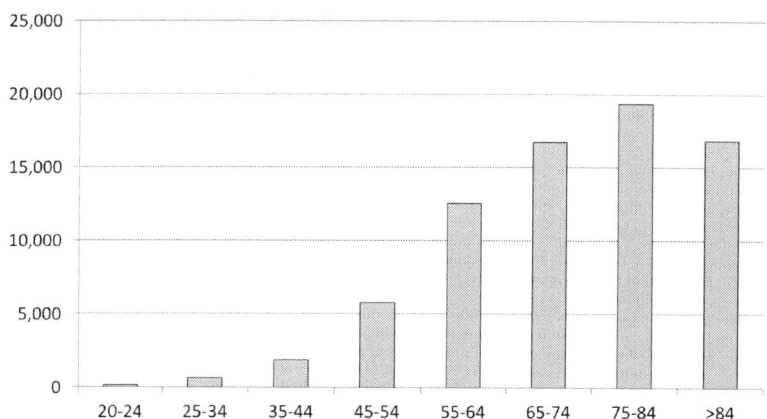

Source: National Vital Statistics Reports, Volume 64, Number 10.

Obesity

Obesity is defined as a disorder in which excess body fat has accumulated to an extent that health may be adversely affected. The most commonly used measure of body fatness is the Body Mass Index (BMI) calculated as weight in kilograms divided by height in metres squared. Adults with a BMI greater than 25 kg/m² but less than 30 kg/m² are considered overweight. Adults with a BMI greater than 30 kg/m² are considered obese. An adult who is more than 45 kilos (100 pounds) overweight or has a BMI greater than 40 kg/m² is considered morbidly obese.

Being overweight significantly increases the risk of death from hypertension, dyslipidemia, Type 2 diabetes, stroke, osteoarthritis and coronary heart disease. Other dysfunctions include gallbladder disease, sleep apnea, respiratory problems and breast, prostate and colon cancers.

The impact of psychology on physiology

In recent years, obesity has reached epidemic proportions in the US and the UK. Figure 13.17 shows the percentage of the population considered obese in the US from 1960 to 2010.

Figure 13.17: Percentage of population in the US considered obese.

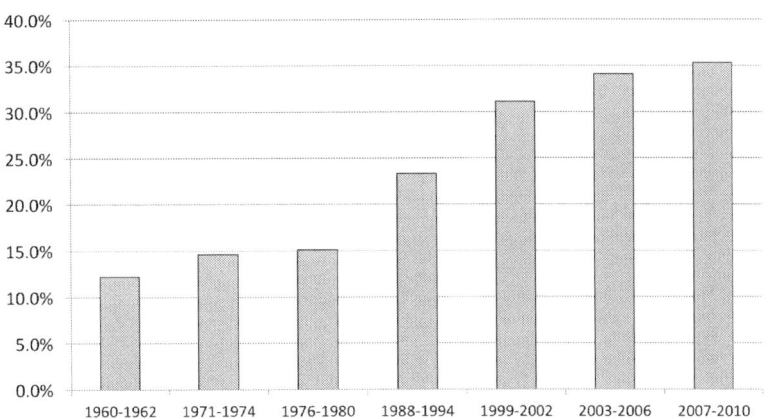

Source: National Centre for Health Statistics.

The epidemic of obesity is not limited to adults: in the US, the percentage of young people who are overweight has more than doubled in the past 20 years. Figure 13.18 shows the percentage of people different age groupings in the US in 2012 considered obese.

Figure 13:18: Percentage of population in the US considered obese by age grouping in 2012.

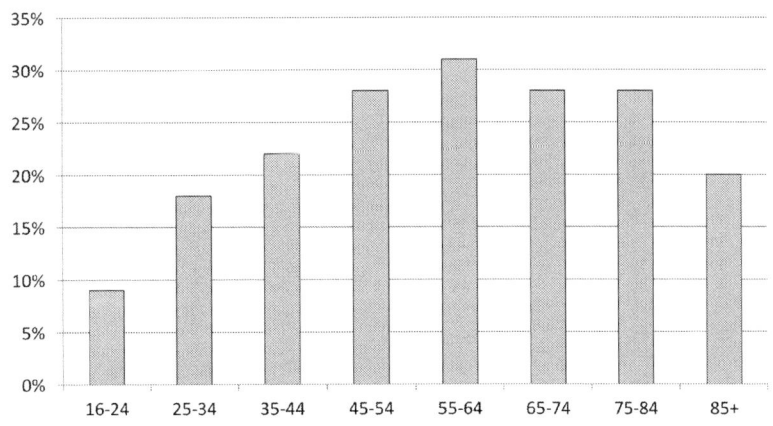

Source: National Centre for Health Statistics.

Those suffering from obesity not only have low levels of self-esteem, but they also have low levels of discipline and self-control. I believe obesity is a problem of recognition. People with obesity take in more food than they need to compensate for the lack of recognition they get in their lives. They use food as a substitute for the energy of appreciation, something that nurtures them.

In feeding the stomach, they are attempting to fill the emptiness of the low self-esteem they feel in this layer of their energy field. They lack discipline and self-control because they have given up caring about being recognized. Obesity is a sign that the solar plexus chakra is underactive.

The recent explosion in obesity suggests that young people are suffering from a lack of acknowledgement and recognition from their parents, peers and teachers. This lack of acknowledgement shows up in spending too much time on their own, not getting nutritious meals (too much junk food), not being supervised and a breakdown in family relations.

Anorexia nervosa

Anorexia nervosa is characterized by a fear of weight gain and an unreasonable and unhealthy restriction of food. Research suggests that about 1 percent of female adolescents in the US suffer from anorexia, and it is estimated that 20 percent of people suffering from anorexia will prematurely die from complications related to their eating disorder.[15]

People with anorexia can suffer potentially fatal medical conditions, including heart disease, kidney and liver disease, and potassium and magnesium imbalances that can lead to heart failure. Also, they often suffer from osteoporosis (thinning, brittle bones), low blood pressure, ulcers, dizziness and fainting, irregular heart rhythm, headaches, nausea and a myriad of other physical problems. People with anorexia also experience anxiety, depression, and other psychological problems.

Anorexics behave in exactly the opposite manner around food to the obese. Whereas the obese have given up on meeting their self-esteem needs, and therefore, lack discipline around food, anorexics have not given up; they are totally disciplined and controlled around food.

The male parent of anorexics is usually absent from their life or does not pay them much attention. Consequently, they do not get the respect and recognition they need. Anorexics have learned they need to control what they take in from the outside world to preserve and nurture their sense of self-esteem. They tend to nurture their self-esteem through academic excellence.

For most people, anorexia is equated to a loss of appetite. This is not the case. Anorexics only behave as if they have no appetite. In reality, they are controlling their food intake for other reasons.

Some people explain anorexia by giving it a religious spin because asceticism has strong links to eating disorders. Marilyn Lawrence, a UK psychotherapist, specializing in anorexia explains:

> Fasting, self-harm, and self-flagellation have often formed a part of Eastern and Western religious traditions.[16]
>
> The body is viewed, like the external world, as essentially sinful. The mind/soul can achieve perfection only if the body can be subdued and overcome. The body is felt to be an enemy of the soul, which it attempts to keep trapped in sinful imperfection.[17]

In this statement, we not only see a link to discipline and control—the needs of the body must be "subdued and overcome"; we also see a link to the fundamental issue discussed in this book—the issue of ego-soul dynamics and the fundamental purpose of life. Lawrence continues with the religious links to anorexia nervosa:

> Young females, experiencing puberty, view their bodies as uncontrollable. The uncontrollable nature of the body cannot be accepted.[18]
>
> While [modern day] patients are clearly highly motivated to pursue their relentless goal of absolute thinness, they do not seem to know what it is that motivates them ... Medieval saints ... on the other hand, were quite clear and explicit that they were trying to free their souls from the prison of the body. They were aiming for spiritual perfection.[19]

This last statement clearly implies that medieval saints who were "seeking to free their souls from the prison of the body" were seeking spiritual recognition; recognition from their inner world.

No matter what reason young females have for "relentlessly" pursuing thinness, it appears to me that the psychological causes of anorexia, as in all eating disorders is connected to the experiences children and teenagers have in getting the recognition they need during the differentiating stages of development and getting some level of control over their decision-making. This need to exercise control suggests they also have difficulties meeting their needs at the surviving stage of development. The strong control and self-discipline issues of anorexics are some of the factors that differentiate them from bulimia sufferers.

Bulimia nervosa

Bulimia nervosa is characterized by episodes of rapidly eating large amounts of food and then getting rid of the consumed food by vomiting, laxatives or diuretics. Because typically, bulimics do not get as dangerously thin as anorexics, the physical damage to their bodies is not as severe. Bulimics generally suffer from depression and substance abuse. Bulimics, like anorexics, have not given up on getting their self-esteem needs met. The main differences between anorexics and bulimics are:

- Bulimics are not as disciplined and controlled as anorexics.
- Bulimics seek recognition of their body-image (self-esteem) from the outer world; whereas I believe anorexic sufferers seek recognition from their inner and outer worlds.

About 50 percent of people who have had anorexia nervosa go on to develop bulimia nervosa or bulimic patterns. The shift from anorexia to bulimia is usually regarded as a step forward on the journey to healing. More information on the psychological causes of anorexia nervosa can be found in *The Anorexic Mind*, by Marilyn Lawrence.[20]

Conclusion

Apart from suicide, the two leading causes of death linked to difficulties in mastering the differentiating stage of development are liver disease and diabetes. The prevalence of these disorders starts to appear in the early 20s and gradually becomes more important in the following ten-to-fifteen years roughly in line with my hypothesis (see Table 13.3).

The conclusion I draw from this data is that a failure to master the differentiating stage of development frequently leads to diabetes and liver disease.

With regard to eating disorders, the onset of anorexia nervosa, bulimia nervosa and obesity align with my hypothesis—anorexia nervosa and bulimia nervosa mostly affect adolescent girls and young women (12–24 age). Anorexics tend to distribute towards the lower end of this range, and bulimics tend to distribute towards the higher end of this range.

Even though obesity can occur at any stage in our lives, the rapid increase in obesity among children and teenagers suggests that they are not getting the attention and recognition from their parents they so badly need to master the differentiating stage of development.

Eating disorders have the highest mortality rate of any mental illness, and anorexia is the third most common chronic illness among adolescents in the US and the UK.

Physical disorders associated with the conforming stage of development

The conforming stage of psychological development, which begins in childhood, relates to the lower emotional field and the sacral chakra. This stage of development is about finding physical and emotional safety in your life. The area of the body and the homeostatic functions associated with the sacral chakra are shown in Table 13.10.

Table 13.10: Characteristics of the conforming stage of psychological development.

Stage of development	Conforming
Energetic impulses	Emotions and feelings towards self
Energy field	Lower emotional
Developmental task	Safety: feeling safe and protected by staying close to your kin and community and satisfying your need for loving relationships.
Chakra	Sacral
Endocrine system	Gonads

Endocrine function (homeostatic functioning)	Reproductive system
Body parts	Female sexual organs, bladder, colon, bowel, bladder, and prostate, kidneys and spleen.
Body functions	Autonomic Nervous System—parasympathetic system.
Physical and mental issues	Prostate cancer, ovarian cancer, urinary problems, pelvic pain, anorexia, bulimia and obesity
Psychological issues	I am not loved enough.
Negative feelings	Guilt and blame
Positive feelings	Safety and protection
Characteristics associated with balanced chakras	When the sacral chakra is functioning normally, you can form intimate, loving relationships. Your feelings flow freely and are expressed without being overly emotional. You are not afraid of conflict, and you can be passionate and lively. You have no problems dealing with your sexuality and feel comfortable in your body.

The sacral chakra controls the flow of energy to the layer of the energy field that represents the conforming stage of psychological development and the relationship level of consciousness. The parts of the anatomy energized by the sacral chakra are the female sexual organs, the prostate, bladder, colon, bowel, kidneys and spleen.

Conclusion

There are few leading causes of death *directly* related to the conforming stage of development. The leading causes of death *indirectly* related to the conforming stage of development (emotional safety) are prostate and ovarian cancer. Other issues indirectly related to difficulties in mastering the needs of the conforming stage of development include urinary and kidney infections, and bowel issues.

The most profound and long-lasting consequences of struggles to meet the physical and emotional needs of the conforming stage of development are mental disorders. Depending on the severity of the difficulties encountered at this stage of development these disorders can range from neuroses to dissociative identity disorder.

Physical disorders associated with the surviving stage of development

The surviving stage of psychological development relates to the lower etheric field and the root chakra. This stage of development is about staying alive: the ultimate existential issue we face in our lives. The area of the body and the homeostatic functions associated with the root chakra are shown in Table 13.11.

Table 13.11: Characteristics of the surviving stage of psychological development.

Stage of development	Surviving
Energetic impulse	Action
Energy field	Lower etheric
Developmental task	Survival: stay alive and survive. Maintain physical health and vitality. Actions focused on needs of self.
Chakra	Root
Endocrine system	Adrenal glands
Endocrine function (homeostatic functioning)	Stress response and metabolism
Body parts	Rectum, anus, lower spine, legs and feet. Link to reptilian mind/brain (body-mind)
Body functions	Defecation
Physical issues	Arthritis, varicose veins, rectal tumours and lower back pain
Psychological issues	I do not have enough to survive
Negative feelings	Fear and anxiety
Positive feelings	Control and vitality
Characteristics associated with balanced chakras	When the root chakra is functioning normally, you feel grounded and stable—in control of your life. You are present in the here and now; connected to your physical body and trust that things will work out.

The root chakra controls the flow of energy to the layer of the energy field that represents the surviving stage of psychological development and the survival level of consciousness. The parts of the anatomy energized by the root chakra are the hips, legs, feet and the adrenal glands.

The causes of death during the surviving stage of development are varied. One of the most significant is Sudden Infant Death Syndrome (SIDS). Other physiological disorders directly related to this stage of development include arthritis in children.

Sudden Infant Death Syndrome

Medical science has no explanation to offer for the occurrence of SIDS. Thorough autopsies have never revealed any signs of physiological malfunction in deaths attributed to SIDS: the heart just appears to stop beating.

SIDS usually occurs between two and four months of age and tends to affect male babies more than female babies. SIDS occurs during sleep, a time when the dominant conscious awareness is closed down and soul awareness is active. I believe that SIDS is a voluntary action taken by the soul. When the will of the soul to be present in 3-D awareness is not strong, and the soul is overwhelmed by the energetic instability (pain) it experiences in material awareness, it may choose to withdraw from the baby's body. This is the soul's choice and should not be regarded by the parents as a failure to care for the baby.

Arthritis

Although rheumatoid arthritis is most commonly associated with older adults, there is a version of the disease that afflicts children. This condition, called juvenile rheumatoid arthritis (JRA), can vary from being relatively harmless to having permanent and potentially dangerous consequences. According to some sources, nearly 300,000 children in the US suffer from some form of arthritis.

Conclusion

The cause of death *directly* related to the surviving stage of development is SIDS. Other directly related physiological issues include arthritis.

There are many physical disorders *indirectly* related to the surviving stage of development. These include heart disease, blood pressure and cancer. Other related issues arising from difficulties in meeting the needs of the surviving stage of development and survival consciousness include disorders related to the anus, legs and feet.

The most profound and long-lasting consequences of struggles to meet the needs of the surviving stage of psychological development are mental disorders. Depending on the severity of the struggle, these disorders can range from neuroses to different forms of psychoses.

Cancer dysfunctions

What is different about cancer dysfunctions, compared to all other causes of death, is that they are not confined to a specific part of the body. Almost every organ of the body, including the brain, but not the heart, can be affected by cancer. This suggests that cancer is not primarily a developmental issue but a more of an existential issue—a profound inability to prioritize the desires of the soul because of the separation that exists between the ego's motivations and the soul's motivations. For this reason, most cancer dysfunctions do not tend to show up until we reach the second half of our lives.

The risk of cancer increases considerably if the immune system has been compromised by repeated difficulties in meeting our survival, safety or security needs. When we become resigned to not being able to meet one of these needs, the sympathetic nervous system closes down, and the immune system is weakened.

Cancer strikes when there is an inability to meet the desires of the soul and where the energetic instability due to an underactive chakra is the greatest—where the workings of the immune system are most compromised.

For most women, these two issues are found in the same layer of the energy field: the layer that corresponds to the chest area. This layer of the energy field corresponds to the internal cohesion level of consciousness and the self-actualizing stage of psychological development. Energetic instability in the chest area and difficulties in meeting the soul's desire for self-expression lead to breast cancer.

The risk of breast cancer increases if, during the surviving stage of psychological development, the female baby struggled to get its survival needs met and during childhood was taught to put the needs of others before its needs.

> Clinicians often report the impression that many cancer patients have been "givers" for much of their lives, subordinating awareness of their needs to awareness of the needs of others. Learning to be aware of and to articulate what you would like can sometimes be a new and even frightening prospect.[21]

For most men, the two issues—an inability to prioritize the desires of the soul and energetic instability—are found in different layers of the energy field. The highest level of energetic instability in men tends to occur in the lower abdomen area, which corresponds to the relationship level of consciousness and conforming stage of development.

Since this layer of the energy field supports the layer of the energy field associated with the individuating stage of development, when men reach the integrating stage of development their ability to meet the desire of the soul for connection is compromised by the energetic instability they have in the layer of the energy field associated with the conforming stage of development. Consequently, a failure to meet the desire of the soul for connection shows up as prostate cancer.

It is important to remember that cancer cells are not diseased cells; they are cells where the will to cooperate in pursuit of the common good has been suppressed, where the sense of separation from the soul is greatest.

When cells feel this sense of separation they lose their larger sense of identity (every cell is part of an organ) and start to focus on their own self-interest. They grow and develop without concern for other cells. They become thoroughly ego-centric, focused uniquely on their own survival. They have been imbued by the soul with the will to survive and that is what they focus on. Their unique focus on self-interest eventually leads to their demise. This is true in all walks of life: a focus on self-interest always leads to failure.

Using game theory, two evolutionary biology researchers found that: "evolution will punish you if you're selfish and mean. For a short time and against a specific set of opponents, some selfish organisms may come out ahead. But selfishness isn't evolutionary sustainable"[22].

Evolution does not progress by entities becoming the fittest, but by becoming the most inclusive and stable. There is a definite evolutionary advantage in being able to expand your consciousness (your sense identity) to include others; in other words, there is an evolutionary advantage in advancing your psychological development.

What does all this mean?

What I have attempted to show in this chapter, based on data I have gathered from many sources, is that our physiological health is intimately linked to the struggles we have in meeting our ego's needs and our soul's desires. More specifically, our health is a function of our ability to align our ego's motivations with our soul's motivations.

To achieve optimum physical health, we must learn to master each stage of psychological development by letting go of the ego's fears about meeting our survival, safety and security needs and fully embracing our soul's desires for self-expression, connection and contribution. Table 13.12 summarizes the physiological disorders that are linked with difficulties in mastering the different stages of development.

Table 13.12: Stages of development and the onset of physiological disorders.

Stage of psychological development	Physiological disorders
Serving	Alzheimer's disease, strokes and Parkinson's disease
Integrating	Prostate cancer and ovarian cancer
Self-actualizing	Breast cancer, respiratory disorders
Individuating	Heart disease
Differentiating	Liver disease, diabetes, obesity, anorexia nervosa and bulimia nervosa
Conforming	Mostly psychological disorders
Surviving	Mostly psychological disorders and SIDS

My profound hope is that the insights gained by linking psychology with physiology can contribute to a greater understanding of the root causes of physiological disorders, and that by attending to psychological disorders early in life we can increase the level of psychological and physiological well-being later in life.

A summary of key points

Here are the main points of Chapter 13.

1. My hypothesis is that physiological dysfunctions associated with difficulties in mastering a particular stage of psychological development start to become significant 5–10 years after the start of that stage of development and peak 10–15 years later.
2. According to the United Nations, the top three leading causes of death in the world are heart disease (7.4 million per year), stroke (6.7 million per year) and lung disease (3.1 million per year).
3. Because of the linkages that exist between the lower (ego) and upper (soul) etheric, emotional and mental fields, when you reach the upper (soul) stages of development any weakness or impairment in your ability to meet the needs of the corresponding lower (ego) stage of development may put additional pressure (instability) on the lower etheric, emotional or mental layers of the energy field causing physiological dysfunctions at those levels.
4. The leading causes of death associated with the serving stage of psychological development are related to dysfunctions of the brain.
5. The leading causes of death associated with the integrating stage of psychological development are prostate cancer and ovarian cancer.
6. The leading causes of death associated with the self-actualizing stage of psychological development are breast cancer and lung disease.
7. The leading cause of death associated with the individuating stage of psychological development is heart disease.
8. The leading causes of death associated with the differentiating stage of psychological development are liver disease and diabetes.
9. There are no leading causes of death associated with the conforming stage of psychological development.
10. The leading cause of death associated with the surviving stage of psychological development is Sudden Infant Death Syndrome.

11. Cancer is not primarily a developmental issue but a more of an existential issue; a profound inability to prioritize the desires of the soul. For this reason, most cancer dysfunctions do not tend to show up until we reach the second half of our lives.
12. The risk of cancer increases considerably if the immune system has been compromised by repeated difficulties in meeting our survival, safety or security needs.

References and notes

1. Michael A. Lerner, *Choices of Healing: Integrating the best of conventional and complementary approaches to cancer* (Boston: MIT Press), 1994, p. 137.
2. WHO, Health Statistics.
3. In theosophy, a branch of esoteric philosophy, the pineal gland is called the third eye. It is through this "eye" that we access our soul potential and the higher states of consciousness.
4. Dementia, also known as senility, is a broad category of brain diseases that cause long-term and gradual decrease in the ability to think and remember.
5. Norman Cousins, *Anatomy of an Illness* (New York: W. W. Norton & Co.), 1979, p.53.
6. Ibid., p. 79.
7. George E. Vaillant, *The Wisdom of the Ego* (Boston: Harvard University Press), 1993, p. 223.
8. Ibid., p. 224.
9. http://www.alz.org/facts/downloads/facts_figures_2015.pdf
10. Dementia: A public priority, WHO, 2012.
11. Exocrine glands secrete their products into ducts that finish up outside of the body, whereas endocrine glands secrete their products into the bloodstream.
12. University of Toronto. *Link Between Childhood Physical Abuse and Heart Disease.* Science Daily, 23 July 2010.
13. University of Toronto. *Childhood Sexual Abuse Linked to Later Heart Attacks in Men.* Science Daily, 6 September 2012.
14. http://www.lifeclinic.com/fullpage.aspx?prid=521310&type=1

15. http://www.anad.org/get-information/about-eating-disorders/eating-disorders-statistics
16. Marilyn Lawrence, *The Anorexic Mind* (London: Karnac), 2008, p. 7.
17. Marilyn Lawrence, *Anorexic Nervosa—The Control Paradox.* Women's Studies International Quarterly, 2: 93-101.
18. Marilyn Lawrence, *The Anorexic Mind* (London: Karnac), 2008, p. 8.
19. Ibid., p. 9.
20. Marilyn Lawrence, *The Anorexic Mind* (London: Karnac), 2008.
21. Michael A. Lerner, *Choices of Healing: Integrating the best of conventional and complementary approaches to cancer* (Boston: MIT Press), 1994, p. 21.
22. Article, Nature Communications, *Evolutionary Instability in Zero-determinant Strategies Demonstrates that Winning is not Everything,* by Christophe Adami and Arend Hintze, published 1 August 2013.

14

SUICIDE AND THE STAGES OF DEVELOPMENT

Taking your life is the ultimate coping mechanism. When you can no longer bear the pain of living, you can choose to opt out. The majority of people who commit suicide do so when they have given up hope of getting their needs met. Suicide is the ego's way of aborting the soul's desire to experience 3-D awareness.

In the last chapter, I explored the link between difficulties in mastering the stages of psychological development and the onset of physical disorders. I came to the conclusion that to achieve optimum physical health we must learn to let go of our ego's fears about meeting our survival, safety and security needs and fully embrace our soul's desires for self-expression, connection and contribution. In this chapter, I want to explore the link between the stages of psychological development and the incidence of suicide.

When we think of suicide, we often think of failure; a failure to master the vicissitudes of life. But this is not the whole story. It is not just the failure to master everyday living that causes people to take their lives. There are many other reasons. The terminally ill take their lives to avoid the pain involved in the dying process; others take their lives as an act of revenge. In Japan, the practice of Seppuku (Hara-kiri) is a ritualized form of suicide first practiced by Samurai warriors as a means of atonement. In more recent years Hara-kiri has been practiced as a form of protest. Suicide bombers take their lives for the glory of their God.

My intent in this chapter is not to cover the gamut of causes of suicide but instead to limit my focus to suicide as a means of overcoming the psychological pain involved in struggling and failing to meet the needs associated with the stages of psychological development. When we keep on struggling but fail to meet our needs, there comes a point in time where we lose hope, feel trapped, and see no other way to cope with our pain other than taking our life.

From this perspective, suicide represents the ultimate coping mechanism—the last form of control we have in our lives—after all other forms of control are taken from us. Even when we cannot control anything else in our lives, the one thing we can control is whether we live or die; whether or not we end the soul's experiment of attempting to experience life in a 3-D material world.

In focusing on the struggles we have to master at the different stages of development as a cause of suicide, I recognize that I am neglecting the important topic of suicide as a way of coping with the pain of Post-Traumatic Stress Disorder (PTSD). Suicide linked to PTSD can occur at any time in our lives, usually several years after the trauma has occurred. For this reason, suicide as a response to the pain of PTSD does not have a direct link to the stages of psychological development. What I am suggesting instead is that suicide linked to PTSD is caused by a crisis associated with a failure to make meaning of death, torture or significant physical abuse: issues related to our greatest existential fears.

Existential psychologists identify four causes of internal conflict; death, freedom, isolation and meaninglessness. PTSD usually involves two of these conflicts: a confrontation with death and the meaninglessness of life.[1]

My hypothesis

The basic hypothesis I want to test in this chapter is as follows:

> The majority of people who commit suicide do so when they can no longer bear the pain associated with the struggle to get their needs met at the stage of development they have reached.

I would like to suggest that it is not the hopelessness of their struggle to meet their needs, that causes people to commit suicide but their sense of *entrapment in the hopelessness of not getting their needs met.*

The Integrated Motivational-Volitional Model

The Integrated Motivational-Volitional (IMV) Model of suicidal behaviour[2] developed by Rory O'Connor at the Suicidal Behaviour Research Laboratory at the University of Glasgow suggests that there are three phases to suicide—the pre-motivational phase, the motivational phase, and the volitional phase.

- Phase 1: The pre-motivational phase concerns the background factors such as a pre-disposition to suicide, a lack of supporting environment and significant negative life events.
- Phase 2: The motivational phase concerns thinking about committing suicide and the development of intent. These thoughts are brought on by defeat, humiliation and entrapment.
- Phase 3: The volitional phase concerns the actual suicidal behaviour.

Phase 1: Pre-motivation

From a developmental perspective, the pre-motivational phase concerns the imprints, schema and beliefs we learned about our inability to get our needs met while the reptilian-mind/brain (body-mind), limbic mind/brain (emotional mind) and the neocortex mind/brain (rational mind) were forming. In other words, the memories of the struggles we had trying to get our needs met during the surviving, conforming and differentiating stages of psychological development can set us up for the experience of hopelessness in our adult lives. If we struggled to get our needs met when we were young, we will have a storehouse of painful memories that can be triggered whenever we come across similar situations in our adult life. If we did not have to struggle to get our needs met while we were young, we will not have such painful memories.

Phase 2: Motivation

The motivational phase concerns the struggles we have in getting our needs met at the stage of development we have reached. If we continually struggle and fail to get our needs met, the pain of the memories of similar situations will heighten our feeling of not being able to cope and increase the feeling of hopelessness and sense of entrapment.

Phase 3: Volition

The volitional phase only comes into play if the pain of not getting our needs met becomes overwhelming. At this stage, other factors come into play. Chief among them is our impulsivity, ability to plan the suicide, and access to the means of committing suicide, such as guns, poison, etc.

Above all other factors, researchers have found that a high pain tolerance and a high pain threshold correlate strongly with suicide risk. One would think just the opposite: A high pain tolerance and threshold for pain would make us more resilient. It is *because* we have experienced a lot of pain in the past that these indicators are elevated. We have become practiced at tolerating and concealing our pain. That does not make the pain less bearable.

Having identified the factors that influence suicide risk, let us now take a look at how these factors relate to the stages of psychological development.

Suicide and the stages of psychological development

Stage 1: The surviving stage

This stage of development, which occurs from the moment we are born to the time we reach the age of 2, contributes to the pre-motivational stage of the IMV model. Any experiences of not being cared for or nurtured during this period (while the reptilian mind/brain is growing and developing) that causes an imprint to form in our body-mind that struggling to get our survival needs met is useless (learned hopelessness), can significantly weaken our resolve to keep on battling when times are hard, thereby compromising our ability to cope with life's vicissitudes and weaken our resolve to keep on trying to express ourselves at the self-actualizing stage of development.

Stage 2: The conforming stage

This stage of development, which occurs from age 2 to 7, also contributes to the pre-motivational stage of the IMV model. Any experiences of not feeling loved or accepted during this period (while the limbic mind/brain is growing and developing), that causes limiting beliefs to form in our emotional mind, that struggling to get our safety needs met is useless, can significantly weaken our resolve to keep on trying to build loving relationships and compromise our ability to meet our soul's desire for connection at the integrating stage of development.

Stage 3: The differentiating stage

This stage of development, which occurs from age 8 to mid-20s, can contribute to the pre-motivational stage or the motivational stage of the IMV model. Any experiences we have during this period that causes limiting beliefs to form about our ability meet our security (self-esteem) needs, can affect our ability to be respected and recognized by our peers and compromise our ability to meet our soul's desire for contribution at the serving stage of development.

Stage 4: The individuating stage

This stage of development, which occurs from mid-20s to late-30s, contributes to the motivational stage of the IMV model. Any dependencies we have or events that block or prevent us from finding the freedom and autonomy we need to explore who we are can significantly increase the risk of suicide at this stage of development.

Stage 5: The self-actualizing stage

This stage of development, which occurs in the 40s, contributes to the motivational stage of the IMV model. At this stage of development, we are attempting to satisfy the soul's desire for self-expression. Any dependencies or obligations we feel we have towards others that prevent us from finding our meaning and purpose in life significantly increase the risk of suicide at this stage of development. These difficulties in satisfying our soul's desire for self-expression can be exacerbated by any limiting beliefs we have about being able to meet our survival needs.

Stage 6: The integrating stage

This stage of development, which occurs in the 50s, contributes to the motivational stage of the IMV model. At this stage of development, we are attempting to satisfy the soul's desire for connection. Any limiting beliefs we formed during the conforming stage of development about not feeling safe or not feeling loved will make it difficult to connect with others at the integrating stage of development and increase our sense of loneliness. Loneliness does not arise from not having people around, but from holding back, not communicating what is important to you or having views that you feel others cannot accept.

Stage 7: The serving stage

This stage of development, which occurs from the 60s onwards, contributes to the motivational stage of the IMV model. At this stage of development, we are attempting to satisfy the soul's desire for contribution. Any limiting beliefs we formed during the differentiating stage of development about not feeling secure or not feeling respected or recognized will make it difficult to contribute at the serving stage of development and increase our sense of isolation. Isolation does not arise from failing to connect, but from not reaching out and offering to make your skills, gifts and talents available for the well-being of others.

Based on this, we can identify seven key developmental factors that contribute to the risk of suicide. These are learned hopelessness, lack of love for self, lack of recognition, lack of freedom, lack of self-expression (meaning), lack of connection (loneliness) and lack of contribution (isolation). Let's now see how these factors play out in the incidence of suicide in the UK, Sweden and US.

Incidence of suicide in the United Kingdom

The data I am using to look at the incidence of suicide in the UK is based on a survey carried out by the UK Office of National Statistics (ONS) in 2012. The results of this survey are shown in Figure 14.1. Superimposed on this figure are the time periods of the different stages of psychological development.

What is immediately noticeable is that the incidence of suicide increases significantly in the early 20s and again in the early 40s—at the end of the differentiating stage, and at the end of individuating stages of psychological development. The peak incidence occurs in the self-actualizing stage of development. After that the incidence of suicide decreases during the integrating and serving stages of development.

Figure 14.1: Incidence of suicide in the UK by age and gender in 2012.

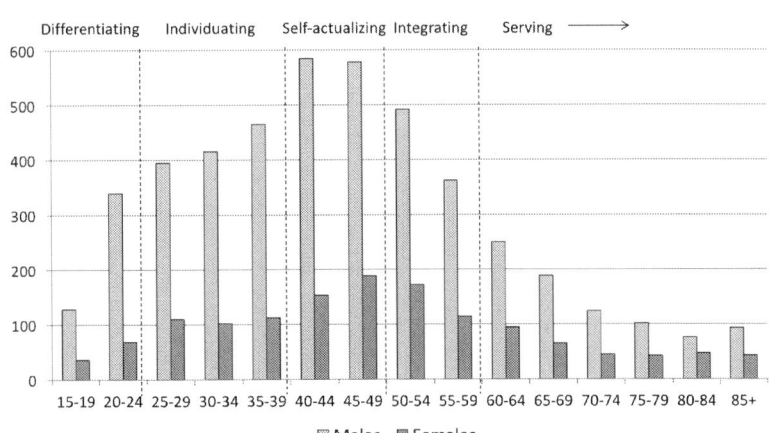

Source: The Office of National Statistics, UK.

The incidence of suicide among males is significantly higher than females, particularly during the late differentiating stage, the individuating stage and the start of the self-actualizing stages of development. These differences raise some important questions about how boys and young men are raised compared to how girls and young women are raised.

In the UK,[3] the highest number of suicides for males is in the 40–44 range, indicating a failure to master the individuating stage of psychological development. The full impact of a failure to master a stage of development usually takes place during the latter part of a stage or the early part of the following stage. For females the age range with the most suicides is slightly higher, the 50–54 range, indicating a failure to master the self-actualizing stage of psychological development.

In other words, generally speaking, males have more difficulty individuating—freeing themselves from their cultural dependencies—while females have more difficulty self-actualizing, expressing who they are at the core of their being so they can fulfil their soul's desire for self-expression. This correlates with the increased incidence of deaths from breast cancer and respiratory problems at the self-actualizing stage of development shown in Figures 13.10 and 13.11.

When we break the UK data down by country—England, Scotland, Wales and Northern Ireland—and gender, we see some interesting differences (see Table 14.1) in suicide rates.

Table 14.1: Highest suicide rates by age range and gender for UK countries in 2012.

Nation	Male Age range (years)	Female Age range (years)
England	40–44	45–49
Scotland	35–44	45–49 and 50–54
Wales	30–34	30–34
Northern Ireland	25–29	50–54

Source: Suicide Statistics Report 2014, Samaritans based ONS data.

As far as males are concerned, the age range with the highest suicide rate in Northern Ireland is 25–29 years, in Wales it is 30–34 years; in Scotland it is 35–44 years, and in England, it is 40–44 years. All of these age ranges, except the one for Northern Ireland, are indicative of a failure to master the individuating stage of psychological development. In Northern Ireland, the 25–29 age range is indicative of a failure to master the differentiating stage.

As far as females are concerned, the age range with the highest suicide rate in Wales is 30–34 years, in Scotland it is 45–54 years, in England it is 45–49 years, and in Northern Ireland, it is 50–54 years. All of these age ranges, except the one for Wales, are indicative of a failure to master the self-actualizing stage of psychological development. In Wales, the 30–34 age range is indicative of a failure to master the individuating stage of development.

I believe the differences speak volumes about the specific challenges that men and women are facing in their respective countries. Why is it that young men in Northern Ireland have great difficulty in mastering the differentiating stage of psychological development, becoming a member of a community where they can be respected and recognized? Why is it that young females in Wales have great difficulty in mastering the individuating stage of psychological development, finding the autonomy they need to let go of their parental and cultural dependencies? In other words, what needs do these two groups have that are not being met in their countries?

Young men in Northern Ireland

A study involving teenagers in Northern Ireland[4] found the key issue was finding a sense of collective identity: the fundamental issue in differentiating. A failure to differentiate means that we are unable to establish ourselves in a group we resonate with where we feel respected and recognized.

What provokes this issue in Northern Ireland is sectarianism. Sectarianism is a form of discrimination or hatred arising from overly attached importance to differences, such as religious affiliations.

Discussions with young people involved in the Northern Ireland study revealed a strong sense of "us and them" or "our area and their area". Young males, more so than young females, feel they are being forced to differentiate themselves from others in a manner that does not align with who they are. This enforced differentiation into one of two groups—Protestant or Catholic, neither of which they fundamentally identify with—causes them to feel trapped, unable to affiliate with a group that respects and recognises who they are. Because of this failure to meet the needs of the differentiating stage of development, their risk of suicide increases.

Many participants in the study were critical about the negative impact that parents and other significant adults had on the formation of their attitudes towards other groups. The great majority of participants said that schools should be integrated to give young people the chance to mix with others from different socio-religious backgrounds from an early age, but that integration should be by choice rather than forced.

Young women in Wales

A study by a women's charity (Platform 51)[5] found that 53 percent of young women and girls in Wales report mental health problems. Thirty-five percent of women experiencing such problems have taken at least a week off work; 22 percent have self-harmed, and 33 percent have lost friends as a result of their issues. The research also found two-thirds did not leave their homes for long periods, 20 percent regularly got drunk, and one in six had built up debt.

The key issue for these young women is their inability to find gainful employment. Because they can't find jobs, they are not able to experience the freedom and autonomy necessary to individuate. This makes them feel helpless, useless and trapped. Consequently, their will to live—to stay present in our physical reality—is weakened.

Incidence of suicide in Sweden

The incidence of suicide in Sweden follows a similar pattern to the UK, except the two peaks—at the end or the differentiating and self-actualizing stages—are more pronounced (see Figure 14.2). The incidence of suicide in males falls significantly during the individuating stage of development. The imbalance in the ratio of male to female suicides is less pronounced in Sweden than in the UK. This may be due to the greater gender equality that exists in Sweden.

Figure 14.2: Incidence of suicide in Sweden by age and gender in 2012.

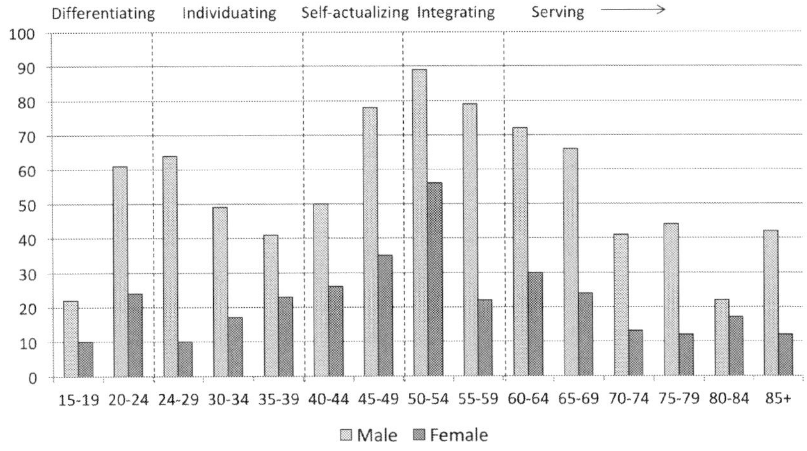

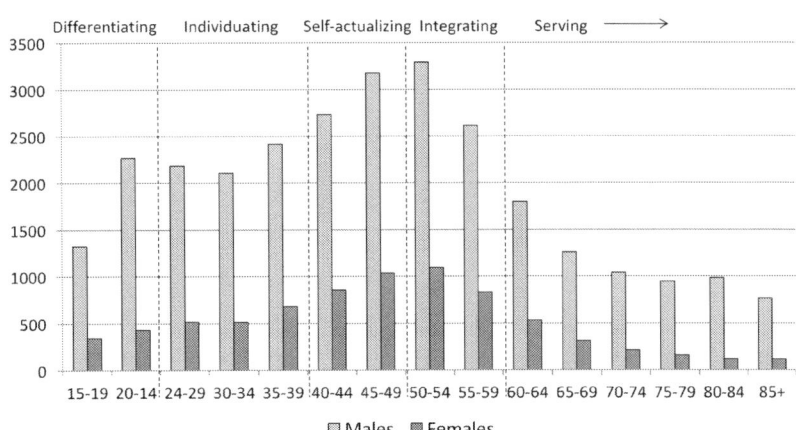

Source: National Board of Health and Welfare, Sweden.

Incidence of suicide in the United States

The results of a survey on suicide by the National Centre for Injury Prevention and Control in 2009 are shown in Figure 14.3. Superimposed on this figure are the different stages of psychological development. The incidence of suicide in the US is similar to Sweden and the UK.

Figure 14.3: Incidence of suicide in the US by age and gender in 2009.

Source: National Centre for Injury Prevention and Control.

The number of deaths by suicide in white US males shows two peaks. The first peak, which occurs in the 20s, represents a struggle to differentiate. The second peak, which occurs in the early 50s, represents a struggle to self-actualize. Between the peaks, the incidence of suicide increases in the late 30s and early 40s, indicating a failure to individuate. As in the UK, the incidence of suicide decreases through the integrating and serving stages of development. After accidents, suicide represents the second leading cause of death at the differentiating and individuating stages of development in the US.

What is also similar between the US and the UK data is that the incidence of suicide among males is significantly higher than females. This imbalance is at its greatest during the differentiating stage. Unlike males, there are no significant peaks in the incidence of suicide among females, just a steady increase up to the early 50s.

Young veterans in the United States

In recent years, the number of young veterans under the age of 30 committing suicide has jumped dramatically: a 44 percent increase in a decade.[6] On average, two young veterans take their lives every day. The National Mental Health Director for Suicide Prevention says the reasons are unclear; they suggest it could be due to a number of factors: readjusting to civilian life, combat injuries and PTSD may all play a role.

It is interesting to note that the increase in suicides applies just as much to young male veterans who were in combat zones as those who were not in combat zones, suggesting trauma may only be part of the reason for the high prevalence of suicide among young veterans. Young female veterans also saw an 11 percent rise in suicides in recent years.

Based on these facts, I believe the high incidence of suicide among young veterans, especially those who did not experience combat—do not suffer from PTSD—is linked to the difficulties they have in mastering the differentiating stage of development, in particular, the reintegration into civilian life.

Most young men enter the military in the late teens or early 20s and come out again a few years later. While they are in the military, they are part of a structured community. They are cared for and usually form part of a cohesive team where each member is dependent on the other members for their success. They become part of group where they have an identity and feel respected and recognized. This is reinforced by a strong "us"—the team—and "them"—the enemy—attitude.

When they leave the military, they no longer form part of a close-knit team. Their lives become unstructured and they lose their community. They need to find a new sense of identity, and a new community where they feel respected and recognized. For many, this proves to be difficult. This failure leads them to consider suicide.

Suicides among gifted writers

In her book, *The Body Never Lies*, Alice Miller (1923-2010), makes the point that the early suppression of a child's inborn talents leads to suicide when these people reach their 40s and 50s: the self-actualizing stage of psychological development.[7]

I described in Chapter 4 how Miller describes the abusive childhoods of ten writers who lived between the mid-eighteenth and the mid-twentieth centuries, all of whom committed suicide in middle age or shortly thereafter. Table 14.2 lists these writers, describes their sufferings, and the relationship they had with their parents or immediate family.

In all cases, the people concerned had childhoods filled with fear: either fear for their survival or fear for their safety. Additionally, most, but not all, had their creative impulses systematically suppressed by their parents. The memory of their fears and the pain of their struggles to survive and feel safe as children created such inner conflicts that when they reached the individuating, self-actualizing and integrating stages of their development—the stages of freedom, self-expression and connection—they could not go on with their lives.

Table 14.2: Suicides among gifted writers.

Writer	Age at death	Physical and mental sufferings	Quality of relationship to immediate family
Arthur Rimbaud	37	Bone cancer in the leg	Harsh and brutal mother Suppression of self-expression

Franz Kafka	41	Lonely, depressed, suicidal. Died of tuberculosis	Abusive father
Anton Chekov	44	Tuberculosis	Abusive father
Yukio Mishima	45	Not known	Self-expression suppressed by grandmother and father
Friedrich von Schiller	46	Suffered in youth from several complaints such as painful convulsions and cramps	Abusive father. Suppression of self-expression
Marcel Proust	51	Asthma	Controlling and over powering mother
Friedrich Nietzsche	56	Suffered in youth from rheumatism, severe headaches, many other complaints	Abusive parents
Virginia Woolf	59	Committed suicide after experiencing depressive states	Sexual abuse at hands of half-brothers
James Joyce	59	Eye problems	Violent and abusive alcoholic father
Fyodor Dostoevsky	60	Insomnia, nightmares, epileptic fits, addiction to gambling	Brutal and abusive father

Suicide in old age

A variety of factors has been implicated in suicidal behaviour in elderly people. These can be broadly described as psychological, physical, and social factors.

Psychological factors

According to psychological autopsy studies of suicides in elderly people, 71–95 percent of them had a major psychiatric disorder at the time of death.[8] Depressive disorders are by far, the most common diagnosis. Elderly people who die as a result of suicide have been shown to have higher levels of neuroticism, lower scores for openness to experience, and a restricted range of interests.[9]

Physical factors

In a study involving residents of a nursing home aged over 85, researchers found that having multiple physical disorders is predictive of increased suicidal feelings and a wish to die. The death wish was also found to be associated with older patients attending their general practitioner for depression, anxiety and at-risk alcohol abuse.[10]

Social factors

Decreased social support and social isolation are associated with increased suicidal feelings in elderly people.[11] Other studies suggest that loneliness and low social interaction are predictive of suicide.[12] In general, widowed, single and divorced elderly people have a higher risk of suicide, with marriage seeming to be protective. Bereavement is also associated with attempted and completed suicide in elderly people: men seem especially vulnerable to the loss of a spouse, their relative risk of suicide being three times that of married men.

Religiosity and life satisfaction have been found to be protective factors against suicidal ideation. Similar findings are reported in the terminally-ill, where higher spiritual well-being and life satisfaction predicted lower suicidal feelings.[13]

Conclusion

This brief overview of suicide and the stages of psychological development shows, I believe, a strong correlation between a failure to meet the needs associated with specific stages of psychological development and the taking of one's life. This correlation is particularly noticeable among young people who are attempting to differentiate, young adults who are attempting to individuate, and people in their 40s who are attempting to self-actualize.

A summary of key points

Here are the main points of Chapter 14:

1. Suicide represents the ultimate coping mechanism, the ultimate form of control we have over lives. Even when we cannot control anything else, the one thing we can control is whether we live or die; whether or not we end the soul's experiment of attempting to experience life in a body in three-dimensional physical awareness.
2. People commit suicide when they can no longer bear the pain associated with not getting their needs met at the stage of development they have reached.
3. It is not the hopelessness of their struggle to meet their needs that causes people to commit suicide, but their sense of entrapment in the hopelessness.
4. The Integrated Motivational-Volitional (IMV) model of suicidal behaviour suggests that there are three phases to suicide: the pre-motivational phase, the motivational phase, and the volitional phase.
5. The surviving stage of development contributes to the pre-motivational stage of the IMV model.
6. The conforming stage of development contributes to the pre-motivational stage of the IMV model.
7. The differentiating stage of development, which occurs from age 8 to mid-20s, can contribute to the pre-motivational stage or the motivational stage of the IMV model. At this stage of development, a lack of recognition and respect significantly increases the risk of suicide.
8. The individuating stage of development, which occurs from mid-20s to late-30s, contributes to the motivational stage of the IMV model. At this stage of development, a lack of freedom and autonomy significantly increases the risk of suicide.
9. The self-actualizing stage of development, which occurs in the 40s, contributes to the motivational stage of the IMV model. At this stage of development, a lack of meaning and purpose significantly increases the risk of suicide.
10. The integrating stage of development, which occurs in the 50s, contributes to the motivational stage of the IMV model. At this

stage of development, loneliness significantly increases the risk of suicide.
11. The serving stage of development, which occurs from the 60s onwards, contributes to the motivational stage of the IMV model. At this stage of development, isolation significantly increases the risk of suicide.

References and notes

1. Irvin D. Yalom, *Existential Psychotherapy* (New York: Basic Books), 1938.
2. Rory C. O'Connor, Stephen Platt and Jacki Gordon, *Towards an Integrated Motivational-Volitional Model of Suicidal Behaviour*, International Handbook of Suicide Prevention (London: Wiley and Sons), 2011.
3. http://www.samaritans.org/sites/default/files/kcfinder/files/research/Samaritans%20Suicide%20Statistics%20Report%202014.pdf
4. http://www.ofmdfmni.gov.uk/voices.pdf
5. http://www.bbc.co.uk/news/uk-wales-12156198
6. http://www.stripes.com/report-suicide-rate-spikes-among-young-veterans-1.261283
7. Alice Miller, *The Body Never Lies: The Lingering Effects of Hurtful Parenting* (New York: W. W. Norton & Company), 2006, pp.43–81.
8. Y. Conwell, P. R. Duberstein, E. D. Caine, *Risk Factors for Suicide in Later Life*. Biology and Psychiatry 2002; 52: 193–204.
9. P. R. Duberstein, Y. Conwell, E. D. Caine, *Age Differences in the Personality Characteristics of Suicide Completers: Preliminary findings from a psychological autopsy study*. Psychiatry 1994; 57: 213-24.
10. E. Rubenowitz, M. Waern, K. Wilelmson, P. Allbeck, *Life Events and Psychosocial Factors in Elderly Suicides—case-control study*. Psychol Med 2001, 31: 1193–1202.
11. J. M. Bertolote, A. Fleischmann, D. De Leo, D. Wasserman, *Suicide and Mental Disorders: Do we know enough?* Br J Psychiatry 2003, 183: 382–383.

12. H. F. Chiu, P. S. Yip, I. Chi, S. Chan, J. Tsoh, C. W. Kwan, et al. *Elderly Suicide in Hong Kong: A case-controlled psychological autopsy study.* Acta Psychiatr Scand 2004, 109: 299–305.
13. C. S. McClain, B. Rosenfeld, W. Breitbart, *Effect of Spiritual Wellbeing on End of Life Despair in Terminally Ill Cancer Patients.* Lancet 2003, 361: 1603–1607.

15

A MODEL OF HUMAN WELL-BEING

> *The root of all well-being lies in the ability to master the tasks involved at each stage of psychological development. You can only begin to flourish when you can give full attention to your soul's desire for self-expression, connection and contribution. We arrive at the pinnacle of flourishing when we can recreate our soul's 4-D reality in 3-D awareness.*

My original purpose in writing this book was to explore Maslow's idea of a larger jurisdiction for psychology: the possibility of building a theory of human well-being that unites science, psychology and spirituality, a theory that integrates body, mind and soul. I believe my investigation turned out to be much more. By finding linkages between the stages of psychological development, the human energy system and the chakras, I believe I have been able to make a contribution to bringing together Western psychology with Eastern medicine.

The theory of human well-being I am proposing, postulates:

1. Humans beings are 4-D energetic souls attempting to live in 3-D material bodies. In reality, our physical bodies are the soul's energy templates viewed through the lens of 3-D material awareness.
2. The soul's purpose in incarnating (willing itself to be present in the 3-D material awareness) is to recreate its 4-D energetic reality in 3-D material awareness. This is sometimes referred to in religious circles as "creating Heaven on Earth".
3. The physical body, which is the soul's energy template, is kept "alive" in 3-D material awareness by an entity known as the

body-mind represented in material awareness by the reptilian mind/brain. The reptilian mind/brain keeps the body alive through a biological process called homeostasis. In 4-D terms, the purpose of homeostasis is to keep the soul's energy template in energetic balance.
4. The soul's three main desires—to fully express its character, connect with others and contribute to the good of humanity—are dependent on the ego's ability to master the surviving, conforming and differentiating stages of psychological development.
5. The learning that is necessary to master these stages of development primarily takes place while the reptilian mind/brain, the limbic mind/brain and neocortex mind/brain are forming and developing.
6. The ego is created by the soul to protect it from the pain (energetic instabilities) it experiences in being in 3-D material awareness.

The energetic instabilities experienced by the soul-mind during its time in the womb, during the birth process, and in the first two years of life, have two sources: physiological pain—the energetic instability experienced by the body-mind when it struggles to maintain homeostatic functioning, and psychological pain—the energetic instability experienced by the body-mind and soul-mind when they struggle to make meaning of the discomforting sensations we call physiological pain.

Around the age of 2 years, shortly after the limbic mind/brain becomes dominant, and the soul begins to feel the pain of separation, when the child realizes that it is no longer living in a state of undifferentiated oneness the soul begins to create the ego to act as a buffer to the energetic instability it is experiencing from being in 3-D material awareness.

The ego-mind protects the soul from the psychological pain involved in being in a physical body in a material world of separation by attempting to provide the soul with a fear-free physical, social and cultural framework of existence from which it can fulfil its desire to recreate its 4-D reality in 3-D material awareness.

When the ego-mind finds it difficult to cope with the pain involved in trying to get its survival, safety and security needs met—the needs that must be met to create a secure foundation for the soul to be fully present in 3-D awareness—the conscious awareness of the ego-mind becomes impaired. To minimize this impairment, the dominant ego-mind (emotional mind or rational mind) represses the pain it is experiencing to its subconscious.

This allows the dominant ego-mind to stay focused on meeting the body's survival needs, the emotional mind's safety needs and the rational mind's security needs, thereby supporting the foundational requirement of the soul to maintain its presence in 3-D material awareness.

Although the pain repressed by the dominant ego-mind is no longer in conscious awareness, it does not go away. The energetic instability associated (pain) stays present in the layers of the ego's energy field that correspond to the survival, relationship or self-esteem levels of consciousness, in the ego-mind's subconscious and unconscious.

The energetic instabilities associated with the ego's unmet survival needs are stored in the lower etheric energy field: the field that relates to the operation of the body-mind and the rational mind's unconscious. The energetic instabilities associated with the ego's unmet relationship (safety) needs are stored in the lower emotional field: the field that relates to the operation of emotional mind and the rational mind's subconscious. The energetic instabilities associated with the ego's unmet self-esteem needs (security) are stored in the lower mental field: the field that relates to the operation the ego's rational mind.

If the energetic instabilities that are stored in the conscious, subconscious or unconscious are not allowed to dissipate—if they are denied, not felt or do not find an emotional outlet—they will show up as mental disorders or physical disorders later in life, first as mental disorders and then as physical disorders. Physical disorders show up later than mental disorders because it takes more time for the energetic instabilities to manifest in the 3-D material world of the body than it does for them to affect the functioning of the conscious awareness of the 4-D energetic mind.

The mental disorders that show up are linked to the level of consciousness and layer of the energy field where the energetic instability is stored, and the physical disorders that show up are linked to the parts of the anatomy that are associated with the chakra that serves the layer of the energy field where the energetic instabilities are stored.

The most significant impact that energetic instability has on our lives occurs during the periods when the reptilian mind/brain (body-mind), the limbic mind/brain (emotional mind) and neocortex mind/brain (rational mind) are growing and developing, between 0–2 years, 3–7 years, and 8–24 years respectively. Of these, the period when the reptilian mind/brain is forming is the most critical because it affects the regulation of our endocrine system and the regulation of the body's organs.

There are two reasons the impact of energetic instability is greatest during the formation of the reptilian mind/brain. First, the reptilian mind/brain is the least sophisticated of the three mind/brains and has the greatest struggle making meaning of the experiences it has when it fails to get its needs met. Hence, the experience of pain during this stage of development is more frequent and acute. Second, the needs associated with survival are significantly more important to supporting the soul in its desire to be present in the 3-D material awareness than the needs associated with safety and security. Hence, the pain (fear and anger) experienced during the first two years of our lives and the time spent in the womb is more severe.

The next most critical period is between 2 and 7 years when the limbic mind/brain is attempting to get its relationship needs met so we can keep safe. The limbic mind/brain is more sophisticated than the reptilian mind/brain but less sophisticated than the rational mind/brain. Consequently, it struggles less to make meaning than the reptilian mind/brain.

Therefore, the struggles we have in getting our survival and safety needs met during our time in the womb, the birth process and from the moment we are born up to the age of about 7 years have the most impact on the imprints and beliefs we create about how to survive and stay safe later in life.

There is a significant amount of evidence to suggest that the most severe mental disorders—clinical and personality disorders, and the most severe physical disorders—coronary heart disease and cancer, can be traced back to these two periods in our lives. These are the periods when we are engaged in rapid emergent learning, when the synapses are forming in our brains, when our meaning-making is least sophisticated and when the fears we have are the greatest.

To understand the source of our energetic instability and the subsequent psychological and physiological disorders that follow, we must unite several branches of psychology, and also unite psychology with spirituality and with science.

Unifying psychological approaches

The branches of psychology that the new psychological theory of human well-being begins to unite are:

- Certain aspects of psychoanalytical psychology.
- Developmental Psychology.
- Existential Psychology.
- Humanistic Psychology.
- Phenomenological Psychology.
- Transpersonal Psychology.

Psychoanalytical psychology

Psychoanalytical Psychology was the first modern psychology. This approach encourages the individual to express verbally his or her thoughts, through free associations, fantasies and dreams. Based on these thoughts and images, the analyst infers the unconscious conflicts that are causing the individual's symptoms and character issues. The new psychology of human well-being recognizes the role played by subconscious and unconscious conflicts in creating psychological disorders.

Developmental psychology

Developmental psychology is the scientific study of how and why human beings develop over the course of their life. Originally concerned with infants and children, the field has expanded to include adolescence, adult development and ageing. In particular, it examines the influences of nature and nurture on the process of human development. Of all the psychologies, this is the one that is most focused on stages of development. The new psychology of human well-being is based on a particular interpretation of developmental psychology, which I refer to as the ego-soul dynamic.

Existential psychology

Existential psychology is a philosophical method of therapy that operates on the belief that inner conflict within a person is due to that individual's confrontation with the "givens" of material existence in a body. The existential givens are death, freedom and its attendant responsibility, isolation and meaninglessness. Of all the psychologies this is the one that is most focused on physical and material reality. The new psychology of human well-being recognizes the importance of meaning-making, isolation, death and freedom in creating psychological disorders.

Humanistic psychology

Humanistic psychology is an approach that emphasizes the individual's inherent drive towards self-realization; the process of realizing and expressing one's innate potential. This approach rose to prominence in response to the perceived limitations of the psychoanalytical theories of Sigmund Freud. Of all the psychologies, this is the one that is most focused on positive psychology. The new psychology of human well-being recognizes the fundamental importance of the drive to self-realization in expressing one's innate potential.

Phenomenological psychology

Phenomenological psychology is an intensely personal approach to psychology that focuses on the subjective experience; about how the individual feels about the events and situations that occur in his or her life and the subjective meaning the individual gives to these experiences. Feelings are regarded as the subjective experience of emotion. This approach has strong links to humanistic and existential psychology. The new psychology of human well-being recognizes the importance of subjective meaning-making and feelings in creating the patient's reality.

Transpersonal psychology

Transpersonal psychology is an approach that integrates the spiritual and transcendent aspects of human experience, in which the individual's sense of identity can expand beyond the normal material sense of self to include humanity, the planet and the cosmos. Of all the psychologies, this is the one that is most focused on spiritual development. By recognizing our essential soul nature, the new psychology of human well-being fully integrates "spiritual" development into the stages of psychological development.

Unifying spirituality with psychology

Although there is no single definition of spirituality, it is generally regarded as the unifying principle that brings together the world's religions. The traditional meaning of spirituality is a process of personal re-formation or transformation whereby an adherent to spiritual principles constantly seeks to attain "higher" levels of conscious awareness. This leads to a reunification with the originating force in the universe—with the soul and through the soul to the universal energy field referred to as the one-mind, which some refer to as God.

The term "higher" in this context means a more inclusive sense of identity. Whenever you assume a larger identity, your sense of self expands to include all those who share that identity. You will still be operating from self-interest, but the self that has the interest will have an expanded sense of identity.

For example, when you shift from being single to being married and have children, you expand your sense of identity to include your spouse and children; you identify with your family. When you find a job that you like, in an organization where you feel comfortable—one that supports your personal as well as your professional growth—you may expand your sense of identity to include the colleagues you work with. As you move into the realms of management or leadership, you may start to identify with the organization itself.

One of the most notable changes that occurs when we assume a higher level of identity is we start caring about the well-being of the members of the group we identify with. When you identify with your family, you care about the well-being of the members of your family. When you identify with a work team, you care about the well-being of the members of your team. When you identify with an organization, you care about the well-being of the members of your organization.

If you fail to care for the members of the group you belong to and stay primarily focused on your self-interest, you will find yourself ignored, marginalized or not included in the activities of the group. The group loses its cohesion, and you lose an aspect of your identity. When you identify with your soul, you identify with and care for the whole of humanity.

Another meaning we often give to "higher" in the context of consciousness is the ability to operate in increasingly complex frameworks of existence. As we progress from being babies to infants, to children, to teenagers, to young adults and then to mature adults the physical and social frameworks of our existence become increasingly larger and more complex. In order to successfully survive and thrive in larger, more complex environments, we must develop more complex minds; our minds must increase their breadth perception (knowledge) and increase their depth perception (understanding), not just about what is happening in our surroundings, but also about how we relate to ourselves and the members of the groups we identify with in our expanded framework of existence.

The moment we stop expanding our consciousness is the moment our life-force begins to close down. When we stop expanding our identity, we deny ourselves the possibility of experiencing the fullness of who we can become. The closing down and shrinking away of the soul's potential shows up in the physical body as a shrinking of the neocortex mind/brain, which leads to various forms of dementia, strokes and Parkinson's disease. The ultimate expansion of identity we can experience is our connection to the one-mind. We must identify with our soul before we can identify with the one-mind.

Some of the natural outcomes of being more inclusive, developing a more complex mind and expanding our identity, are that we increase our level of maturity; we learn to handle ambiguity, we begin to think in longer-term time horizons, and we become less fearful, less judging, and more trusting—more at ease with uncertainty.

Unifying science with psychology

It is widely recognized that science is associated with the evolutionary levels of organization that are found in nature. Physics, the study of the organization of atoms is the most basic level of organization. Chemistry, the study of the organization of molecules comes next. These are followed by biology, the study of the organization of cells and organs; physiology and psychology, the study of the organization of the outer and inner nature of human individuals; and sociology and culture, the study of the organization of the outer and inner nature of humans groups.

Each evolutionary level can be regarded as a plane of being. The energetic plane of being is explained by particle physics and quantum theory; the atomic plane is explained by chemistry; the cellular plane is explained by biology; the plane of creatures is explained by physiology and psychology at the individual level, and sociology and culture at the group level. Each plane of being provides a foundation on which the next plane of being can be built. The evolutionary planes of being and evolutionary scales of organization on each plane of being are shown in Table 15.1.

Table 15.1: Planes of being and scales of organization.

Planes of being	Scales of organization
Humanity	Human race
Creatures (Homo sapiens) Sociology Physiology	Regional groups and global groupings
	Bands, tribes, city-states, nations
	Human beings
Cellular Plane (Eukaryotic cell) Biology	Complex organisms
	Organisms
	Cells
Atomic Plane (Carbon atom) Chemistry	Complex molecules
	Molecules
	Atoms
Energetic Plane Quantum theory	Wave/particle duality

(Evolution ↑)

Each plane of being is divided into three sub-planes, each differentiated by scale and complexity of organization: the scale of existence and organization of an individual entity; the scale of existence and organization of the group structures that are formed when individual entities bond with each other; and the scale of existence and organization of groups of group structures that are formed when group structures cooperate with each other.

One of these higher order group structures thus formed then becomes the entity that acts as a foundation for the next plane of being. At the atomic plane, the entity that evolved to the next plane of being was the carbon atom; at the cellular plane, it was the eukaryotic cell; at the scale of being of creatures, it is *Homo sapiens*. Life, as we know it in our 3-D material world, is built on the foundations provided by energetic particles, carbon atoms, and eukaryotic cells.

Not only do these three entities exhibit higher levels of awareness and organization than their predecessors in the planes of being, the group structures and the groups of group structures they form, display higher levels of awareness and organization than their predecessors. The evolutionary progression we see in Table 15.1 does not just represent physical evolution; it also represents consciousness evolution or in human terms the evolution of "psychological" development. The schema of evolution shown in Table 15.1 raises several questions.

The first question is what is it about the carbon atom, the eukaryotic cell and *Homo sapiens* that make them the key links in the chain of evolution? The answer is as simple as it is profound: because the carbon atom, the eukaryotic cell and *Homo sapiens* all exhibit the highest propensity for bonding and cooperation among all the other entities that exist in their respective planes of being.

The second question, which builds on the first, is since each plane of being forms the foundation for the next higher order plane of being, and each organizational scale forms the foundation for the next higher order organizational scale, what happens when the operation of a plane of being or a level of organization is compromised? In other words, what happens when an entity loses its ability to bond and cooperate? When it becomes energetically unstable?

Once again, the answer is as simple as it is profound. The answer is: when the ability of an entity to bond and cooperate is compromised, the operation of that scale of being and all the higher order planes of being that depend on that scale of being is also compromised.

Issues of functioning at the cellular level in a human being will also compromise the functioning of the organ and the body the cell belongs to. For example, when cancer, which starts at the level of the individual cell, is left unchecked, it will eventually compromise the functioning of the organ it belongs to and the functioning of the whole entity at the physiological level.

The same is true at the level of the human individual. When an individual fails to bond and cooperate in a family or community setting, the functioning of the family or community is compromised. Similarly, when nations fail to cooperate, the functioning of higher order entities such as the United Nations or World Bank is compromised.

The third and fourth questions, which are perhaps the most important of all to our present inquiry, are as follows. What is the fundamental cause of the failure of physical entities—atoms, cells, and *Homo sapiens*—to bond and cooperate? How did the concept of bonding and cooperation arise in the first place?

To answer these questions, we must remember that every physical form and every physical group structure in the chain of 3-D material evolution—atoms, cells, creatures and their group structures—represents an energetic field in 4-D consciousness. Only when the "soul" of an entity takes on 3-D awareness does it perceive the energetic fields of other entities as 3-D material forms. In other words, what my 4-D soul perceives when it takes on 3-D awareness is the 3-D material aspect of the 4-D energetic fields of other souls. When our souls look at each other through the lenses of 3-D awareness they see physical bodies, when they look at each other through the lenses of 4-D awareness they see energy fields.

At the level of 4-D awareness, everything is connected: we are all individuated aspects of the same universal energy field. At the level of 3-D awareness, everything appears to be separate. What we perceive as bonding and cooperation in our 3-D reality is simply 4-D entities attempting to recreate their 4-D reality of connectedness in 3-D conscious awareness.

3-D physical evolution is the history of how souls, who chose to manifest in 3-D awareness, are attempting to recreate the reality they experience in 4-D awareness, a field of energetic connection that we refer to in our 3-D material world as a field of love. Love conquers all because it brings us into alignment with the energetic reality of our souls and the universal energy field.

Energy as the link to psychology

Viewed from this perspective, the Seven Stages of Psychological Development can be viewed as stages in the recovery of the 4-D reality of the soul in 3-D consciousness.

First, the soul wills itself into 3-D awareness where it creates an ego to protect itself from the pain of being in a body and the pain of separation. The ego, acting as protector of the soul, learns how to become viable and independent in the physical, the social and cultural framework of its 3-D material world and filters out its true identity—a soul—in the process. This occurs during the first three stages of psychological development.

To reconnect with the soul, the ego has to disembed itself from its material identity, let go of its false self and embrace its true self. It lets go of its false self at the individuating stage of development, and bonds with the soul (its true self) at the self-actualizing stage of development. The soul then attempts to recreate its 4-D reality by connecting and cooperating with other souls in communities at the integrating stage of psychological development and supporting other souls in their journey into 4-D awareness at the serving stage of development.

At each critical stage in this process, the key to success is energetic alignment: The energetic alignment of the ego with the soul, the energetic alignment of souls with other souls, and the energetic alignment of souls with the one-mind.

The only factor that prevents energetic alignment is fear. The only way to overcome fear is through trust. You overcome fear at the self-actualizing stage by learning to trust your soul; you overcome fear at the integrating stage by learning to connect with and trust others. When you have completed these stages of development, you are ready to trust the universe to supply all your needs.

If the energy of fear is present in any layer of the ego's energy field, then the ego will find it difficult to bond with the soul: the ego's energy field will not be in energetic alignment with the soul and the soul will not be able to cooperate with other souls. This is the work of the individuating stage of psychological development.

Psychological development is all about the energetic balancing and aligning of the layers of the human energy field. Wherever there is in energetic instability, there is a lack of energetic alignment due to the presence of fear. Wherever fear is present, there is the possibility of psychological and physiological disorders.

Redefining healing

In the 3-D materialistic approach to correcting physiological and psychological disorders, the focus is on restoring the patient back to health and *curing* the impairment of functioning that prevented the patient from leading a normal life.

In the 4-D energetic approach I am proposing here, the focus is on *healing* rather than curing. A successful healing intervention is focused on restoring the patient back to wholeness and releasing the energetic disturbances that are causing the ego-mind to be out of alignment with the soul-mind. You restore yourself back to wholeness when you overcome your sense of separation and establish energetic alignment between your ego and your soul. When you heal this split, by letting go of your fears and uniting your ego with your soul, you become one with your soul. In *Loyalty to Your Soul*, Ron and Mary Hulnick describe healing in the following way: "Healing is the application of loving to the places inside that hurt".[1]

In short, healing is about caring for the life of the soul. Caring for the life of the soul means three things: supporting the soul in fulfilling its desire to express its creativity and fulfil its potential; supporting the soul in developing unconditional loving connections; and supporting the soul in living a life of service for the good of humanity.

This approach is not new. It is as ancient as shamanism. Shamans were, and still are, spiritual healers.

> One of the deepest teachings of shamanic healers was that the shaman, to be of the greatest possible assistance to the patient should be less concerned with the maintenance of physical health and more concerned with the safeguarding the patient's soul.[2]

Caring for the soul results in the healing of the body because the physical body is the 3-D expression of the soul's 4-D energetic template.

Safeguarding the soul is also one of the central and common traditions of the perennial philosophy.[3] If you look towards safeguarding and expressing your unique character, expressing your unique gifts and talents, and making those gifts and talents available to the world, you will live a healthy and joyful life well into old age.

Redefining well-being

Based on the preceding, we now have a way of redefining human well-being that gets to the core of who we are. As I indicated earlier in Chapter 4, the factors that influence well-being are different at each stage of development. During the first three stages of development, the ego experiences well-being as happiness. The opposite of happiness is the stress and worry associated with the fear we have of not getting our needs met.

The happiness the ego feels arises from its ability to satisfy its survival, safety and security needs. During the last three stages of development, the ego experiences well-being as meaning. The meaning the ego feels arises from its ability to satisfy the soul's desire for self-expression, connection and contribution.

The greatest lack of well-being occurs around mid-life (the self-actualizing stage of development) because the ego has entered a zone of chaos: the transition from a life focused on happiness to a life focused on meaning; from a life where the ego is the dominant decision-making authority to a life where the soul is the dominant decision-making authority.

Elliott Jacques (1917–2003), a Canadian psychoanalyst and organizational psychologist, referred to the behavioural symptoms associated with a failure to navigate this critical phase in human development as a mid-life crisis. Not everyone experiences a mid-life-crisis, and those who do may not experience it in the same way. It depends on the type of fears (survival, safety or security) the ego is still holding onto, the unmet needs it still has. Some people experience mid-life-crisis in their 40s, others in their 50s. A mid-life crisis in the 40s usually has to do with survival and finding meaningful work. A mid-life crisis in the 50s usually has to do with relationships and finding a meaningful and loving sexual (intimate) connection.

We can conclude, as I indicated in Chapter 4, that the root of all well-being lies in the ability to master the tasks involved at each stage of psychological development. You can only begin to flourish when you have mastered every stage of development and can give full expression to your soul's desire for self-expression, connection and contribution. In other words, we flourish when we can recreate our soul's 4-D reality in 3-D awareness.

The reason you were born was to fully express who you are and explore your soul's potential. Call it personal development, personal growth, self-actualization or whatever you want, your life in this 3-D material world is your soul's attempt to evolve, grow and develop. If you want to be happy and fulfilled, do not think of your life in terms of achievement and success, but in terms of being the best person you can become.

A summary of key points

Here are the main points of Chapter 15.

1. Humans are 4-D energetic souls attempting to live in physical bodies in a 3-D material world.
2. The soul's purpose in incarnating (willing itself to be present in the 3-D material awareness) is to recreate its 4-D energetic reality in 3-D material awareness.
3. The physical body, which is the soul's energy template, is kept "alive" in 3-D material awareness by an entity known as the body-mind: the reptilian mind/brain. The body-mind keeps the body alive through a biological process called homeostasis. In 4-D terms, the purpose of homeostasis is to keep the soul's energy (body) template in energetic balance.
4. The soul's three main desires—to fully express its character, connect with others and contribute to the good of humanity—are dependent on the ego's ability to master the survival, relationship and self-esteem levels of consciousness.
5. The ego is created by the soul to protect the soul from the pain (energetic instabilities) it experiences in being present in 3-D material awareness.
6. The ego protects the soul from the psychological pain involved in being in a physical body in a material world of separation by attempting to provide the soul with a fear-free physical, social and cultural framework of existence from which it can fulfil its desire to recreate its 4-D reality in 3-D material awareness.
7. The theory of human well-being proposed in this book not only unites several branches of psychology; it also unites spirituality with psychology and science with psychology.
8. Caring for the soul results in the healing of the body because the physical body is the 3-D expression of the soul's 4-D energetic template.
9. The root of all well-being lies in the ability to master the tasks involved at each stage of psychological development.
10. You can only begin to flourish when you have mastered every stage of development and can give full expression to your soul's desire for self-expression, connection and contribution. In other

words, we flourish when we can recreate our soul's 4-D reality in 3-D awareness.
11. Do not think of your life in terms of achievement and success, but in terms of being the best person you can become.

References and notes

1. H. Ronald Hulnick and Mary R. Hulnick, *Loyalty to Your Soul: The Heart of Spiritual Psychology* (Carlsbad: Hay House), 2010, p. 174.
2. Michael A. Lerner, *Choices of Healing: Integrating the best of conventional and complementary approaches to cancer* (Boston: MIT Press), 1994, p. 122.
3. Aldous Huxley, *The Perennial Philosophy* (London: Harper Press), 1945.

Annex 1

Loyalty to your soul: key principles[1]

1. We are not human beings with souls; we are souls having a human experience.
2. The nature of God is Love.
3. Direct experience is the process through which belief or faith is transformed to knowing.
4. Since we are all part of God, our nature also is love, and we have the opportunity to know our loving nature experientially, here and now.
5. Physical-world reality exists for the purpose of spiritual evolution.
6. Spiritual evolution (growth) is a process, not an event.
7. All of life is for learning.
8. An unresolved issue is anything that disturbs your peace.
9. Every time a single person resolves a single issue, angels rejoice and all of humanity moves forward in its evolution.
10. All "becauses" are merely triggers to internal unresolved issues inviting completion.
11. Inner disturbances are themselves a major component of the spiritual curriculum you are here to complete.
12. Unresolved issues are not bad; they are just part of your spiritual curriculum and are an opportunity for healing.
13. Personal responsibility is the foundational key that opens the door to freedom.
14. Nothing outside of you causes disturbances.
15. You create your future by how you respond to experiences now.

16. How you relate to an issue is the issue, and how you relate to yourself while you go through an issue is the issue.
17. What you believe determines your experience.
18. A life filled with acceptance is a life devoid of unnecessary emotional suffering. It's a life filled with love.
19. Your primary goal is not to change the school; your primary goal is to graduate.
20. Healing is the application of loving to the places inside that hurt.
21. Loving, healing and evolving are all the same process.
22. Judgement is self-condemnation. Self-forgiveness is redemption; and compassion, acceptance, peace and joy naturally flow.

Source: H. Ronald Hulnick and Mary R. Hulnick, *Loyalty to Your Soul: The Heart of Spiritual Psychology* (Carlsbad: Hay House), 2010.

Annex 2

A Decathlon of Flourishing, from Age 60 to 80

1. Included in Who's Who in America.
2. Earning income in the study's top quartile.
3. Low in psychological distress.
4. Success and enjoyment in work, love and play since age 65.
5. Good subjective health at age 75.
6. Good subjective and objective physical and mental health at age 80.
7. Master of the Eriksonian task of Generativity.
8. Availability of social supports, other than wife and children, between ages 60 and 75.
9. In a good marriage between ages 60 and 75.
10. Close to children between ages 60 and 75.

Source: George E. Vaillant, *Triumphs of Experience* (Boston: Harvard University Press), 2012.

ANNEX 3

CULTURAL WORLD VIEWS

In thinking about culture, let us not assume cultural evolution is the driving force behind personal evolution. I believe it is more of a symbiotic interaction: advances in personal evolution yield opportunities for cultural evolution, and advances in cultural evolution yield opportunities for personal evolution. Let me explain how this dynamic works by describing a theory of cultural evolution called Spiral Dynamics.

Spiral Dynamics

The theory behind Spiral Dynamics, which was developed by Professor Clare Graves (1914–1986), was originally known as The Emergent, Cyclical, Double Helix Model of Adult Human Bio-psycho-social Systems.[1] At the core of Grave's theory is the idea that human evolution is the product of two forces: changes in the existential problems of living, and changes in the neuropsychological equipment/software for decision-making. These two forces are continually interacting with each other. When the problems of living become too acute, new world views emerge that solve the problems that previous world views precipitated.

The evolution of human world views from our earliest ancestors to modern day times is shown in Table A2.1. The names of the world views are shown in the first column. In brackets is the colour classification that Don Beck and Chris Cowan, who worked with Clare Graves, gave to each world view. Beck and Cowan gave the next world view to emerge after Turquoise the colour designation of Coral. Graves did not describe this world view because it was not emergent while he was alive. I believe it is now becoming emergent and have provided a very brief description of what it might look like based on the information presented in this book.

Table A2.1: The evolution of cultural world views.

Stages of cultural evolution	Key features	Focus	First appearance of world view
Energetic* (Coral)	Energetic Self: self as an individuated part of a universal energy field contributing to the evolution of human consciousness.	Cosmic Unity	Now appearing
Holistic (Turquoise)	Holistic Self: self as part of a larger, conscious, spiritual whole and global community that serves self and the good of all living entities.	Humanity	30 years ago
Integrative (Yellow)	Integral Self: personal freedom for all without harm to others or the physical environment. Limit the excesses of self-interest. Focus on self-expression and systemic approaches.	Interconnected States	50 years ago
Communitarian (Green)	Sensitive Self: explore inner self and community. Share resources among all. Reach decisions through consensus. Liberate humans from greed and dogma.	Social States	150 years ago
Achievist (Orange)	Rational Self: search for success and enhance living through science and technology. Seek independence and autonomy. Play to win and enjoy competition.	Economic States	1,000 years ago
Purposeful (Blue)	Rule/Role Self: bring order and stability to all things and control impulsivity through a higher authority. Sacrifice now for later rewards.	Religious States	5,000 years ago

Impulsive (Red)	Power Self: gratify impulses and senses and fight remorselessly to survive and defend reputation so as to avoid shame and achieve respect.	City states	10,000 years ago
Magical (Purple)	Magical Self: bond together to endure and find safety by living in harmony with each other and the forces of nature.	Tribal Groups	50,000 years ago
Survivalist (Beige)	Instinctive Self: focus on human biological needs through instincts with little awareness of self as distinct from the environment.	Hunter/ Gatherer Bands	100,000 years ago

* My interpretation.

What is noticeable about the evolution of new world views is the significant acceleration that has taken place over the last 150 years since the arrival of the Communitarian World View. This world view had its genesis in the Industrial Revolution, which freed people from the land and levelled the playing field in terms of providing opportunities for people to accumulate wealth. This development, along with the evolution of equality and democratic practices, provided people with an opportunity to meet their survival, safety and security needs, thereby freeing them from their deficiency needs and the need to focus on their self-interest.

Figure A2.1 plots the number of years ago that each world view began to emerge. The survivalist world view emerged with the birth of the genus *Homo sapiens* 250,000 years ago (I have not shown this in Figure A2.1). The magical world view (tribal) emerged about 50,000 years ago. The impulsive world view (city states) emerged 10,000 years ago, and so on. In more recent times the communitarian world view emerged 150 years ago, the integrative world view 50 years ago and the holistic world view 30 years ago. The philosophy behind the Coral world view is now beginning to emerge.

Figure A2.1: The emergence of new world views (years ago).

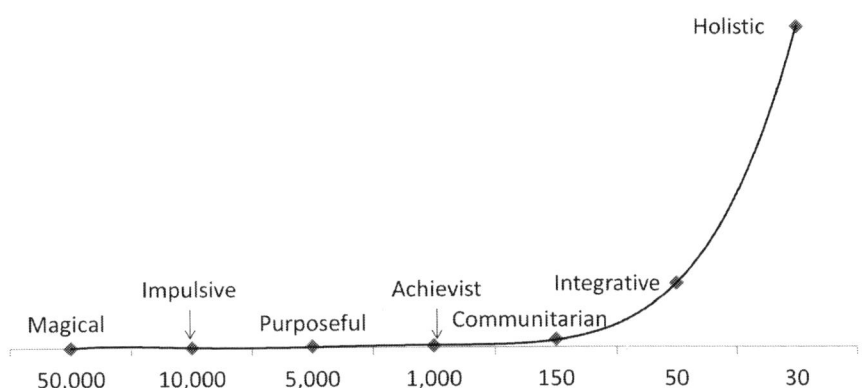

What causes cultural world views to change?

A world view only stays dominant in a culture as long as the culture can maintain internal stability. When a critical mass of people within a culture is no longer able to meet its needs, cultural entropy begins to increase, and internal stability begins to decrease. Once this happens, the world view is contested. Eventually, a tipping point[2] is reached, and a new world view emerges. The new world view responds to the needs that were not being met by the old-world view, but in turn, it eventually creates new problems of existence that make it become increasingly dysfunctional and a new cycle begins.

World views are distinctly cultural rather than ethnic in origin. The magical world view that initiated tribalism is still found in many parts of Sub-Saharan Africa, and the purposeful world that initiated monarchies and religious states is still prevalent in the Middle East. The more advanced, mostly Western democracies, such as the Scandinavian countries are mostly operating with a Communitarian world view. The remaining democracies—countries such as the USA, UK, France, Germany and Italy—are mostly operating from an Achievist world view.

As yet, there are no nations that have embraced the integrative world view, but it is showing up in a few small urban and rural communities, and also in some small and medium-sized organizations run by enlightened leaders.

What's next?

Given the rapid acceleration in world views that has occurred since the advent of the industrial revolution, it is highly likely we will see another world view emerging in the coming decades. The precise form of this world view is still in question. I believe the next world view (Coral) will be a reflection of the principles governing the serving stage of psychological development—a shift towards a more expansive sense of inclusion and the desire to make a personal contribution to the evolution of human consciousness.

How does the spiral relate to seven levels?

Having introduced the Spiral Dynamics Model, I think it is important that we explore how this model (of cultural development) relates to the Seven Levels Model (of personal development). I believe the easiest way to explain the relationship between the two models is as follows:

- We operate at levels of consciousness.
- We grow in stages of development.
- We live inside world views.

The level of consciousness we operate from will normally be the same as the stage of development we have reached. If we have any unmet needs from earlier stages of development, then we can be triggered into operating from those levels of consciousness. Similarly, if our life circumstances change and we can no longer meet our deficiency needs we will temporarily revert to the lower levels of consciousness.

Enculturation

The world views of the culture we live in have a strong influence on the beliefs and behaviours we adopt while we are growing up. By the time we reach our 30s we are fully enculturated either by the world view of our parents or by the world view of the peer group within which we have learned how to survive, stay safe and find security.

In former times, let's say more than 150 years ago, the world views of our parents would have been the same as the world views of our peers. This is because world views took centuries to emerge, develop and decline. This is no longer true. New world views are emerging at a rapid pace. The cultural world views adopted by the peer group of the children born today could be significantly different from those of their parents born thirty to forty years ago. This is why there is so much interest it the attitudes and behaviours of the so-called millennial generation.

One of the reasons for the rapid evolution in world views is because democracy and capitalism not only brought stability to our lives, they also brought freedom. For the first time in human history, the masses and the disadvantaged were able to meet their deficiency needs. Having learned how to survive, stay safe and feel secure in their framework of existence, the masses were free to pursue their freedom and independence (the individuating stage of development) and most importantly began to align more closely with the values of their souls, the values that promote self-expression, connection and contribution.

From a historical perspective, we can say that the emergence of the Communitarian world view was an evolutionary turning point that is giving large numbers of people, the world over, the possibility of aligning their ego motivations with their soul motivations.

I believe the next world view to emerge—the Integrative world view—was a cultural reflection of the needs associated with the self-actualizing stage of psychological development—the bonding of the ego with the soul. It gave people the freedom to express themselves within a value system that transcends physical, racial, and religious differences.

I believe the Holistic world view is a continuation of this trend: It is a reflection of the Integrating stage of psychological development. It focuses on our global connectedness. In this world view, we become part of a global conscious spiritual community that serves the good of all living entities.

ANNEX 3

This is why I also believe the next world view to emerge will reflect the needs of the serving stage of psychological development. It will be a world view that supports individuals in focusing on their individual contribution to the evolution of human consciousness.

This leads me to the conclusion that the progression of world views defined by the Spiral Dynamics Model is a cultural reflection of the Seven Stages of Psychological Development. What we have been witnessing over the past quarter of a million years is the emergence of a new type of human: one who is centred in soul consciousness. This evolution was made possible by the Communitarian world view and the Individuating stage of psychological development.

The correspondence between the Seven Levels of Consciousness and the cultural world views of Spiral Dynamics is shown in Table A2.2. The colour designation given in the third column is that of Beck and Cowan, who worked with Graves. The colour designation in the fourth column is that of Ken Wilber.[3]

Table A2.2: Stages of individual psychological development and cultural world views.[4]

Stages of individual development (Seven Levels Model)	Stages of collective development (Spiral Dynamics Model)	Colour designation (Graves)	Colour designation (Wilber)
Serving	Energetic (Energetic self)	Coral	Indigo
Integrating	Holistic (Holistic self)	Turquoise	Turquoise
Self-actualizing	Integrative (Integral self)	Yellow	Teal
Individuating	Communitarian (Sensitive self)	Green	Green
Differentiating	Achievist (Rational self)	Orange	Orange
Differentiating	Purposeful (Rule/Role self)	Blue	Amber
	Impulsive (Power self)	Red	Red
Conforming Magical self	Magical (Tribal self)	Purple	Magenta
Surviving Instinctive self	Survivalist (Clan self)	Beige	Infrared

You will immediately notice from Table A2.2 that apart from the Impulsive, Purposeful and Achievist world views, which represent different facets of the differentiating stage of development, there is a one-to-one correspondence between world views and the stages of psychological developmental.

I would like to draw your attention to what I feel are the most important dependencies that exist between the personal development model and cultural development model.

First, no matter what world view a person is embedded in, they will always grow and develop in accordance with the stages of psychological development. Second, there are certain world views that support access to the higher stages of psychological development and certain world views that inhibit access to the higher stages of development. Let me explain.

The world views situated above the dotted line in Table A2.2 are increasingly supportive of the individuating stage of development, the portal through which we access the higher stages of development. The world views situated below the dotted line are increasingly suppressive of the individuating stage of development.

As far as the UK is concerned, this boundary was first breached with the signing of the Magna Carta in 1215, although it took another 713 years, until 1928, for women in the UK over the age of 21 to be granted the right to vote in elections and become a member of parliament.

The Magna Carta is regarded as an important symbol of liberty, held in great respect by the British and American legal communities. It is often cited by politicians and campaigners. Lord Denning (1899–1999) describes it as "the greatest constitutional document of all times—the foundation of the freedom of the individual against the arbitrary authority of the despot"[5]. The Magna Carta represented a concept that heretofore had never been institutionalized into law.

Any governance regime that is less than democratic in nature will tend to suppress individual psychological development. I say "tend" because it is not true of all non-democratic regimes. Bhutan is a notable exception. Throughout history, that is until recently, Bhutan has been a kingdom; a kingdom that embraced the philosophy of Buddhism. This religious philosophy has always encouraged personal evolution for everyone. Consequently, individuation was not suppressed but actively encouraged. This was not true in the former USSR, nor is it true in China today. Both countries actively suppress free thinking. Intellectuals are quietly removed from society and are left in prison to rot or are never heard of again. It takes immense courage to embrace your personal evolution in non-democratic regimes.

Clare Graves recognized that something of strategic importance happens during the evolution of the Communitarian world view. He noticed that the next world view that cultures step into—the Integrative world view—showed similar characteristics to the first world view—the Survivalist world view. Instead of focusing on survival at the local level we began to focus on survival at the global level. He also noticed a similarity between the second world view—the Magical world view—and the Holistic world view. Instead of learning how to become a member of your ethnic tribe, you learn how to become a member of the human tribe. This same correspondence, between the lower stages of development and the higher stages of development, also occurs in my stages of psychological development model.

Based on these observations, Graves hypothesized that the Integrative world view (yellow) was the starting point for a higher order of world views; the lower order focusing on subsistence (deficiency) needs and the higher order focusing on being (growth) needs. This caused him to label the first six world views, First Tier and the emerging world views, Second Tier.

I completely share Graves view concerning the strategic importance of the Integrative world view (and its individual counterpart, the individuating stage of psychological development.) The shift that occurs culturally and the shift that occurs individually, both move us towards the possibility of manifesting the value system of the soul's 4-D energetic reality in our three dimensional physical world.

According to the Economic Intelligence Unit, there were only 24 full democracies in 2012—nations that operate with Communitarian or Integrative world views. There were 52 flawed democracies—nations that operate with an achievist world view—and 39 hybrid and 52 authoritarian regimes—nations that operate with a Purposeful or Impulsive world views.[6]

To accelerate the evolution of human consciousness, we need to do two things: enable people to satisfy their deficiency needs by eliminating poverty and disease and promoting education; and enable people to satisfy their growth needs by promoting freedom of expression.[7]

References and notes

1. www.clarewgraves.com/articles_content/1981_handout/1981_summary.pdf
2. A tipping point is a critical point in an evolving situation that leads to a new and irreversible development. The term is said to have originated in the field of epidemiology when an infectious disease gets out of control and can no longer be prevented from spreading. A tipping point is often considered to be a turning point. The term "tipping point" is now used in many fields and can be equally applied to social phenomena, medical phenomena, psychological and energetic phenomena.
3. For an overview of Ken Wilber's take on the Spiral Dynamics Model see ww.awaken.com/2014/04/ken-wilber-summary-of-spiral-dynamics-model/
4. This table is slightly different from representations you may find in my earlier publications. This is simply because my ideas have evolved.
5. Danziger and Gillingham, *1215: The Year of the Magna Carta* (London: Hodder), 2004, p. 268.
6. http://en.wikipedia.org/wiki/Democracy_Index
7. Richard Barrett, *Love, Fear and the Destiny of Nations* (Bath: Fulfilling Books), 2012.

Index

A

Abraham Maslow and Maslow ix, xvii, xxx, 1, 2, 3, 5, 7, 8, 9, 10, 12, 13, 14, 16, 17, 18, 19, 23, 32, 56, 101, 113, 129, 130, 131, 132, 134, 169, 170, 171, 182, 271
Alan Watkins 15, 18, 82
Albert Einstein 21
Alice Miller 63, 67, 192, 202, 265, 269
Alzheimer's disease 60, 61, 204, 205, 212, 214, 216, 217, 218, 249
Amit Goswami 91, 100
Andrew Bernstein 18
Anger xxxiv, 36, 45, 49, 50, 53, 106, 111, 112, 115, 116, 117, 118, 119, 120, 122, 123, 124, 126, 132, 135, 136, 140, 141, 143, 146, 147, 149, 151, 152, 153, 154, 156, 158, 162, 163, 164, 165, 166, 173, 176, 193, 199, 231, 232, 233, 274
Anorexia nervosa 210, 220, 237, 240, 241, 242, 243, 249
Anoxia 159
Antonio Damasio 115, 126
Anxiety v, 2, 53, 85, 106, 109, 116, 117, 118, 122, 123, 124, 126, 135, 143, 149, 154, 160, 162, 163, 164, 169, 172, 176, 240, 245, 267
Arthritis 245, 246, 247
Arthur Janov 58, 65, 66, 67, 150, 153, 159, 165, 179, 181, 182, 202
Astral field 191, 192, 198, 213, 231
Attention deficit hyperactivity disorder 38, 39
Autonomic nervous system 160, 163, 184, 185, 201, 220, 244

B

Barbara Brennan 189, 193, 202
Barbara L. Fredrickson 59, 179
Barrett Values Centre iii, iv, xix, 6, 136
Beatles 107
Bernardo Kastrup 21, 32
Bessel van der Kolk 150, 153, 174, 182
Big bang xxxiii, xxxviii, 39, 40, 41, 50, 51
Birth process 45, 149, 159, 160, 161, 166, 272, 274
Birth trauma 161, 231
Brain in the gut 198, 236
Breast cancer 205, 209, 210, 213, 225, 226, 227, 228, 229, 230, 248, 249, 250, 260
Brow chakra 194, 195, 197, 212, 219, 220, 221
Bulimia nervosa 210, 220, 237, 242, 243, 249

C

Cancer dysfunctions 247, 251
Carl Jung and Jung ix, xvii, xxxv, 3, 9, 10, 13, 18
Chakra or chakras xxxiv, 183, 184, 185, 186, 187, 188, 189, 190, 191, 192, 193, 194, 195, 196, 197, 198, 201, 202, 203, 212, 213, 214, 215, 219, 220, 221, 222, 224, 225, 226, 230, 231, 232, 235, 236, 240, 243, 244, 245, 246, 247, 271, 273
Clare Graves 290, 291, 298
Coherence 14, 15, 16, 17, 18, 82, 124, 126, 192, 199, 230, 232
Collective unconscious 9, 10
Comb analogy 26
Creativity v, xxv, xlii, 12, 34, 49, 54, 55, 59, 60, 65, 79, 80, 83, 89, 90, 91, 99, 100, 119, 186, 190, 194, 215, 216, 283
Crown chakra 195, 196, 197, 212, 213, 214, 215
Cultural Transformation Tools 6
Cultural world views 290, 292, 293, 295, 296, 297

D

Dan Buettner 61, 67
David Harper 57
David R. Hawkins 123, 126
Decathlon of flourishing 289
Decision-making xxiv, xxxvi, xxxviii, xxxix, xl, xlii, xliii, 4, 16, 37, 92, 141, 142, 143, 146, 147, 148, 152, 175, 176, 185, 242, 284, 290
Deficiency sensation xxxiii, 103, 104, 105, 106, 112, 113, 116
Defining desires 106
Defining requirements 104
Definition of a need 106

Dementia 60, 204, 205, 211, 212, 214, 216, 217, 251, 278
Depression v, 15, 36, 55, 63, 66, 86, 109, 112, 119, 120, 165, 169, 214, 220, 226, 240, 242, 267
Developmental focus 73
Developmental psychology 275
Developmental task 72, 73, 83, 214, 219, 225, 230, 236, 243, 245
Diabetes 60, 205, 208, 210, 211, 213, 236, 237, 238, 239, 243, 249, 251
Dissociative Identity Disorder 167, 168, 181, 245
DNA xlii, 21, 139
Dominant mind 137, 138, 144, 145, 146, 147, 149, 152, 170, 176
Dualism xxx, xxxi, xliv, xlv, 19

E

Early Maladaptive Schema 132, 134, 163, 170, 171
Edward O. Wilson 28
Ego awareness 3, 47, 48
Ego development 69, 72, 137
Ego-soul alignment 70, 81, 137
Embryo 45, 51, 139, 154, 155, 157
Enculturation 295
Energetic instability xxxiv, xxxvi, 15, 36, 45, 49, 51, 53, 103, 111, 112, 135, 136, 142, 143, 144, 145, 147, 148, 149, 150, 151, 152, 153, 154, 155, 156, 157, 158, 159, 161, 162, 164, 165, 166, 167, 168, 172, 175, 176, 180, 184, 246, 247, 248, 272, 273, 274, 282, 285
Ervin László 22, 32
Existential psychology 275, 276

F

False needs 105, 106
Feeling deficiencies xxxiii, 103, 104, 112, 116

Filtering 34, 35, 36, 38, 39, 41, 43, 44, 45, 46, 50, 95, 137
Flourishing ii, xxxiv, 271, 289
Foetus xxxvii, 39, 45, 51, 74, 139, 149, 154, 159, 160, 165, 166
Frequency of vibration 22, 23, 40, 47, 121, 123, 124, 183

G

George Land 89, 100
George Vaillant xxii, xxiii, 58, 91, 216
Gerald L. Schroeder xlv, 51
Glueck Study xxiii
Grant Study xxi, xxii, xxiii, 58, 60, 62, 180, 216

H

Happiness i, xxi, 15, 16, 53, 57, 58, 66, 100, 115, 116, 117, 119, 122, 123, 128, 133, 140, 169, 180, 284
Healing xxix, xxxii, xxxiii, xlv, 59, 109, 111, 114, 135, 149, 153, 185, 189, 201, 202, 204, 242, 251, 252, 282, 283, 285, 287, 288
Heart chakra 191, 192, 193, 198, 230, 231, 232
Heart disease 15, 112, 161, 204, 205, 207, 208, 209, 210, 211, 213, 231, 232, 233, 234, 235, 239, 240, 247, 249, 250, 252, 274
Hermann Ebbinghaus xxix
Hierarchy of needs 2, 3, 5
Homeostasis 146, 151, 165, 272, 285
Human energy field xxxiv, 23, 111, 116, 183, 188, 189, 196, 198, 199, 200, 202, 203, 212, 282
Humanistic psychology xxx, 275, 276

I

Incidence of suicide in Sweden 262, 263
Incidence of suicide in the United Kingdom 259
Incidence of suicide in the United States 263
Irritable Bowel 109, 213, 236
Isolation xix, 85, 120, 166, 254, 258, 259, 267, 269, 276
Ivan Petrovich Pavlov xxix

J

Jeffrey Young 170
John James 23, 32
Joy i, 8, 17, 29, 55, 57, 60, 71, 84, 115, 116, 117, 119, 122, 123, 124, 128, 129, 133, 159, 170, 177, 178, 214, 289

K

Ken Wilber 82, 297, 299

L

Lee Raby 62, 67
Levels of consciousness xxxiii, xxxiv, xliii, 2, 3, 5, 6, 7, 16, 70, 78, 83, 84, 85, 86, 137, 187, 188, 189, 203, 273, 285, 294, 295, 296
Limbic mind/brain xl, xli, xliii, 45, 75, 111, 136, 137, 139, 140, 141, 142, 143, 148, 152, 162, 164, 166, 175, 177, 178, 180, 185, 201, 220, 221, 255, 257, 272, 273, 274
Liver disease 205, 210, 211, 213, 236, 237, 238, 240, 243, 249, 251
London School of Economics 62
Loneliness 85, 120, 166, 178, 179, 258, 259, 267, 269
Longevity xxiii, xxvii, 61, 62
Lord Kelvin 26
Lord Richard Layard 62, 67
Lower emotional field 190, 191, 194, 200, 219, 221, 243, 273

Lower etheric field 189, 190, 191, 193, 199, 226, 245
Lower mental field 191, 195, 200, 215, 235, 273
Lung disease 204, 205, 211, 229, 250

M

Marc Gafni and Gafni iv, 11, 18
Mary Hulnick xxvi, 283
Max Planck 22
Meaning-making xxxiv, 40, 102, 146, 147, 148, 169, 170, 171, 175, 177, 178, 185, 274, 276
Michael Shermer 30
Millennials 98, 99, 100, 295
Mindfulness 3, 35, 97, 186, 202
Monism xxxi, xlv, 19
Motivations of the ego xxxiii, 50, 52, 53, 102
Motivations of the soul xxxiii, 50, 52, 54, 55, 102

N

Neocortex xxxviii, xli, xliii, 46, 75, 128, 133, 136, 137, 140, 141, 142, 148, 151, 152, 164, 172, 175, 178, 179, 180, 197, 212, 214, 236, 255, 272, 273, 278
Neuroscience xxv, 15, 117, 143
Neurosis xxx, 148, 169, 171, 172
Newtonian mechanics 26, 47
Niels Bohr 27

O

Obesity 60, 210, 213, 220, 237, 238, 239, 240, 243, 244, 249
Obsessive compulsive disorder 38
Omnipresence 47, 48
One-mind 42, 44, 45, 50, 125, 136, 137, 277, 278, 282
Ordering of stages 83
Ovarian cancer 213, 220, 221, 222, 224, 225, 228, 244, 249, 250

Overactive chakra 186, 202

P

Parasympathetic nervous system 185, 186, 187, 201
Parkinson's disease 212, 214, 216, 218, 249, 278
Personal conscious xxxviii
Personal subconscious xxxviii
Personal unconscious xxxix, 9
Peter Ouspensky xxvi, xxvii
Phenomenological psychology 275, 276
Physiological pain xxxvi, 135, 142, 143, 151, 152, 155, 159, 162, 272
Placebo 108, 109, 113, 114
Planes of being 279, 280
Plato's cave 28
Pneumonia 29, 204, 205, 229
Primary motivations 52, 54, 65, 83, 86, 87, 99
Progression through the stages 127
Prospective Studies xxii, xxiii
Prostate cancer 205, 209, 211, 213, 220, 221, 222, 223, 224, 225, 244, 248, 249, 250
Psyche xxxi, xxxv, xliv, xlv, 149
Psychoanalytical psychology 275
Psychological pain 135, 143, 144, 145, 147, 151, 152, 153, 154, 155, 156, 158, 164, 166, 172, 232, 254, 272, 285
Psychosis 168, 169, 171, 173, 182
Psychosomatic disorders 14, 162, 163
PTSD 172, 173, 174, 175, 182, 254, 264

Q

Quantum mechanics 26, 27
Quantum theory 22, 27, 48, 108, 279

R

Rapid emergent learning xli, 72, 84, 128, 133, 138, 139, 146, 148, 154, 171, 185, 186, 201, 202, 274
R. D. Laing 10, 18
Real needs 105
Reptilian mind/brain xl, xli, xliii, 39, 45, 74, 111, 136, 137, 138, 139, 140, 141, 148, 149, 151, 152, 157, 158, 160, 175, 177, 180, 185, 201, 213, 225, 226, 232, 245, 257, 272, 273, 274, 285
Richard Barrett i, ii, iii, iv, v, vi, vii, 5, 17, 18, 100, 153
Robert Kegan 94, 100
Roberto Assagioli and Assagioli ix, 13, 18, 87, 96, 100
Ronald Hulnick xxvii, 286, 289
Root chakra 189, 190, 197, 212, 245, 246
Rumination 36, 120, 126

S

Sacral chakra 190, 197, 212, 219, 220, 221, 222, 224, 243, 244
Sadness xxxiv, 53, 55, 63, 112, 114, 115, 116, 117, 119, 120, 122, 123, 140, 154, 156, 158, 165, 176, 177, 178, 214, 220, 226
Secondary motivations 52, 54, 65, 83, 86, 87, 99, 100
Self-witness 35, 83, 97, 100
Shadow 28, 37, 231
Sigmund Freud xxix, 276
Solar plexus chakra 191, 197, 212, 235, 236, 240
Soul activation 71, 72, 81, 137
Soul awareness 47, 48, 246
Soul-mind xxxvi, xxxix, xlii, xliii, 23, 25, 32, 41, 44, 45, 46, 47, 51, 102, 116, 121, 122, 136, 139, 140, 141, 143, 145, 146, 147, 149, 151, 152, 153, 154, 155, 157, 158, 159, 160, 165, 177, 178, 179, 180, 192, 272, 283
Species blueprint 139
Spiral dynamics 290, 294, 296, 299
Strokes or stroke 15, 60, 61, 67, 161, 204, 205, 208, 209, 211, 215, 216, 217, 218, 233, 239, 249, 250, 278
Sudden Infant Death Syndrome 161, 246, 251
Suicide xxxiv, 86, 120, 127, 161, 174, 182, 206, 207, 208, 209, 210, 229, 235, 236, 237, 242, 253, 254, 255, 256, 258, 259, 260, 261, 262, 263, 264, 265, 266, 267, 268, 269, 270, 271
Sympathetic nervous system 145, 160, 163, 185, 201, 247

T

Terman Study xxiii, 59, 91, 216
Thalidomide 157, 158
Throat chakra 193, 194, 197, 212, 225, 226
Transpersonal Psychology xxx, 23, 275, 276
Trauma xxxvi, xl, 62, 63, 65, 77, 149, 150, 154, 160, 161, 162, 166, 167, 169, 173, 174, 175, 182, 185, 201, 231, 254, 264

U

Underactive chakra 184, 186, 247
University of Santa Monica iii, xxv
Upper emotional field 194, 198, 219
Upper etheric field 158, 193, 198, 225
Upper mental field 195, 198, 213, 215

V

Value priorities 83, 87, 88, 89
Vedic philosophy 2, 3
Veterans 174, 175, 182, 264, 269

Viktor Frankl 11

W

Well-being theory 57
Wilhelm Wundt xxix
William H. Murray 13, 18
William James xxix, 13, 18
Womb 39, 65, 74, 149, 159, 161, 166, 199, 232, 272, 274

Printed in Great Britain
by Amazon